A NEW TYPE *of* WOMANHOOD

NATASHA KIRSTEN KRAUS

A NEW TYPE *of* WOMANHOOD

Discursive Politics and Social Change
in Antebellum America

Duke University Press   Durham and London   2008

© 2008 Duke University Press

All rights reserved

Printed in the United States of America
on acid-free paper ∞

Designed by Heather Hensley

Typeset in Minion Pro by Achorn
International

Library of Congress Cataloging-in-
Publication Data appear on the last
printed page of this book.

For my family—
Wendy, David, Krupskaya, Wilma, and Jon—who have kept me grounded, given me support and love through hard times, and an awful lot of joy. With love and gratitude, and plenty of squalor.

In memory of Tanya Ciszewski,
whose strength, sweetness, and righteous outrage suffused her very being, giving her no choice but to live as an activist—a difficult journey that was a gift to her family, her friends, and the world itself.

Woman must put herself into the text—as into the world and into history—by her own movement.

—HÉLÈNE CIXOUS, *THE LAUGH OF THE MEDUSA*

The important thing is to give the monotonous and empty concept of 'change' a content, that of the play of specified modifications . . . to show that discontinuity is not a monotonous and unthinkable void between events, which one must hasten to fill with the dim plenitude of cause or by the nimble bottle-imp of mind (the one solution being the symmetrical twin of the other), but that it is a play of specific transformations, each one different from the next . . . , linked together according to schemes of dependence. History is the descriptive analysis and the theory of these transformations.

—MICHEL FOUCAULT, *POLITICS AND THE STUDY OF DISCOURSE*

There is a demand now for a new type of womanhood. We are daily assuming new positions—taking upon us new duties, and claiming the exercise of our civil and political rights.

—ELIZABETH CADY STANTON, *LETTER FROM MRS. ELIZABETH C. STANTON TO THE WORCESTER CONVENTION,* NOVEMBER 1851

CONTENTS

TABLES

ACKNOWLEDGMENTS

THIS BOOK'S GENESIS HAS SPANNED SOME FIFTEEN YEARS and unusual circumstances. During that time, I have lived what seems like a number of completely distinct lives. But across that time and my experiences, certain people have provided deep and unquestioning support of my work, my thinking, and my life. Although illness forced a rupture of sorts in both my life and this work, the strength of the support flowing from these friends, family, and colleagues has been indispensable to me; in great part, it is because of them that I have been able to continue to push forward. Lengthy serious illness is an incredibly isolating experience. As Laura Hillenbrand has written, "My world narrowed down to my bed and my window. . . . Most of the people around me stepped backward" (2003, 59). Often the compassion and belief that sustained me was communicated through the ether, as it were, as people tended to their own lives, partners, children, work. My knowledge of their care, my ability to trust that it was there and would be there when we could communicate, is a testament to the strength of their support and friendship. I count my life, my thoughts, my politics, my meanings as richer and intensely shaped by their caring and interlocution, whether explicit and present nearby or implicit and hailing from afar. For all this, I am deeply grateful to Jorge Arditi, Claudia Center, Tanya Ciszewski, Patricia Clough, Shana Cohen, Naheed

Islam, Wendy Kraus, Krupskaya V, Jon Kraus, Wilma Kraus, Ellen Kraus, Charles Lemert, John Levi Martin, David Modersbach, Jesse Palmer, Avital Ronell, Jeff Soukup, Roel van den Oever, Judith Wise, and madgrrls. Additionally, over the course of the past fifteen years and several iterations of this book, I was lucky to have numerous people read drafts in their entirety or in part and provide insightful and helpful commentary. For this undertaking, I thank many of the people above as well as Nancy Chodorow, Troy Duster, Peter Kilby, Eyal Rabinovitch, Eleanor Townsley, Christina Weber, and members of the Great Barrington Theory Group. Jorge Arditi in particular read every page of this book's first iteration, offering critical commentary that pushed me to go as far as I could and should theoretically and historically. And he believed avidly in my work even when I had doubts. Judith Butler gave constructive criticism and encouragement at an early stage of the project. Peter Evans and Michael Burawoy offered general support at the same stage. The Bay Area activist communities that I called home through the mid-1990s—especially the anarchist and antiracist communities and my two affinity groups—impacted this work and all of my thoughts dramatically, and continue to do so. In my two years at Wesleyan University, ly.nn owens, Kay Owens, Eyal Rabinovitch, and Roel van den Oever provided much-needed comraderie and collegiality. Over the past year, Jeffrey Alexander and the Center for Cultural Sociology at Yale University have provided a welcoming and stimulating intellectual community. During the final production push, Bernhard Giesen joined me in thought-provoking conversation, and Mila and Aki supplied moments of joy and relaxation as well as the opportunity for recuperative, ambling chats with Aki's parents, Jessica and Anthony.

Appreciation beyond the measure of words goes to a few of these people for their commitment to me, my work, my life. Charles Lemert, Avital Ronell, and Patricia Clough have gone far beyond the bounds of what anyone could dare expect or even ask of senior scholars. Each has aided me in finding institutional support and academic environments in which to do my work as I return to health. Charles Lemert in particular has been a consistently nurturing force—incredibly generous with his time and his space. He has provided intellectual and institutional support at pivotal times as well as his friendship, always with an eye toward my growth both as a scholar and in life. I have benefited immeasurably from his efforts as a mentor and his presence as an extended family member and friend. Avital Ronell taught me the joys of close reading and reaffirmed my passion for rigorously pursuing theory into the social and political. She has continued to provide needed institutional and warm collegial support from afar over the years and has helped to ensure that my theoretical pursuits had a place to call home. Patricia Clough affirmed the use of (re)writing history at a time when I was uncertain, and I thank her for nurturing my book through some difficult moments.

As chosen family members, David Modersbach and Krupskaya V have been with me in body or spirit from the inception of this project to the present. And their presence and love have affected everything. Krupskaya lived this with me 24/7 for fourteen years; and David is still the truest anarchist I know, inspiring me daily. My biological family members' strength is what one could only wish for. They have been the ones present and nearby, helping me through unexpected years of illness and struggling with me to return to health, work, life. They are there no matter what time of day or night, whether for emotional support, helping me get groceries, paying outlandish medical bills, or talking analytically about the social world. I first learned politics, history, activism, and community strength and interdependence from my parents—marching at civil rights demonstrations as a toddler, learning a counterhistory of the United States and the world as I grew up, and living in a household suffused with the belief that the promise of democracy must be continually fought for. In addition, my father, Jon, provided helpful, critical commentary on my writing of history and political economy. And my mother, Wilma, critiqued numerous chapters with an eye toward making the theory more easily readable. My sister, Wendy, continues to be one of my very best friends, in every sense of the word. I'm incredibly lucky to know her, and by some wonderful accident she's actually my sister. On top of this, she's an editorial and sociological reader *extraordinaire.* For a decade, her lucid and detailed comments have improved my writing skills. And she's been an important interlocutor on sociological and broad theoretical terrain, as well as in sharing daily life. This book and, in fact, I would not be without her.

Finally, I am grateful to the editors at Duke University Press, who remained committed to this project over an unexpectedly long development period and who marshaled it through the process even while providing the flexibility that I needed. My thanks go to Raphael Allen for initially acquiring the project and to my editor, Reynolds Smith, who entered the process at a later point than usual, for fully taking on the project and treating it as his own. In the final stages, the Editorial Board made some suggestions for my introductory chapter that proved to be crucial interventions. My appreciations go to Sarah Deutsch in particular, who generously spent her time discussing the framing of my work and pointed me to some previously unnoticed sources. Needless to say, any remaining problems with the text are my responsibility.

The Departments of Sociology at the University at California, Berkeley, University at Buffalo-SUNY, and Wesleyan University provided institutional support and community at various points in this work, as have the Center for the Humanities at Wesleyan University and the Center for Cultural Sociology at Yale University. The following libraries were essential to the book as sources of primary documents: the Rare Books and Manuscripts and Special Collections Room at the Library of Congress, the Manuscripts and Special Collections at the New York State Library, the Manuscripts and Special Collections Room at Vassar College Library, the New York Public Library, the Schlesinger Library of Women's History at Radcliffe University, and the John Hay Library at Brown University. Working at these libraries in the company of other scholars also intensely reaffirmed my faith in and love of books, texts, and documents as society's records through the centuries.

INTRODUCTION

THIS BOOK CAN BE READ IN (AT LEAST) TWO WAYS. IT can be read as a general retelling of the antebellum woman's rights movement, specifically in terms of the rights of property and contract, with a focus on how that movement deployed and refigured social meanings of Womanhood, contract, the economy, and the nation. Or it can be read as the elaboration of a new theoretical frame that can be used to analyze moments of societal rupture in past, present, and future history by paying close attention to the particulars of how systems of social meanings and institutions are intricately interwoven in any given social order, with the antebellum woman's rights movement as a case study of its use. For me, the latter reading is the more important one, and it is my hope that the theory I propose will provide insights into today's political and theoretical projects (as pointed to in the conclusion), including, but not limited to, queer activism and theory, disability activism and theory, antiracism activism and theory, feminist activism and theory, and postcolonial and anti-imperial activism and theory. Still, readers always determine in great part how any text will be used and what it will become. I hope that both academics and activists find an interest in transforming this text.

I began this work at the end of the first Gulf War, which coincided with the government's decimation of much of progressive activism and many progressive activist links across the United States after years of protracted struggle. The "Vietnam syndrome" (repeatedly invoked by the first George Bush to suggest that America had allowed its Vietnam experience to maim its will, to provoke internal fear of any war, and to distort its understanding of any military demonstration of might into one of morally questionable, imperial right) had indeed been demolished. And my work on this project is ending in the midst of a second Gulf War, whose specific and devastating trajectory was certainly aided by that earlier decimation. During this time, progressive communities have grappled with serious questions of social movement, most centrally: How to think about, or rethink, progressive political action. What would a progressive politics for the new millennium look like? What issues would be salient, and what approaches to politics, to social change, to standing institutions, would tactically be useful? How might the relations between the social order as it exists—in daily practices, institutions, identities, understandings—and social movements best be understood? And where might that lead us?

These questions raise, in turn, questions of citizenship and the nation, questions of community and beyond-the-nation, questions of who is a legitimate civil or political subject and how legitimacy is determined, and questions of how communities' parameters and delimitations get drawn. I believe that a theory of structural aporias, as defined and described in the following pages, will point us in new, useful directions when considering these questions.

In practice, conservatives in the United States have been much better discursive theorists than progressives for the past several decades—not just better rhetorically, but discursively. I mean that they have been better at analyzing the complex and imbricated operations of (a) the systems of social meanings that figure subjecthood and (b) central societal institutions (such as economic and legal institutions). All theorists, policymakers, academics, and activists need an analysis of how the social order operates through discourse and how discourse and institutions operate through each other, particularly in constituting moments and sites of political conflagration and the processes through which they play out. We need to become smart discursive theorists and actors, whether as analysts or activists.

For this reason, in this book I ask how the social sciences, particularly sociology, might learn from poststructuralist and deconstructionist understandings of language—in specific, understandings of its operations and its force, including its historical force. I ask how modernist feminist histories and theories might be reread through classic, not necessarily feminist, post-structuralist and deconstructionist frameworks. I ask how feminist post-structuralism and deconstruction might usefully be reread from a social scientific, particularly sociological, point of view. Finally, I ask what sociology can learn about the subject of social movements, who is also of course the subject of history, from these interdisciplinary, perhaps postdisciplinary, meldings. In all these questions, I hope to engage the social theorist, the cultural critic, the social historian, the political economist, and the activist.

Language and its vagaries demand a quick note here. In order to remain true to the distinctness of the social realm, I rely on variations of the verb "imbricate" to denote how the social sphere is crucially constituted by an inextricable interweaving of both webs of social meanings and institutional matrices at any given time. Very few satisfactory substitutes exist for the meaning of "imbricated" evoked here—a sense of "so structurally and conceptually intermeshed that the social sphere is in fact one structure from which it is impossible to differentiate or disentangle systems of social meanings and institutions; and yet such a social structure is in no way a monad, but a complex and contingent social architecture." Hence, "interwoven," "intertangled," "overlapping," "layered," and "combined with" do not suffice because they all imply a separability of parts. Whereas the theory of structural aporias described here reconceptualizes precisely how social meanings and social institutions are entirely co-constitutive and inseparable in the founding and continued functioning of any social order. That said, "interimplicated" provides a close synonym, and slight simplifications such as "intertwined" and "embedded in a complex web" are sometimes used, with the caveat that the impossibility of untwining these matrices lies at the heart of my analysis.

PART I

PRODUCTIVE ECONOMIES, BOTH FAMILY AND PUBLIC, were in transition from the 1820s through the 1860s. At the same time, and clearly related, significant changes in women's social position and daily practices took place. Successive waves of feminist historians have narrated these changes in ways that speak as much to the analysts' historical moment as to the on-the-ground mid-nineteenth-century realities. Feminist historical narration of this period can be usefully approached by recognizing the centrality of both institutional practices and regulations and the understandings and operations of systems of social meanings to the maintenance, reproduction, and disruptions of any given social order. In other words, the mid-1800s rise of True Womanhood and the "cult" of domesticity holds a dual history: their socially and historically embedded construction throughout the nineteenth century and their socially and historically embedded reconstruction as the symbols of historical subjects by feminist historians from the 1960s to the present. The question of how true a hegemonic concept is to historical subjects' "real, material" daily lives continues to haunt feminist history. It is, perhaps, the wrong question. As historical forces entirely imbricated with daily practice, systems of social meanings are cultural actors that daily affect and effect a society's reproduction and disruption, whether or not they are 'accurate.'

From the late 1960s through the early 1980s, feminist historians by and large understood mid-nineteenth-century changes in production and labor as creating a rigid gendered division of labor, positioning men and women in separate spheres of both economic and social life. Their narrative went as follows: As men's labor became overwhelmingly market-oriented and increasingly occurred in public venues rather than at home, women's work became not only different from men's, but invisible and therefore less valued. In their relegation to the home, women suffered a loss in the status of their labor. At the same time, their status increased and solidified in the moral realm. As "angels of the household," women provided a respite and sanctuary from the market's encroachment. This narrative focuses on changes in institutional practices and regulations. That is, it focuses on changes in daily gendered practice that demarcate and are delimited by changes in the contemporary institutions of the family and the economy. Systems of social meanings are broached solely as tools existing to promote the already given institutional structure. Four typical and well-respected versions of this familiar narrative follow, each one slightly different:

> Family and economy began to emerge as distinct spheres characterized by distinct relationships. Each had a positive content of its own and was recognized as an important and integral part of social life. The sphere of commodity production was characterized by exchange relationships between property owners; it was a sphere in which individuals sought their fortunes and determined themselves, a sphere of impersonal, *quid pro quo* relationships and competition. The home became a familial sphere; it became the sphere of personality formation and of the emotional bond of love, the sphere where particular personalities mattered and were appreciated, the sphere of sharing rather than competition. (Matthaei 1982, 114)

> By the middle of the nineteenth century the . . . middle-class northern woman had seen a . . . transformation occur in her home: formerly an important part of a communal productive process under her direction, it had become a place where her children stayed before they began to work and where her husband rested after the strain of labor. Once her family had looked to her quite literally to clothe and feed them; now they expected a complex blend of nurture and escape from her "voluntary" care. (Douglas 1977, 48)

Women's dependence was the basis for the nineteenth-century ideology of female submission. If women were to accept that subservience, it was necessary that they internalize male dominance, rather than simply obeying men out of fear of withdrawal of economic support or the sanctions of the law. . . . [The urbanization and industrialization] process was accompanied by a gradual shift in the kind of work performed by women in the home. They continued to cook and to clean and to perform the other tasks that went into the running of a household, but the time and energy that had once been spent on directly productive work were transferred to more emotional tasks: helping their children learn the social skills that would enable them to deal with a more complex society and giving their husbands the support they demanded. Mere brandishment of male power was not enough to make women accept domesticity; they needed also to be convinced of its importance. This was the task of the guidebooks to marriage and motherhood and, more generally, of the ideology of femininity. The central elements of this ideology were, first, that children required full-time, undivided adult attention; second, that women were especially endowed to provide this care (and to create the homes that their husbands needed as well); and finally, that domesticity would shield women from the evil of the outside world and bring them status and power, mediated through their families. (Epstein 1981, 80–81)

During the years when farm households which were self-contained productive units prevailed, . . . women's economic dependency was one strand in a web of interdependence of men's and women's typical work. It was when commercial farm production augmented subsistence, master craftsmen became bosses of journeymen and replaced custom work with work for the market, and wage earning or profit taking became characteristic ways of "providing" that women's economic role appeared singular, their dependency prominent. (Cott 1977, 22)

From the mid-1980s on, feminist historians complicated this narrative. First, they noted women's active and socially acknowledged participation in shaping their family's economic and labor trajectory. Second, historians noted women's entry into an arena located between the home and the market in the new urban centers: the arena of civic associations (Ryan 1981). While welcome, both of these observations only complicated the analytic realm of

institutional practice: first, by demonstrating that activity within and between the already given institutions of the family and the economy was more
complex than previously understood; second, by introducing a new intermediary institution. The historical details of civic associations' practices forced
scholars to record the realm of social meanings, since their many cultural
events clearly navigated this space. Descriptions of civic associations' institutional practices inevitably and repeatedly mentioned their interaction with
contemporary systems of social meanings. For instance, Ryan's (1990, 173)
cogent summary of women's position in public culture from the 1820s to 1860
intertwines inextricably with the contemporary social meanings of Womanhood, especially with those of True Womanhood:

> Between 1825 and the outbreak of the Civil War, gender made a progres-
> sively more distinct and consequential impression on a remodeled public
> life. The female gender stood out in sharpest relief on ceremonial occa-
> sions, where she paraded not simply as a sexualized mark of exclusion
> but as a symbol of newly feminine civic values—chastity, sobriety, passiv-
> ity, domesticity. The new gendered typography of public culture evolved
> at a time of democratic insurgency. . . . The vast majority of the new po-
> litical actors were male and emphatically masculine—the soldiers on pa-
> rade, the manly Democrats of Tammany Hall, the breadwinners out on
> strike. But the elaboration of public politics also opened up territory for
> the expression of women's opinions, most fully enunciated by the female
> moral reformers of New York in the 1830s and 1840s. . . . The increasing
> visibility of women in public was not, however, a discrete display of pure
> sexual difference. Rather, women as a category were tightly linked with
> other social groupings, political identities, and cultural categories. . . .
> By the 1850s, gender difference was distinct and public enough to figure
> prominently in the most vitriolic local conflicts—it became intertwined
> with . . . nativism, class antagonism, and partisanship. . . . By 1860, gen-
> der had appeared on the public stage as something far more complicated
> than the simple representation of the female sex.

This description of gender on the public stage recognizes True Womanhood's national relevance to men and women alike. But it offers no way to
consider the historical effects of symbols of Womanhood apart from their
institutional deployments, even as it underscores their extra-institutional

significance. That is, it lacks any way to think about systems of social meanings as autonomous actors in and on history, and thereby falls short of its subject.

Earlier analyses of separate spheres did not sufficiently address the complexities that Ryan documented in either her pathbreaking study of Utica, New York, or her study of urban public space. But, while Ryan remarked on the "doctrine" of separate spheres and True Womanhood as cultural and historical realities, she still did not systematically integrate social meanings into the analytic framework used to narrate social change. The earlier, common argument that the diminished status of women's labor resulting from its invisibility under separate spheres led, presumably by an inherent human need for positive status in some realm, to a heightening of their moral status was unsatisfactory. And the connected argument that this moral status was accorded women because men needed a refuge from the market was simply functionalist. On the other hand, Ryan demonstrated that the reality, as opposed to the doctrine, of separate spheres was institutionally muddy, by showing that (a) women's labor was clearly still somewhat visible and critical to the present and future class position of the family and its members and that (b) women were not entirely relegated to the home. But Ryan did not ask how systems of social meanings, such as those encoded in the doctrine of separate spheres and True Womanhood, interacted with, on, and through institutional practices to generate a complex historical reality. Nonetheless, she continued to document their significant presence in civic associations' operations during this time period: "A closer look along the sidelines, at minor ceremonies, and in the iconography of parades reveals a pivotal reconfiguration of gender during the 1840s and 1850s. . . . First, women became references for the kinship ties that marked ethnic differences within the polity. Second, women were vehicles for representing incipient feminine values, especially the tenets of an emerging cult of domesticity" (1990, 53).[1]

Ryan's more complex analysis marked changes in historiographic practices that rejected earlier simplistic views of cultural or ideological forms as true measures of historical reality, "giving more attention to questions about the social relations of the sexes and treating the language of separate spheres itself as a rhetorical construction that responded to changing social and economic reality" (Kerber 1989, 21). But language, in this case expressing the doctrine of separate spheres and domesticity, does not just respond to material reality, but is inextricably entangled and interwoven with it. How humans conceive of themselves and their world shapes material reality as socioeconomic forces shape their conceptions. Women's moral existence in the domestic realm did not simply stave off the brutalities of the capitalist market. For an unsettled people, it signified the continued existence of social order in precarious socioeconomic times, allowing them the sense of social stability necessary to get through the next day. Women's discursive residence in the domestic sphere provided a last and important attachment to an earlier and much more stable social order, during a transition from agrarian domestic production to urban market reliance. And women's civic role in associations upheld and sustained True Womanhood, providing communal expressions of societal order by invoking the common values Womanhood signified.

The popular discourse of True Womanhood moored men and women alike. As a set of meanings and relations through which women and men conceived of women's existence in the social world, it was a powerful force shaping material reality, just as it is an insufficient measure of what daily life and practice actually looked like. True Womanhood was also a concept subject to change. Its social meanings were embedded in the contingencies of its own historical emergence and in its play with other contemporary concepts, such as contract, property, the economy, and the nation, which themselves were historically and discursively embedded.

In renarrating the conceptual relations of Womanhood in the antebellum United States, I consider the analytical and political implications of understanding social meanings as societal structures that are as important as and entirely interimplicated with institutions and daily practice in the travels and travails of contingent history and social movement. I propose an analytical framework of structural aporias, or a structural aporetic analytic, as a way to read history for the embedded and interwoven cultural and institutional structures while paying equally close attention to the always existing supplement of any structure—the step beyond societal structures into an abyss that is constitutive of those very structures. A careful reading of the discourse of antebellum Womanhood demonstrates the myriad ways that what have conventionally been understood as "material" social movements and social histories cannot exist distinct from "cultural" relations embedded in a society's conceptual systems. Part I provides an overview of the terrain of antebellum Womanhood: its social meanings; its legal, economic, and familial practices; its deployment by the antebellum woman's rights movement; and the dramatic changes it underwent between the mid-1840s and the early 1860s. It also provides an overview of the analytical and political claims at stake in this sociological study and lays out my concept of structural aporias.

Chapter 1

TRUE WOMANHOOD, THE ECONOMY, AND WOMAN'S RIGHTS

> We might share, with the late Theodore Parker, a
> prejudice against woman's occupancy of the so-
> called manual fields of production; but we should
> still have to be informed of the impropriety of her
> holding in her hand a clean bank note, and hold-
> ing it in her own name, if she pleases, and on the
> NATIONAL WOMAN'S RIGHTS BANK. I would not
> have her hold it as gracelessly as the male miser,
> but with sufficient firmness to be able to "keep in
> her own proper sphere," and save herself from the
> possible lordship of man or the rights of a privi-
> leged angel; from the contingency of being driven
> into the streets for bread, and thus becoming ei-
> ther a female drudge, or a gilded prostitute.
>
> —BRYAN J. BUTTS, *MATERIAL INDEPENDENCE
> OF WOMAN,* 1871

THIS BOLD CALL FOR WOMAN'S ECONOMIC INDEPEN-
dence, issued in 1871,[1] declares a distinctly new conception of
Womanhood—a version of Womanhood just taking hold on a
wider historical canvas. Previously, in the antebellum United
States, the very idea that Woman might engage in independent

economic activity was anathema to any understanding of her "keep[ing] in her own proper sphere." The reigning conception of Womanhood implicitly but significantly placed her outside of the economic and market spheres—spheres crucial to a new social order being defined by the rise of industrial capitalism in the Northeast. The popular imagination could not conceive of a reputable Woman who paid attention to financial or business matters, even domestically. Any suggestion that Woman might engage with economic matters required that its very possibility be demonstrated in surrounding arguments, constructing an understanding of how a Woman might take economic action and yet remain reputable—how she might remain a True Woman. But Butts's 1871 declaration includes no such argument. In fact, he positions Woman's financial independence and economic action as central to maintaining her dignity in daily life, claiming that she should "[hold] in her hand a clean bank note, and [hold] it in her own name . . . with sufficient firmness to be able to . . . save herself from the possible lordship of man . . . [and] from the contingency of being driven into the streets for bread." His implicit, and accurate, assumption that the public could make sense of this juxtaposition without further discussion marks a social change of great significance.

For the last decade of the antebellum era, from 1848 to 1860, a woman's rights movement demanded women's rights of contract and suffrage. While defined as a national movement by both contemporaries and its own literature, its members were primarily northern women, though the southern Grimke sisters were just two among many exceptions. In demanding property rights, broader rights of contract, and suffrage, it fought for women's and Woman's right to be a legitimate economic and civil actor and a legitimate political actor. Resisting and reshaping the figure of Woman inscribed in an increasingly national discourse of True Womanhood—usually described by historians as a belief system that prescribed and proscribed respectable femaleness during the antebellum and postbellum periods (see, for instance, Newman, 1999, 32)—comprised an integral but often ignored portion of the movement's struggle. The antebellum woman's rights movement's entwined challenge to the figure of the True Woman and fight for women's economic and contractual rights would prove as revolutionary as contemporary challenges to the tenets of slavery.

To a great extent, the mid-nineteenth-century nation drew on the cultural site of True Womanhood and, specifically, its placement of Woman outside the market economy as one of the few stable points in a time of dramatic social changes—a time during which social disorder seemed a constant danger.[2] Accordingly, the cultural legibility of Butts's pamphlet and others like it suggests that popular codes of Womanhood had been at least partially rewritten by 1871. His line of argument assumes a popular imagination that could conceive of economic conduct and self-sufficiency as aspects of reputable Womanhood. Butts assumes that a relationship between a True Woman and the economy is no longer unthinkable in and of itself, and instead that the critical issues to be considered are how exactly this relationship will be defined and what its delimitations and demarcations will be. Further on, he addresses the ubiquity and scale of questions regarding the boundaries of Woman's reputation and economic action: "It is our purpose to put into the mouths of all the women in the nation the effectual reply: '*We will support ourselves, Gentlemen!*' To this end, we hail an increase of wages and time for self-culture for both sexes, which will tend to render labor honorable" (Butts 1871, 13).

In this woman's rights agenda, not only would women become economically self-sufficient across the country, but the very status of labor performed outside of the domestic arena—the form that labor was increasingly taking in a burgeoning capitalist economy—would become honorable for all, men and women alike. The moments that would define Woman's new relation to the economy would also redefine the economy's relation to humanity by making ignoble industrial and commercial work reputable. Reshaping the relations between Womanhood, contract, and the economy so that women could hold an acceptable place as both laborers and autonomous economic agents would, by definition, necessitate a restructuring of the nineteenth-century economy and concomitant systems of social meanings, reordering both the political economy and the moral economy of the times. Redefining Woman's position would reorder the capitalist economy, the disorienting rise of which had thrown society in and out of financial panics and thrown families and individuals in and out of poverty throughout the 1800s. Butts's address recognizes True Womanhood's centrality to contemporary understandings of the nation and the economy. It further recognizes that changes in the social meanings of any one of these categories would implicate the others and would effect significant changes in the meanings of people's daily lives and the broader social world.

The antebellum woman's rights movement tacitly recognized the same complexities of social meaning surrounding Womanhood in its various forms of activism, and, as a result, it had already effected important shifts in Womanhood's relation to the economy and the nation by 1871. Butts's pamphlet handily lays out crucial aspects of the terrain on which these social meanings had played out and would continue to play out. But his clarity was possible only because certain underlying assumptions of the antebellum social order—assumptions that required that they remain unspoken for their effectiveness—had already been explicitly challenged and powerfully rewritten by the antebellum woman's rights movement. And the movement's success was possible only because a fortuitous concatenation of social forces and events joined it in applying pressure to the stabilizing, yet inherently unstable, gendered assumptions that lay at the heart of modern democracy and capitalist economy. In combination, these forces produced interimplicated ruptures in social meanings and institutions of the time, reshaping the complex relations between Womanhood, property, contract, the economy, and the nation.

READING HISTORY ASUNDER

The antebellum United States was a place of dramatic social transformations. People across what we now understand to be the United States— states and continental territories alike—reaped the benefits of new railroad and canal transportation. New forms of manufacturing provided increased material wealth and access to the basics of subsistence. At the same time, industrialization and the new forms of transportation dramatically transformed cities, towns, and rural areas in other ways. Not only people traveled by rail and waterway; consumer goods, foodstuffs, raw materials, and cultural goods, such as newspapers, pamphlets, magazines, and novels, also did. These reading materials—combined with traveling speaker circuits and a greater ability of the general citizen to travel from place to place— transmitted cultural ideas and beliefs from region to region at a rate and intensity unprecedented in American history. In the midst of this growth and change, and in fact because of it, the country was repeatedly shaken by economic crises. In addition, social movements such as woman's rights and abolition took root in this rich climate and were ultimately successful. To anyone versed in the time, this is a familiar tale told in a familiar fashion—

a story of change driven by industrial and technological innovation. Social histories are generally framed, as most stories are, for narrative coherence. But structuring a narrative in this way holds particular implications when the stories are histories. It means that histories are usually written in a way that makes society's changes from one point in time to another seem cohesive when they may not be and favors a history of progressions—whether of rationality, Western-style democracy, or human ethics. While understandings of history as progressive have fallen out of fashion over the past several decades and sociologists and historians have accepted that discontinuous shifts and ruptures play a crucial role in the path societies take, nonprogressive history remains difficult to narrate. In this book, I propose a new conceptual approach to thinking about society—one that seeks out moments of rupture in imbricated social meanings and institutions, and through it renarrates the successful struggles of the 1850s woman's rights movement. This renarration approaches history by what, in another context, Jonathan Arac (2006) calls "reading asunder."[3]

The familiar history of the antebellum period is, in part, a product of the conceptual and theoretical frames through which it has been viewed and told. In the following pages, this familiar history is retold; it is reimagined with a different narrative focus and a different conceptual frame. On a broad scale, I ask, What happens if we renarrate histories to focus on social rupture instead of social coherence and to emphasize the interimplication of shifts in the conceptual and material underpinnings of society? On a narrower scale, I probe the historical minutiae of a particular societal moment of transformation—the northern United States from 1848 to 1860—for insight into how processes of societal rupture and transformation work through systems of social meanings and institutions that are intertwined at the level of their very constitution. Specifically, I renarrate the place in antebellum America of the 1850s woman's rights movement, paying attention to the economic, industrial, and legal changes of the day as well as the movement's entanglement with the language of True Womanhood and popular conceptions of Womanhood, contract, the economy, and the nation. Focusing on the space occupied by white women of the middling-classes, I plumb New York State legislative debates as well as pamphlets, speeches, petitions, and newspaper reports of the 1850s woman's rights movement. By reviewing this historical information in a new conceptual context—through a theory of what I call structural aporias—we can see shifts and ruptures in the antebellum social order taking place before our eyes. While the historical "facts" are not always new, exploring them from this new theoretical perspective lays bare social processes operating during one moment of historical rupture in a way previously unnarrated.

Until the past twenty years, studies of feminist movement and organizing left the 1850s woman's rights movement largely unwritten or treated it as a minor footnote to later efforts. Histories of feminism had tended to assimilate all nineteenth-century woman's rights struggles into a progressive trajectory of struggle for suffrage, influenced in great part by the early and voluminous *History of Woman Suffrage,* a history of women's struggles from 1838 to 1920 compiled by leading female activists in the late nineteenth and early twentieth centuries once suffrage had become their central battle (E. C. Stanton, Anthony, and Gage 1889/1970).[4] As late as the mid-1980s, most studies of women's nineteenth-century activism focused on narrowly defined antecedents to woman's suffrage, including these activists' abolition work (Berg 1978; Bolt 1993; DuBois 1978, 1998; Flexner 1959; Kugler 1987; Melder 1964; O'Neill 1969), and mostly neglected the 1850s movement. In the 1980s, scholars in a number of fields began to write subtle social histories of women in the nineteenth century. Their detailed analyses of the importance of women's complex inter- and intraclass relations to nineteenth-century social transitions provided a much needed historical backdrop to any study of how women's activism affected antebellum social meanings and institutions (Baker 1984; Epstein 1981; Ginzberg 1986, 1990; Hewitt 1984; Ryan 1981). In addition, several legal histories of women's antebellum struggles for economic rights provided the minute details of how marriage law fit into the legal system's day-to-day operations and the specific ways women had to engage the legal system in their attempts to change property laws, as well as how those narrowly legal battles progressed (Basch 1982; Chused 1983, 1985; Rabkin 1975, 1980; Shammas 1994; Speth 1982; Thurman 1966; Warbasse 1987).[5]

Over the past decade, scholarship began to refocus on the antebellum woman's rights movement. In resurrecting the movement as worthy of sustained attention on its own terms, scholars analyzed the philosophical antecedents in play in the movement's claims to individual freedom, equality, and rights (Hoffert 1995); examined women's legislative petitions for economic rights from before 1848 as a case study in the relationship between civic membership and legal rights (Ginzberg 2005); traced the international origins and networks of the movement (Anderson 2000); depicted how antebellum women's acts of petitioning served as a way of writing themselves into legitimate political subjecthood (Zaeske 2003); emphasized the broad political and cultural critique at the movement's core (Isenberg 1998); and compiled useful texts combining overarching analysis with primary documents from the time period that were not previously easily accessible (McClymer 1999; Sklar 2000). Reva B. Siegel (1994) worked to reclaim the radical nature of the movement's economic arguments by analyzing external demands and internal discussions.

Still, the 1850s woman's rights movement has not fully gained recognition as not only one among many moments of women's organizing, but one that forced a fundamental shift in foundational societal structures—in imbricated social meanings and institutions—and one without which suffrage could not have been achieved.[6] I aim to refocus attention on the antebellum movement from this perspective. In doing so, my work stands on the conceptual shoulders of scholars whose work did not speak directly or solely to the 1850s, but provided a foundation for rethinking the importance of refiguring social meanings of womanhood, and its crucial imbrications within a larger web of social meanings, to our daily lived experience and the structures of the societal institutions in which we live that experience. Denise Riley (1988, 1992) persuasively demonstrated how meanings of "woman" or "women" not only differ by time and place but always exist only in relation to an entire discursive field of social meanings. Carroll Smith-Rosenberg (1985), Linda K. Kerber (1980, 1997), Joan B. Landes (1988), and Joan Scott (1989, 1992) traced reconstitutions of conceptions of womanhood and examined the discursive operation of gender in historical context. Avery Gordon (1997) and Robyn Weigman (1995) powerfully showed how these historically constructed discursive fields daily haunt the social meanings and institutional practices of our lives and matrices of desire. Equally important, Amy Dru Stanley (1998, ix) traced the nineteenth-century rise of and changes undergone in "contract as a worldview ... [that] transcended the boundaries of law as a basic participatory act and meaning in daily social life." Others examined the gendered intertwining of marriage, citizenship, and the nation in United States history (Cott 2000; Kerber 1998) and intricately traced some of the imbrications of womanhood, race, empire, and nation in the late nineteenth-century United States (Newman 1999). Through their labors, these scholars, as well as many others, have helped to create a space from which this work could arise.

In renarrating the historical moment of the antebellum woman's rights movement, a number of implications unfold:

1. The successful social movements of the antebellum United States—here, the antebellum woman's rights movement and the subsequent movement for suffrage—did not progressively extend democratic right or principle or humanitarianism to those previously excluded by the terms of the social contract. In fact, an analysis using a theoretical framework that specifically locates and traces moments of historical rupture demonstrates that a dramatic reordering of society was required for women to gain economic and contractual rights and, in turn, suffrage.

2. In successful social movements, cultural goals and tactics are entirely imbricated with material goals and tactics; they are so interimplicated as to be inseparable. In my terms, successful social movements are fully discursive. From this perspective, struggles over social and collective meanings must always be conceptualized as an integral and interwoven part of social movements rather than as separate "cultural politics." The 1850s movement for Woman's economic rights had explicitly material goals. Yet, a renarration of its history demonstrates that it fully interimplicated the cultural with the political economic. *In other words, the 1850s woman's rights movement was not simply engaged in a material and legal struggle, as a battle for economic rights is usually understood, but was necessarily engaged in a discursive struggle over the very conception of Womanhood and its relation to contract, the economy, and the nation—that is, the popular conception of Woman's place in the daily social order.* This renarrated history speaks to cultural analysts, social movement strategists, and political economists. It reveals the importance of an imbricated analysis of culture and political economy to a greater understanding of the parameters of and faults in a polity, in which all of these social thinkers are critically interested.

My analytic framework—a theory of how structural aporias found social meanings and institutions—borrows notions of how language acts or performs from the humanities and from literary theory to focus on the role of discursive politics. The resulting interdisciplinary theory frames the very questions I ask of the historical material with respect to antebellum gendered social orders, disorders, and reorderings, thereby reshaping the familiar historical narrative. In many ways, the interdisciplinary theory proposed in this book is specifically sociological, as understood since Emile Durkheim wrote in the 1700s. That is, it recognizes that society operates on a level distinct from its individual subjects and, in fact, partially constitutes their individuality through its very workings. While political and economic institutions and social meanings make up the moments of our daily lives and are established, in some sense, by us, they operate apart from us and according to very different rules or parameters. A structural aporetic analytic performs a close reading of social systems understood as entities unto themselves, but with a focus on rupture and discontinuity rather than on social coherence. A number of the book's further implications extend from this theoretical frame:

3. Societies are necessarily built on impasses, or 'structured-in' gaps, in both their systems of political and economic relations and the systems of meanings that make the world understandable and livable on a daily basis. Foundational impasses necessarily stabilize and undergird societies, even in their very instability. A societal unconscious of sorts is located in these 'structured-in' gaps—a societal unconscious that is not a generalized psychology, but a space where the social meanings and political and economic institutions that found and hold together a society turn back on themselves as a necessary condition of that society's very existence. These might also be sites where social hauntings take hold. In my terms, societies are founded on structural aporias.

4. Potential points of rupture can be located for a given polity through a close reading of the polity's foundational impasses—specifically, the foundational impasses inherent in congruent social meanings and political economic institutions. In other words, the relation between a society's systems of social meanings and its political economic institutions crucially affects where its historical and future points of rupture—irruptive and disruptive—are located. For instance, such a reading demonstrates that, in Anglo-based constitutional democracies, fundamental

impasses relevant to women's economic rights inhere in the founding myths of the social contract and the legal and economic founding of marriage and contracts. In addition, (a) both cultural and material conditions of possibility must pertain at a given time for a social movement to have the potential for success. Further, (b) these necessary cultural and material conditions of possibility are fully interimplicated. In other words, (a) how social meanings are related to each other at the time—through the contemporary systems or webs of social meanings— is as important to a particular movement's potential for success as the relations between economic and political institutions. Further, (b) at a particular historical moment, systems of relations between social meanings are entirely imbricated with political and economic institutional systems. More specifically, (a) for the antebellum woman's movement, the popular understandings of Womanhood, property, contract, the economy, and the nation and the relations between these conceptual systems were as important as how the legal and economic structure of marriage, the gendered industrial and domestic economy, and the operations of a constitutional democratic political system were interrelated at the time. This is because (b) the relations of meanings between Womanhood, property, contract, the economy, and the nation were fundamentally interwoven with the relations between the legal and economic structure of marriage, the gendered industrial and domestic economy, and the operations of a constitutional democratic political system.

5. Conditions of possibility for a social movement's success can be historically understood by seeking the shape taken by a society's 'structured-in' gaps, or foundational impasses, at the particular time of interest. Foundational impasses shift and irrupt over time in response to societal pressures, such as social movements. While the social meanings and political and economic institutions fundamental to the stability of a particular society can be ascertained through a close reading of that society's foundational impasses, their relations to each other take different shapes over time, as pressure is placed on and plays through the impasses. Analyzing conditions of possibility for a social movement's success requires a careful historical reading of these relations. In other words, the conditions of possibility for the success of the ante-

bellum struggle for Woman's economic rights can be understood only by analyzing the effects of numerous contemporary social pressures playing on both the social meanings and political and economic insti- tutions, and thereby shaping the relations between Womanhood and the economy. For instance, the effects of increased regional and inter- state commerce on legal definitions of the family economy; the effects of a legislative reform movement on legal understandings and regula- tion of contract, property, and marriage relations; the effects of a gen- dered morality underlying the conceptual stability of the nation on the consequences of increased commerce and the legislative reform move- ment; the effects of increased ease of transportation on interstate re- gional and national trade in raw materials and industrial products, and also on the spread of an interstate regional and national web of social meanings.

Careful structural aporetic analysis of specific historical moments allows greater understanding of how various historical ruptures have reshaped a society's foundational impasses and thereby shifted current conditions of possibility for disruptive change, providing a useful "history of the present" to current social movement strategists, social historians, political econo- mists, and cultural critics.

ANTEBELLUM SOCIAL MEANINGS: TRUE WOMANHOOD,
THE ECONOMY, AND THE NATION

From the 1820s to the 1860s—a period notable for the rise of capitalist econ- omies of production, labor, and trade—the northern United States experi- enced dramatic economic, social, and legal restructurings as well as rapidly shifting cultural meanings and practices (Berthoff 1971; Brownlee 1988; Cook 1981; Douglas 1977; Horwitz 1977; Lebergott 1984; Lerner 1967, 1979; McGrane 1924; North 1961; Rabkin 1980; Ryan 1971, 1975, 1981; Temin 1969; Van Vleck 1967). Concomitant with drastic societal change in so many are- nas, a stabilizing conception of gendered identity—True Womanhood— gained increasing cultural hegemony. In a period of dramatically expand- ing cultural media, women's magazines, books, and religious tracts, as well as speeches and sermons, inculcated a perception of the True Woman's morality as the one remaining stable, even sanctified site in a nation rocked by change, while industrialism came to be understood as endangering the honor previously imparted by labor and business (Douglas 1977; Ryan 1971, 1975; Welter 1966, 1976).

Ever since Barbara Welter's first salvo in 1966, when she defined a nineteenth-century "cult of True Womanhood" as having prescribed women's continued cultivation of "four cardinal virtues—piety, purity, submissiveness and domesticity" (152), historians have asked: Was True Womanhood real? And, if so, in what sense? What power did these antebellum and Victorian social meanings wield? Over the years, True Womanhood has been evaluated as an ideology against the daily lived reality of women's lives (Cogan 1989; DuBois, Buhle, Kaplan, Lerner, and Smith-Rosenberg 1980; Kerber 1989; Lerner 1979; Norton 1979; Rosenberg 1982; Ryan 1971, 1981; Sklar 1973). Regardless, antebellum literature across genres bears witness to the definitional parameters of the True Woman as described by Welter—characteristics whose amalgam, I contend, formed a Morality of Durkheimian proportions. That is, this morality—the system of social meanings embedded and embodied in the True Woman—served as a fundamental site of social cohesion for the burgeoning nation. And this social cohesion operated through the congruent 'structured-in' gaps apparent in the social meanings of Womanhood and the legislation of women's legitimacy as economic, civil, and political subjects and actors. True Womanhood's position in the contemporary system of social meanings meant that how it was figured and refigured played a crucial part in potential and actual societal ruptures during this period. I simply use Welter's original discussion and the ensuing debates as a touchstone from which to begin renarrating gender, contract, the economy, and the nation in the 1850s rather than engaging with them intensively (although a few points are taken up in greater detail below).

During the antebellum era, the True Woman was popularly conceived as a specifically raced and classed reputable Woman: white and of the middling or upper classes. Nonetheless, this understanding of Womanhood maintained a powerful sway even over those excluded from its definitional matrix, particularly in their attempts to stake a claim to social legitimacy and the political, economic, and cultural agency it afforded. For instance, Hazel Carby (1987, 6) documents how African American women used slave narratives and fiction to recharacterize both their own lives and conceptions of True Womanhood, thereby enabling (self-)perceptions of themselves distinct from those propagated by the dominant discourse and "produc[ing] an alternative discourse of black womanhood." The explicitness of the rhetoric of True Womanhood shocks today, from the perspective of a post–civil rights and post–women's movement era that uses more subtle linguistic forms of racism, sexism, and classism. To *truly* be a woman, one had to display certain qualities of character and, at the same time, embody certain delimited racial and socioeconomic positions. Contemporaries deployed this discourse not simply to define some as more or less womanly than others, but to define some as Woman and others as *not Woman*. For instance, in 1853, when prostitution among urban working-class women was believed to be a flourishing occupation that supplemented meager incomes (Dall 1867/1972), woman's rights activist Theodore Parker preached a sermon destined to be published and widely distributed as a *Woman's Rights Tract*. In it, he describes Womanhood's sacred and color-demarcated circle while explicitly removing prostitutes from it: "Look at the riches, and the misery; at the 'religious enterprise,' and the heathen darkness; at the virtue, the decorum and the beauty of woman well-born and well-bred—and at the wild sea of prostitution, which swells and breaks and dashes against the bulwarks of society—every ripple was a woman once!" (21–22). His language is telling. Even this staunch woman's rights advocate juxtaposes what is a Woman—the *virtue and decorum* defining Womanhood itself—against what *was a woman once:* an illicit sexuality, a *heathen* nature, and a *darkness.* And he notes that these waves of fallen once-women threaten society's very existence; society must protect itself against their intrinsic onslaught as they *break and dash against its bulwarks.* He also specifically names the three markers of an evolving American understanding of race, which opposed sexual, heathen, colored races to a pure, Christian, white race (Jordan 1969), and which opposed the growing, immigrant-based working class to the nativist middling and upper classes. In doing so, he produces an understanding of Woman's rights as a particular amalgam of race- and class-based Womanhood by deploying the popular understanding of True Womanhood, or of Womanhood at all.

At the same time, there occurred both vast transformations in the gendered economic order—as men took on the economic roles of laborer, clerk, entrepreneur, or professional, and women's labors at home continued apace but with decreasing visibility as productive labor—and an increased emphasis on the domestic realm as a specifically female-created *moral* realm (Matthaei 1982; Ryan 1981). Although overly simple, the idea of separate spheres is a useful starting point here, as the most popularly known framing of antebellum women's relation to the economy (or lack thereof). Its basic idea, professed and advised in women's literature and asserted with vitriol in response to woman's rights claims, was shaped by the economic and demographic changes of the time: Men would leave the home to labor, often in industrial or new commercial service settings, and women would maintain the home as a blissful, domestic refuge for the men to return to, allowing them to escape the evils of the new order—that is, the evils of industrial and commercial capitalism (Christ 1977; Conway 1982; Cott 1977; Degler 1980a, 1980b; Douglas 1977; A. D. Gordon and Buhle 1976; Ryan 1971; Sklar 1973; Welter 1966, 1976). In recent work, feminist historians have clearly documented the ways in which these separate spheres were actually not so separate, even in white middling-class households (see, for instance, Ryan 1981, 1990). Women's productive labor distinctly altered family members' life courses, and often what constituted the domestic sphere would today be called a business: running a laundry or a boardinghouse. In addition, women actively participated in the public sphere in both benevolent and civic associations.

But 1850s discourse defined the home as the preeminent moral realm and the True Woman as the purveyor of its morality. (Just to be clear, throughout this book, the term "discourse" does not mean "rhetoric" as commonly used—that is, ways of speaking and forms of language in and of themselves. Discourse refers here to the complex and interimplicated operations of (a) central societal institutions [in this case, economic and legal institutions], and (b) the systems of social meanings that figure subjecthood in any given social order.) In a time of insecurity amid wrenching social change, contemporary discourse constructed the domestic sphere as the sole respite from a social order that had otherwise strayed from traditional moral strictures and structures and the True Woman as its sole possible sustainer. In these times of social turmoil, the social meanings of True Womanhood were perhaps much more important than whether individual women filled specific physical domiciles with domestic bliss. And what a True Woman could not do was participate in the economy, in the economic realm. It is important to note: The relation between contract and property resides at the center of capitalist democracy as we understand it today and as it was coming into being in the 1800s. No one could or can participate economically unless they had or have full rights of contract, not just the right to own property or just the right to participate. The rights of contract that underlie legitimate economic, civil, and political participation in this social system were precisely the rights that a True Woman could not exercise and that women did not legally hold. This delimitation was even more notable for its unspoken status in the vast literature on social meanings of True Womanhood.

An 1832 sermon delivered by Reverend Joseph Richardson served as an early paean to the developing economic and moral divisions of labor:

> The pursuits and enterprizes of life necessarily call men abroad and demand their attention. They are formed for a different sphere of duty and care. Beyond the domestic circle they have many hardships and conflicts to endure, which the utmost prudence and forethought can not render always easy to meet. God and nature designed that there should be a faithful "keeper at home," where are weighty cares. . . . Keepers at home—presiding angels of the sanctuary of virtue, and love, and peace! . . . "Keeper at home," of the refuge of the partner often worn down with toil; of the weary and sorrowful; keeper of the refuge, where the bleeding heart may find healing from God, administered by the kindest hands and holiest affections. (10)

We can usefully imagine the antebellum white, middling-class family as inhabiting a domicile that had been dislodged from the solid earth of traditional practices and understandings, pitching and rocking as it lurched forward in the rapids of an uncharted river toward untold rocks, outcroppings, and cliffs ahead. Their only foreseeable hope for survival was that the sheer force of the culture of True Womanhood could hold the home's construction together. In this way, the prevailing powers of True Womanhood did much more than simply prescribe or proscribe women's proper constitution and behavior. Rather, the shared meanings and culture of True Womanhood comprised one of the strongest threads in contemporary understandings of the nation's fabric. Equally, any challenge to the reigning tenets of True Womanhood constituted much more than an attack on appropriate behavior for women. Much of the antebellum population truly experienced such challenges as dangers to the nation.

A Woman, suffused with True Womanhood, cumulatively affected the nation through the mechanism of her Woman's Influence. Whereas men exercised their authority and power politically and economically, women were understood to exercise their power appropriately through the moral and emotional aspects of personal relations, culminating in their influence on those with whom they interacted. Of necessity, a Woman's Influence affected primarily her family and relatives, but it also operated on friends and their families as well as, importantly, those visited in acts of benevolence (Alcott (1850); Douglas (1977); Sigourney 1836/1841; Tuthill 1848). Woman's Influence extended the postrevolutionary ideology of Republican Motherhood, under which women should educate themselves in order to exercise political power by raising their sons to be good and active citizens (Anon. 1840; Douglas 1977; Hoffert 1995; Kerber 1980). In the 1840s, Catherine Beecher, an early advocate of women's education and an active force in the creation of women's seminaries and the training of female teachers to be sent west, emphasized that women's education would afford the True Woman the ability to have an even more intelligent and moral effect on the national population than she already did:

> Now, Providence ordains that, in most cases, a woman is to perform the duties of a mother. Oh, sacred and beautiful name! How many cares and responsibilities are connected with it! And yet what noble anticipations, what sublime hopes, are given to animate and cheer! She is to train young minds, whose plastic texture will receive and retain each impress for eternal ages, who will imitate her tastes, habits, feelings, and opinions; who will transmit what they receive to their children, to pass again to the next generation, and then to the next, until a *whole nation* will have received its character and destiny from her hands. . . . Now every woman whose intellect and affections are properly developed is furnished for just such an illustrious work as this. (1846, 11)

Beecher also understood domesticity, one of the founding moral traits of True Womanhood, not only as a refuge from the new masculine-gendered morality of commercialism and acquisition, but also as a model that would re-create the very values of True Womanhood in the national sphere. Representing popular conceptions of Womanhood, she averred that the True Woman's submission to her husband provided an ideal framework for men's relation to their government that would further stability in a democratic social order (Sklar 1973, 161). Similarly, Lydia H. Sigourney (1838, 17–18), in her *Letters to Mothers,* proclaimed that as a True Woman's Influence flowed through a mother's labors, it would reproduce in her children the very aspects of Woman's morality appropriate to all—that is, piety and purity: "As the termites patiently carry grains of sand, till their citadel astonishes the eye, as the coral insect toils beneath the waters, till reef joins reef, and islands spring up with golden fruitage and perennial verdure, so let the mother, 'sitting down or walking by the way,' in the nursery, the parlour, even from the death-bed, labour to impress on her offspring that goodness, purity and piety, which shall render them acceptable to society, to their country, and to their God." In other words, through Woman's Influence, True Womanhood not only created a moral and safe home environment but also perpetuated and sustained morality throughout the generations. Viewing the social meanings of True Womanhood in this light gives new meaning to Welter's (1966, 152) claim that "it was a fearful obligation, a solemn responsibility, which the nineteenth-century American woman had—to uphold the pillars of the temple with her frail white hand." Under the prevailing system of social meanings, the hope for a future not bereft of values rested with the True Woman. Her protected character sustained the larger morality of the nation, its very social cohesion. In fact, postbellum middle-class white women would effectively use their status as "the symbolic representatives and upholders of civilization" to make their Influence understood as key to the success of U.S. colonization efforts—whether of Native Americans, freed African Americans, Mexicans, or unfavored European immigrants—by positioning themselves as what Newman (1999, 25) calls "civilization-workers."

On the other hand, by 1850 the woman's rights movement was underway, with its beginnings usually dated from the Woman's Rights Convention held at Seneca Falls, New York, in 1848—although historians have recently broadened the scope of its inception from the mid-1840s to 1850 (Ginzberg 2005; McClymer 1999). In most states at this time, married women were not legally entitled to control their personal or real (landed) property; in those states where legislation had recently enabled them to own or inherit such property, they were still not entitled to ownership of their earnings or to make contracts regarding the property they did own (Basch 1982; Hoff 1991;

Rabkin 1980; Thurman 1966; Warbasse 1987). A central goal of the 1850s woman's rights movement was for women to gain control over their property and earnings, as well as to ensure their access to earnings through access to employment. These claims to economic and property rights necessarily entailed a claim to a legitimate civil position for women through rights to contract. The movement's success would result in the passage of married women's property acts throughout the northern states. History read asunder discloses that women could not have gained economic and contractual rights without simultaneously having addressed and transformed the figure of True Womanhood, which defined Woman as one who existed solely in a moral and domestic sphere and specifically as uncontaminated by economic interest or activity. Popular fear of the slightest economic contamination of the True Woman, and the expected resultant moral disorder, had reigned since earlier in the century. As early as 1830, Sarah Josepha Hale's distressed review of Lydia Maria Child's advice book for women, *The American Frugal Housewife,* provided a typical example. Child's book firmly kept Woman in the domestic sphere, but suggested actions she might take to help her family remain economically sound in difficult times. But Hale worried that a True Woman's purity would be tainted by even considering the diseased economic sphere: "'Our men are sufficiently money-making,' Hale argued. 'Let us keep our women and children from the contagion as long as possible'" (cited in Douglas 1977, 57). The 1850s woman's movement's response to this fear and what it represented—both a moral stricture and social structure—exhibits the address of entangled social meanings and political and economic institutions that constitutes fully discursive social movements.

A few brief examples are in order. Modeled upon the Declaration of Independence, the *Declaration of Sentiments,* as presented and signed at the 1848 Seneca Falls Convention, held that Woman's economic and property disabilities were among the chief wrongs done to women (Woman's Rights Convention 1848/1870b, 2). Additionally, the *Declaration* listed a number of other disabilities brought into existence at the moment of marriage, at the same time as economic and property disabilities. In doing so, it highlighted the fundamental and systematic relation between gendered economic and property relations and all gendered relations based in the marriage contract in modern Western democracies. The *Declaration* explicitly spoke to the marriage contract at length:

The history of mankind is a history of repeated injuries and usurpations on the part of man toward woman, having in direct object the establishment of an absolute tyranny over her. To prove this, let facts be submitted to a candid world. . . .

He has made her, if married, in the eye of the law, civilly dead.

He has taken from her all right in property, even to the wages she earns.

He has made her, morally, an irresponsible being, as she can commit many crimes with impunity, provided they be done in the presence of her husband. In the covenant of marriage, she is compelled to promise obedience to her husband, he becoming, to all intent and purposes, her master—the law giving him power to deprive her of her liberty, and to administer chastisement.

He has so framed the laws of divorce, as to what shall be the proper causes of divorce; in case of separation, to whom the guardianship of the children shall be given; as to be wholly regardless of the happiness of women—the law, in all cases, going upon a false supposition of the supremacy of man, and giving all power into his hands. (2–3)

One of the earliest National Woman's Rights Conventions was held in Syracuse, New York, in 1852. Participants proffered numerous resolutions as statements of their sentiments and avowed activist energies. Aside from denouncing taxation without representation, they insisted on economic and property rights:

Resolved, that the right of human beings to their own persons, their own earnings and property, and to participate in the choice of their civil rulers, are rights which belong as naturally, absolutely and fully to woman as to man. . . .

Whereas, modern society is such that human freedom, in its best sense, can only be secured by pecuniary independence,

Therefore—

Resolved, That every woman should engage herself in Literature, the Fine Arts, Professions, Agriculture, Commerce, or whatever honorable occupation best adapted to her capabilities, that she may thus remove the stain from labor, and work out her own emancipation. (Woman's Rights Convention 1852b, 16, 23–24)

During the same convention, Abby Price, a well-known activist, invoked and refigured True Womanhood to argue for woman's rights outside of the domestic sphere: "Doomed, as girls are, to a frivolous, objectless existence, how can we expect to see any where flourishing the sterling qualities of a true and aspiring womanhood? We know that our religious nature must be injured, for especially does the religious element need freedom of action. * * * Aid us, then, husbands, brothers, fathers, to achieve this our noble destiny. Give us, as you yourselves possess, the full possession of *all* Human Rights. Give us a chance to exercise all our varied capabilities. Allow our peculiar characters to blend with yours, socially, civilly, and religiously, for mutual benefit" (Woman's Rights Convention 1852b, 55).

Here Price claimed that Woman could reach her *noble destiny,* her *true and aspiring womanhood,* only once she was granted full *social, civil, and religious* equality. Throughout the 1850s, the woman's rights movement refigured the True Woman in speeches, petitions, resolutions, and pamphlets. In this way, woman's rights activists fought a dual and yet unified battle: (a) for economic, property and contractual rights; and (b) for a change in cultural meanings of Womanhood that would allow for their legitimate and respectable civil existence with these rights. Two decades later, Butts no longer finds it necessary to clothe his call for the *Material Independence of Woman* in the language of True Womanhood, in her moral and pious nature. He approaches the issue directly, even discussing the difficulty of doing so (which can be read as an aside on the two prior decades of discussion and the forms it had taken): "There is no cause which can take precedence of the material independence of woman; none which can more justly be clothed in the similitude of a mountain, which it is much easier to address, in eloquent apostrophe, than directly to ascend, or to penetrate with the tunnel of persistent and skillful enginery" (1871, 1–2). In his call, Butts recognizes and draws upon many of the forces that had stabilized early nineteenth-century northern society and that had become increasingly volatile as the century progressed. While he clearly refers to capitalism's power to reorder and fundamentally disorder society, he just as clearly speaks to the gendered forms political economy and moral economy took in the early to mid-nineteenth century and their roles in the process of disordering and reordering society. He invokes the True Woman's intrinsic morality and piety by crediting her movement into the economic sphere with overcoming modernity's evils by *rendering labor honorable*. And yet, in this deployment Butts assumes a radically refigured Womanhood as already culturally legible. Woman's ideal link to the moral and domestic sphere and distinct remove from capitalism's economic sphere had recently been central to any thought of Womanhood; this was the only social position in which Woman existed, from which she could sustain her required piety and purity. As the last bastion of a corroding social order, Woman's Influence grounded a stable moral order in the domestic arena, buffering the familial institution—and through it the nation itself—from the economy's encroaching disorder. But the 1850s woman's movement had successfully shifted these gendered understandings and relations, allowing Butts to assume a newly shaped Womanhood whose clearly defined autonomous position in the economic realm will dramatically undercut capitalism's inherent evil. And while this new Woman's effect on capitalism and the nation will, in part, result from the stabilizing force of her moral and pious character, it will stem from her grounding in the economic realm rather than the domestic and lead to increased wages and education for all. In other words, while Butts still draws on themes of gendered morality, he no longer needs to argue against notions either of the economy as dangerous to Womanhood or of Woman's link to the economy as a danger to the nation. Rather, he asserts the very opposite—Woman's definitional grounding in economic activity will recuperate a disordered nation—without the need to explicitly justify a dramatically refigured Womanhood.

In fact, in one instance, Butts refigures Womanhood to claim that even in the earlier popular conception of Woman's essential idealized existence she was directly linked to the economy as a material producer. In this distinctly rewritten version of the True Woman, she actually *produced* worldly *material prosperity* in her position as the moral healer of mankind: "If the husband is stimulated, as he toils in the corn field or the factory, to increased and sustained effort by visions of the approving smiles or tearful sympathy of the 'angel of the household' who will greet him at the threshold on his return from labor, *who is the chief producer?* If the coarsest muscle of the country is paralyzed in the absence of motive, or the leadership of the capitalist, what a paralysis would fall upon the very springs of material prosperity in the absence of the finer magnetism of woman!" (15). Butts then sets this idealized vision of Woman, *of the "angel of the household,"* against *the staunch woman's rights reformers* whom he names *Angels of Deliverance,* and whose economic and civil actions name them saviors of the nation:

> They will assume the reins of material as well as political power by which alone will capital be forced to take its relentless heel from the palpitating forms of the thousands of toiling women, sensitive to the woes that betide them, and trembling at those which cast their shadows before, but all unconscious of the causes of their ills, and scarcely hearing the faintest footsteps of the Angel of Deliverance! discerning the arm of the *real* oppressor, they will not shrink . . . from the sterner duty of wielding a material arm of their own, if thus they can restore the "balance of power" and hasten the footsteps of Freedom. (7–8)

In this new understanding, Woman as *Angel* will own herself and, from her new position, enable other women to own themselves. She implicitly requires the right of contract and her active existence will result in a reordered "balance of power" that genders spheres of political and moral economy in a distinctly new form. The cultural legibility of Butts's argument—one that addresses questions of *what* Woman's relation to the economy will be and *how* it will be defined rather than questions of *whether* Woman might have a different relation to the economy *at all*—powerfully demonstrates the achievements of the antebellum woman's rights movement in fundamentally redefining the cultural meanings attributed to Womanhood.

Note on Social Meanings and Social Movement: Womanhood

Social meanings of "women," or any other subject position for that matter, are neither arbitrary nor freely constructed. Similarly, a woman experiencing herself as "woman" enters into a relation with these predetermined meanings of "woman" and "women." These discursively constructed meanings are simultaneously shifting and epistemologically always already there. In other words, at the historical level they fluctuate even as they are imbricated with other historically fluctuating social concepts; whereas, at the level of the singular actor's experience and claiming of these collective identities, of these sets of social meanings and understandings, they exist as reified social objects that the actor (or movement) can accept or resist. Consequently, transformative movements are usually analyzed, in great part, as attempts to intervene in actors' predefined relations to already-existing identities and institutions. But this is a weakness of the analysis, whether by intellectuals, pundits, or activists. Denise Riley (1988, 111) demonstrates this flaw in the case of "modern feminism, which in its sociological aspects is landed with the identity of women as an achieved fact of history and epistemology, [and consequently] can only swing between asserting or refusing the completeness of this given identity." But there are more options.

Social movements in general, and feminism in particular, engage in complex discursive transformation of social orders as well as simpler identity resistance and straightforward political and economic reform. Often, they not only challenge the epistemologically "always already there" social identity that subjects claim or resist, but also challenge the historical fluctuations and figurations of these collective identities by not accepting them as always already there—perhaps especially a possibility in times of social disorder. Riley maintains that feminism ought to "suggest that 'women' don't exist—while maintaining a politics of 'as if they existed'—since the world behaves as if they unambiguously did" (112). In over a decade's worth of speeches, conventions, pamphlets, journals, and petitions, the antebellum woman's movement followed precisely this strategy in practice. They consistently challenged the culturally practiced conception of Womanhood—of True Womanhood—a shared meaning that was vital to the nation's sense of stability. At the same time, they challenged the "naturalness" of larger systems of meaning that made Womanhood a socially meaningful concept at all, threatening its fixity in a constellation that included "the nation," "the economy," "property," and "contract." The 1850s woman's rights movement not only countered contemporary definitions of Woman, but attempted to effect historical shifts in the systems of social meaning that Womanhood was "posed against, as well as established by . . . which by no means form a passive backdrop to changing conceptions of gender" (7). Woman's rights activists certainly believed that women and Woman existed, but not unambiguously; they used contemporary ambiguities of Woman to refigure Womanhood in such a way that women might legitimately participate in an emergent social world of capitalism.[7] In fact, their language, actions, and tactics can usefully be read as if they strategically practiced Riley's politics of the signifier; that is, their language, actions, and tactics had this "strategic effect," and analyzing them through this lens provides useful historical insight.[8]

The 1850s were certainly the first time in U.S. history when such broad-based cultural warfare occurred, for it was made possible only by the existence of the new modes of transportation, in particular the railroads and the Erie

Canal, that enabled speakers to travel on extensive tours of New England and New York; women and men to travel to conventions throughout New England, New York, Pennsylvania, and Ohio; and the diffusion of print media throughout New England and New York with an influx of journals, pamphlets, magazines, and books with every arrival of trains and barges. Cultural upheaval dovetailed with a general disordering and reordering of so many societal realms: economic, demographic, and legal. In this time of dramatic societal transformation, interimplications of all these changing conceptions of the social world opened up space from which a social movement might force a concomitant transformation of Woman and Womanhood.

ANTEBELLUM INSTITUTIONS: LAW, ECONOMICS, AND MARRIAGE

New legislation affecting married women's property and economic rights began to be passed throughout the northern states in the same years that the antebellum woman's rights movement became active. One of the earliest married women's property acts was passed in New York State in 1848, just months prior to the Seneca Falls convention. In the years and decades to come, other states would copy this act verbatim in their legislation (Basch 1982; Thurman 1966; Warbasse 1987). The 1848 Married Women's Property Act and its many copies gave married women the right to own real (landed) property that they brought to the marriage or inherited or were given during the marriage. Even as they owned the property, though, they could not legally manage it in any way; they could not buy or sell their property on their own, nor make any contracts regarding it. They also did not retain legal possession of any personal property, which included all monetary property and basic personal possessions such as clothing (Basch 1982; Rabkin 1980; Thurman 1966; Warbasse 1987). But by 1860, a considerably different type of property act was passed in New York State; again, it was one of the earliest of its sort. Known as the 1860 Earnings Act, it provided married women significantly more rights of property focusing on their right to contract, including legal ownership of their earnings and the rights to control their earnings and to make contracts regarding both their earnings and any other property they might own.[9]

In the United States throughout most of the nineteenth and twentieth centuries, women were expected to marry, to participate in the marital contract;

and most women did.[10] But as late as the second decade of the twentieth century in many states, when women entered into the marital contract, they lost their right to make any further legal or economic contracts. Prior to 1848, the specific and extreme disabilities of married women were very similar in states and territories that had been English colonies and stemmed directly from English common law. This is why, as state legislatures decided to address women's legal disabilities, they were often able simply to copy other states' property acts. Generally, marital law dictated that all of a woman's real and personal property, wages, rents (in the economic sense), profits, and debts became her husband's sole property at the moment of marriage.[11] A husband immediately came into complete control of the management of his wife's realty, or landed property, and could charge against it, but he could not transfer its ownership by grant or sale. Only the woman could transfer its ownership, but she needed the explicit consent of her husband to do so. And if she did transfer it with his consent, all proceeds or exchange received were legally defined as personal property (as was almost any form of property that was not landed property: finances, personal and family belongings, and even crops grown on landed property once harvested) and therefore belonged to her husband outright. When she married, a woman also lost her legal capacity to sue, contract for necessary items such as food, borrow money, obtain credit, or make a will—or she could do so only with the consent of her husband. But a single woman, or *feme sole,* could do any of this under her own name. Crimes committed by a married woman were legally assumed to be committed under the husband's influence; he was held responsible. Additionally, legal custody of children went to the husband when the couple separated or divorced, the latter of which was rare. In fact, in 1855 the U.S. Congress passed a law that effectively expanded the gendered legal state of coverture to regulate national immigration and citizenship. Approved "with no ceremony and little debate," the act's explicitly gendered particulars "declar[ed] that any woman who had married or would marry an American man gained American citizenship in doing so . . . [and] affirmed the American citizenship of children born abroad to U.S. citizen fathers, not to mothers" (Cott 1998, 1457, 1456).

Finally, benefits and responsibilities after spousal death were just as gender-differentiated. If the husband died, his widow received only one-third of all property real (landed) and personal (almost all else), even of everything she brought to the marriage or earned or inherited herself while married.

(With great generosity, the law also entitled her to what was termed "para-phernalia": a minimal amount of clothing, cookware, a bed, sewing necessi-ties, etc.) A widow was entitled to keep her one-third of the estate, however, only as long as she did not remarry; if she married again, it reverted to her deceased husband's family. Custody of the children, along with the remain-ing two-thirds of the property, was dispensed with as per the husband's will and automatically went to the husband's family if he died intestate. In stark contrast, if a married woman died, her widower continued to hold all of her personal property and realty for life, although he still could not trans-fer the title of her landed property. If and only if children had not been born into the marriage, the realty reverted back to the woman's immediate fam-ily when he died. If there were children, the widower retained custody, and her landed property remained in his family when he died.[12]

Certainly the 1848 Married Women's Property Act in New York State and all similar acts in other states—allowing women to own but not con-trol real property—served as an important legal entrance into the economic or market sphere for married women. Equally certainly, the 1860 Earnings Act in New York State and all similar acts in other states—granting mar-ried women ownership and control over and the right to contract regarding real property, personal possessions, and earnings—furthered and widened that entrance and its impact. But does this mean that the period from 1848 to 1860 witnessed the gradual entry of women into the economic realm, the sine qua non of capitalism? Not necessarily. In fact, New York legisla-tors were vehemently and vocally opposed to giving women rights to ei-ther their earnings or contract during the 1840s and much of the 1850s. How, then, did legislative opinion, economic rights, and social meanings all change dramatically in such a brief time span?

HISTORY'S SUBJECT

When read asunder, rather than for narrative coherence, the historical pe-riod from 1848 to 1860 does not exhibit a simple change in legislative opin-ion, but much more. During this time period, New York State experienced a telescoping of a much longer process occurring across the northeast-ern United States. When political and economic change came much more quickly to New York State than to the rest of the Northeast, as the Erie Canal opened and quickly transformed frontier towns into centers of commerce, contemporary gendered political and moral economies also experienced more rapid disorganization. The 1850s woman's movement existed, not co-incidentally, during these moments of dramatic disordering and reorder-ing of political, economic, and legal institutions and related systems of social meanings. And during this time it applied critical pressure to social meanings of gender, of Womanhood. These conjunctions—which both re-lied on the existence of a social movement and enabled effects of a social movement that might not have succeeded without the imbricated political, economic, and moral conditions of the moment—performed a disruptive transformation in the very conception of Womanhood, effecting a change in the daily existence of women, men, and the nation alike. This was change wrought by a social movement that was not simply material, but discursive through and through.

In my concept of a fully discursive social movement, societal-level forces connect with individual-level performativity—as elegantly conceptualized by Judith Butler—through which we each continually remake ourselves and our social world and which holds the potential for individual resistance to normative social regimes. As Butler (1995c, 136) notes, if "gender performa-tivity involves the difficult labor of deriving agency from the very power regimes which constitute us . . . this is, oddly enough, *historical work,* re-working the historicity of the signifier." And so the historical work un-folds, beginning, in this case, with an analysis of the antebellum woman's rights movement as a fully discursive social movement and using an ana-lytic framework focused on the portions of social movements in which de-mands for institutional changes and changes in social meanings are fully interimplicated—beginning with an analysis that fruitfully reevaluates the role that women's changing economic, property, and contract rights play in the history of women's social movements and women's social existence in modern Western society.

What was previously seen as a fairly insignificant, somewhat reformist, and purely economic aspect of the history of women's movements proves ac-tually to have provoked disruptive changes in the very conception of what it might mean to legitimately be a Woman in the social world. In a groundbreak-ing and complementary study of the course of economic demands in the an-tebellum woman's rights movement,[13] Reva B. Siegel (1994, 1151) shows that a new claim had arisen by the 1870s: Woman's rights activists "increasingly argued that the deplorable state of marital property law illustrated women's need for the vote." This claim would have been culturally illegible in the 1850s. Its very rise stands as witness to the disruptive changes that the antebellum movement had been able to force in the relation between Womanhood, property, contract, the economy, and the nation. Perhaps submitting other social movements to similar scrutiny, to reevaluations focused on fully discursive struggle, will bring to light other previously neglected yet crucial historical transformations and critical present trajectories.

In chapter 2, I delineate the analytic framework of structural aporias—a framework useful in understanding the power of language to act socially—by drawing on classic deconstructionist theory as well as modernist and poststructuralist feminist theory. I use this framework to explore the discursive constructions of social orders, consisting of their foundational imbrications of social meanings and institutions along with their social origin myths. I then trace the consequent potential sites of rupture in social orders in modern Anglo-based capitalist democracies. Chapters 3 and 4 explore the gendered moral, political, and legal economies of the early- to mid-1800s United States, paying particular attention to the rise of a hegemonic discourse fully interimplicating Womanhood, property, contract, the economy, and the nation. Chapter 3 focuses more heavily on their social meanings in its presentation of the sociological panorama of Womanhood and the economy in the 1850s United States, including the pressures exerted by industrial capitalism. Chapter 4 focuses more heavily on their institutional embeddedness in its summary of the legal codification movement's effects on legal constructions of marriage and contract. Both chapters continually point to how the imbrication of these social meanings and institutions founds the antebellum social order. Chapter 5 considers the antebellum woman's rights movement's simultaneous effective refiguring of Womanhood and success in gaining women's legal rights of property and contract. As a fully discursive social movement, the 1850s woman's rights movement actively deployed and redeployed the complex sets of relations intertwining Womanhood, property, contract, the economy, and the nation in order to radically transform a modern society's foundations. My discussion draws extensively on historical and archival materials covering the antebellum woman's movement's activities (including speeches, petitions, conventions, memorials to legislatures, pamphlets, and newspapers) and contemporary legislative records (including speeches, debates, committee reports, and votes) as well as local newspaper coverage of both. This material reveals, with historical specificity, an instance in which the "material" and "cultural" struggles of a social movement were necessarily entirely interimplicated, both theoretically and practically. Finally, the conclusion considers the implications of this history, further questions arising from a structural aporetic analytic, and social movement today.

Chapter 2

READING ANTEBELLUM HISTORY APORETICALLY
Renarrating Womanhood, Property Rights,
and the 1850s Woman's Movement

DO USEFUL, ALBEIT ALTERNATIVE, SOCIOLOGICAL TALES
arise from considering the social world to consist of interimplicated institutions, practices, and webs of social meaning, or
textuality? Unequivocally, yes. To this end, I cull theories of
textuality from literary criticism, creating and deploying the
concept of structural aporias, an analytical framework that
takes seriously the effects of language upon social orders. This
is a distinctly sociological task, following in the footsteps of
Emile Durkheim (1915/1965), Durkheim and Marcel Mauss
(1963), and Michel Foucault (1972, 1970/1973, 1973/1975,
1980b, 1977/1988), who all investigated how the conjoining of
material practice and language, or material practice and representation, generates social orders.

I begin by laying out some of the concepts that sociology
can usefully garner from contemporary literary theory and
continental philosophy; in particular, I suggest that sociology
appropriate their analytic use of the concept of aporia and apply it to the underlying symbolic and institutional structures
of social orders in the guise of the structural aporia. Then I analyze a structural aporia particular to modern Anglo-based democratic social orders, focusing on private and social contracts

and their relations to legal institutions, societal origin myths, marriage, the economy, and social meanings of Womanhood. I pay special attention to the marriage contract and its relationship to the social contract and women's societal position historically. Finally, I investigate what implications arise from a historical analysis that focuses on underlying structural aporias. In particular, how does such an analysis affect our understanding of the antebellum woman's movement in New York State? And, in general, how does it affect our understanding of the relationship between social movements, historical processes, and social orders?

ENTERING THE APORETIC SPACE:
FUNDAMENTAL IMPASSES IN LANGUAGE

The terms "aporia" and "aporetic" have long-standing use in the humanities, particularly in philosophy. The word "aporia" can be traced in classical philosophy to Aristotle's *Physics IV* (Derrida 1993, 13). The word "aporetic" was declared obsolete by the *Oxford English Dictionary* in 1933, with the most recent examples given dating from the 1600s, but it was brought back to life in the 1972 *Supplement* via philosophical discussions of Plato's "aporetic dialogues" dating from 1949 (Burchfield 1972, 110). Both the definitions provided and etymological references are helpful in discerning how the term is presently used. The *OED* defines "aporia" as literally "impassable," or "to be at a loss." Elsewhere, we learn that it derived from "the Greek 'poros', passage, with preceding privative a-, meaning: without passage, blocking the flux, undecidable. Aporia has come to mean undecidability" (Godzich 1983, 39, n. 6). Philosophical arguments understood an aporia as an impasse in a logical system, an undecidable or unbridgeable space in the system of the argument, in its underlying construction.

Contemporary literary criticism and deconstruction appropriated these terms to refer to fundamental impasses in philosophical, linguistic, and textual systems. Deconstruction locates its most intensive analysis precisely in these aporetic spaces or moments. While both Paul de Man and Jacques Derrida engage in rigorous and minutely detailed textual readings, "the thread of logic leads in both cases into regions which are alogical, absurd," J. Hillis Miller writes. "Sooner or later there is the encounter with an 'aporia' or impasse. . . . In fact the moment when logic fails in their work is the moment of their deepest penetration into the actual nature of literary language, or of language as such" (cited in Culler 1982, 23). Derrida (1993, 15), in turn, has referred to his analytical terrain as "aporetology or aporetography" and has explicitly defined deconstruction "as a certain aporetic experience of the impossible." What exactly, then, do these usages of "aporia" mean in terms of literary theory, and how might they be usefully applied to sociological theory?

The simplest linguistic example of aporetic form, as utilized by deconstruction, exists wherever the literal and figural meanings of language do not coincide. The figural meaning of language can be understood as "the divergence between grammar and referential meaning" (de Man 1979, 270). In other words, a statement's grammar may produce a literal abstracted meaning that is not necessarily the same as its meaning when the statement is understood as referring to contextualized specifics. The figural dimension of language is not the specific, referential meaning of the statement, but is the *impassable gap* that exists between the statement's systematic, literal, and abstract grammar and its specific referents. The figural dimension of language comprises an *impassable gap* that is 'structured into' the working of language. It is unavoidable and yet impassable. The aporetic moment arises when, as language turns back on itself and interacts with this 'structured-in' gap, its figural meaning denies its grammatical meaning. In this case, language plays (or struggles) in the aporetic space as it continues to produce both literal, abstract, grammatical meaning and specific signification—even as the structured-in space of the multiple meanings' coexistence is not only *impassable* but also makes their coexistence *impossible*. Consequently, the aporia is a space of dynamic flux; it is an impassable space that *blocks the flux* from moving cleanly across it, keeping meaning and flux forcefully at play within it.[1]

The reader's or participant's interaction with this impassable gap in language—her interaction with the figural dimension of language—is a difficult moment and constitutes her experience of the aporia. Since aporias' impassability is structured into linguistic systems, the reader or participant necessarily experiences them as fundamental. At a fundamental level, the aporetic space engenders for the reader or participant a *radical unknowability of meaning* that, in turn, and this is crucial, is *generative of meaning*—a meaning that can be provided only from *outside of the text*. Because of its clarity and elegance, I quote Paul de Man's (1979, 9–10) explication of the aporetic rhetorical question at length:

I take [my] example from the sub-literature of the mass media: asked by his wife [, Edith,]² whether he wants to have his bowling shoes laced over or laced under, Archie Bunker answers with a question: "What's the difference?" Being a reader of sublime simplicity, his wife replies by patiently explaining the difference between lacing over and lacing under, whatever this may be, but provokes only ire. "What's the difference" did not ask for difference but means instead "I don't give a damn what the difference is." The same grammatical pattern engenders two meanings that are mutually exclusive: the literal meaning asks for the concept (difference) whose existence is denied by the figurative meaning. As long as we are talking about bowling shoes, the consequences are relatively trivial; Archie Bunker, who is a great believer in the authority of origins (as long, of course, as they are the right origins) muddles along in a world where literal and figurative meanings get in each other's way, though not without discomforts. But suppose that it is a *de*-bunker rather than a "bunker," and a debunker of the arche (or origin), an archie De-bunker such as [Friedrich] Nietzsche or Jacques Derrida for instance, who asks the question "What is the Difference"—and we cannot even tell from his grammar whether he "really" wants to know "what" difference is or is just telling us that we shouldn't even try to find out. Confronted with the question of the difference between grammar and rhetoric, grammar allows us to ask the question, but the sentence by means of which we ask it may deny the very possibility of asking. For what is the use of asking, I ask, when we cannot even authoritatively decide whether a question asks or doesn't ask?

The point is as follows. A perfectly clear syntactical paradigm (the question) engenders a sentence that has at least two meanings, of which the one asserts and the other denies its own illocutionary mode. *It is not so that there are simply two meanings, one literal and the other figural,* and that we have to decide which one of these meanings is the right one in this particular situation. *The confusion can only be cleared up by the intervention of an extra-textual intention,* such as Archie Bunker putting his wife straight; but the very anger he displays is indicative of more than impatience; it reveals his despair when confronted with *a structure of linguistic meaning that he cannot control* and that holds the discouraging prospect of an infinity of similar future confusions, all of them potentially catastrophic in their consequences . . . *open[ing] up vertiginous possibilities of referential aberration.* (emphasis added)

The space between literal and figural meanings requires *extra-textual intentions* in order to understand it. The fundamental impasse requires *intervention* to provide it with meaning, but in and of itself provides only unknowability as to what the meaning will be this time. Only intervention from outside of the text—from outside of the question "What's the difference?"—sustains meaning in the interaction, whether the intervention consists of Edith's assumption or Archie's anger. From within the fundamental impasse itself, from within the inherent instability of Archie's question, only the *extra-textual intention* of the moment—an accident of history—determines the meaning at any given time. In fact, de Man suggests that every text generates such a conflict between rhetorical structures (269). He then defines "text" as "any entity that can be considered from such a double perspective: as a generative, open-ended, non-referential grammatical system and as a figural system . . . that subverts the grammatical code to which the text owes its existence" (270).

De Man's definition widens the aporetic realm beyond traditionally understood linguistic forms and into the space intimated by Derrida when he famously declared, "There is nothing outside of the text" ("Il n'y a pas de hors texte"; cited in Culler 1982, 157). Both theorists repeatedly stake strong claims for the power of textuality in general and of aporias in particular. They understand aporetic forms as not only interesting features of language, but as primary sites of generation and creativity within texts. For Derrida, the "general text" consists of language and history, including all human efforts to inscribe ourselves into the world (Culler 1982, 130). For de Man (1979, 272), an aporia "illustrates the practical consequences of a linguistic structure in which grammar and figure, statement and speech act do not converge." In fact, de Man claims of Jean Jacques Rousseau's *Social Contract,* "Textual allegories on this level of complexity generate history" (277). Detouring further through literary theory, I consider this relation between language and history—or, more traditionally, language and "materiality"—with help from de Man and Derrida.

NAVIGATING STRUCTURAL APORIAS: THE ETHICAL
CALL OF FUNDAMENTAL IMPASSES IN SOCIAL
MEANINGS AND INSTITUTIONS

De Man argues with persuasive clarity that while language must not be confused with the "materiality" of life, linguistic workings may fundamentally order our world. Therefore, literary theory may be consequential in understanding the social orders in which we live.

> It would be unfortunate, for example, to confuse the materiality of the signifier with the materiality of what it signifies. This may seem obvious enough on the level of light and sound . . . ; no one in his right mind will try to grow grapes by the luminosity of the word "day," but it is very difficult not to conceive the pattern of one's past and future existence as in accordance with temporal and spatial schemes that belong to fictional narratives and not to the world. *This does not mean that fictional narratives are not part of the world and of reality; their impact upon the world may well be all too strong for comfort.* What we call ideology is precisely the confusion of linguistic with natural reality, of reference with phenomenalism. . . . Those who reproach literary theory for being oblivious to social and historical (that is to say ideological) reality are merely stating their fear at having their own ideological mystifications exposed by the tool they are trying to discredit. They are, in short, very poor readers of Marx's *German Ideology*. (1986, 11; emphasis added)

Indeed, pursuing de Man's call for a careful analysis of language's engagement with the historical is one way of taking seriously the "effects of power peculiar to the play of statements" (Foucault 1980, 113).[3]

For de Man, by definition, "textuality" consists of the space of interplay—the aporetic space—between the grammatical and figural dimensions of language. Textuality, or the aporetic space, results from a complex turning back on itself that is structured into language. It occurs whenever there exists a gap between the abstract and systematic meanings produced by grammar's structure and the specificity of referential meanings alluded to when language is not read as a system (1979, 270). This gap itself—between grammar's structural meanings and referential meaning derived from the same language—is not the aporia but is what de Man refers to as the figural dimension of language. This gap, or the figural dimension, is an inevitable result of linguistic structure since "the logic of grammar generates texts only in the absence of referential meaning, but every text generates a referent that subverts the grammatical principle to which it owed its constitution" (269). The figural dimension, this gap, is a system in itself; it is the structure taken by referential meaning playing against the grammatical system and being closed off by it at once. The figural dimension comprises an abyss that is 'structured-in' by *the play of statements*. While produced by the mechanical workings of the grammatical system, what de Man refers to as a text, by definition, turns back on and troubles the relation between the grammatical system and the figural dimension of language (a 'structured-in' gap in meaning). Also by definition, the figural dimension of language is already turned back on the grammatical. This doubled turning-back-on and turning-in—this detour into a structured gap and further into an abyssal relation between the structured gap and the continued functioning of the system of language—is precisely the generative site in language for de Man. It is the aporetic space and the space of the *text*. It is the tension between the system itself and its structured-in turning-back-on itself, rhetorically understood by de Man as the tension between a grammatical system and its figural dimension. To be precise, the aporetic space—textuality—is the troubled and troubling relation between a system and its own gaps.

Expanding de Man's insight that a crucial generative, incoherent, and unstable space is structured into the foundations of the text, the concept of structural aporias seeks this site in Derrida's *general text,* in language and history. In the simplest terms, a structural aporia exists when a fundamental impasse is structured into (a) a social order's defining systems of social meaning as well as corresponding material practices and, simultaneously, (b) its corresponding institutions. In other words, a structural aporia exists when a fundamental impasse is structured into a society's discursive order. A structural aporetic analytic begins from the premise that the existence and maintenance of social orders inherently rest on such structurally unstable foundations. Underlying foundational impasses, or structural aporias, are understood to be generative. As aporetic spaces, they are at all times potential sites for disruptive discursive struggles over and against the social order's premises. Structurally, they are the sites where such struggles can take place. When and how these discursive struggles actually occur—the timing and form they take—relies on *extra-textual intervention,* on historical convergences or historical accident. Consequently, a structural aporetic analytic calls for careful analysis of social orders' foundations and the bases of political and discursive irruptions that have occurred and might occur.

A structural aporetic analytic provokes the question, What are potential *sites* of political rupture in given social orders? It shifts analytic focus from the *timing* of political rupture to the sites of political rupture, since timing is unpredictably determined by the vagaries, specificities, and particularities of history. Via the framework of structural aporias, a careful analysis might accurately locate a particular society's discursive spaces for potential disruptive social change. Forceful struggles over social order and disorder have occurred and will occur again at, in, and through these aporetic sites. Or these are precisely the sites through which, as Nietzsche (1967/1969, 77) wrote, "whatever exists, having somehow come into being, is again and again reinterpreted to new ends, taken over, transformed and redirected."

Within this formulation, a society's systems of meaning play as important a part in sociohistorical movement as its institutions do. Systems of meaning are as important to the social order's maintenance and reproduction as are daily material practice and institutions, such as the legal structure. How systems of daily material practice, or institutions, and systems of meaning are imbricated with each other—the particularities of how systems of daily material practice and systems of meaning conjoin to form a specific social order—is what I call a discursive structure. A structural aporia consists of the troubled relation between a site of impasse in the foundations of a society's discursive structures and the discursive structures themselves. As with de Man's explication of the workings of a linguistic text, the interplay of the abstract systems found in a discursive structure and the specificity of its institutional systems and systems of meanings turns back on itself in the space of the structural aporia: a site of impasse and impossibility, the site of textuality of language and history.

A structural aporetic analytic understands social orders to be built on systems of meaning and practices that have structured-in fundamental unbridgeable impasses—a base that has instability and movement inherent in its makeup. Although all social orders, by definition, have strong integrative and socially reproductive characteristics, the concept of structural aporias shifts analytic focus away from social integration. While social orders appear and often remain stable for extended periods of time, they are here understood as having potentials for political irruption structured into themselves, which can be analytically defined and examined. Social orders' inherent sites of instability and movement are analytically locatable in their structural aporias. Radical changes in social orders—in the literal sense of changes at their roots—are then understood as discursive historical shifts that flow through the sites of structural aporias. The potential for political rupture at the site of a structural aporia expands and wanes as historical specifics interplay and struggle through "structured-in" discursive impasses. In other words, discrete analyzable structures exist within any given social order that define the sites through and in which historical transformations will move or have moved. But the specifics of how and when historical transformation might move through these sites are not structurally analyzable. In their impasse and impossibility, structural aporias hold a radical unknowability, a *confusion that can only be cleared up by the intervention of an extra-textual intention.* The social structural site through which transformative historical movement might occur can be analyzed, but the specifics of historical transformation itself are occasioned by extra-textual intervention, by the vagaries of history, or historical accident. This is not ultimate theoretical nihilism, but quite the opposite; the concept of structural aporias motivates a call for careful analysis of social orders' discursive foundations, a call for a careful genealogy of social orders.[4] By locating both historical and contemporary societal fault lines, sociological studies of ruptures and potential ruptures can contribute to an understanding of past history that might "writ[e] a history of the present" rather than "writing a history of the past in terms of the present" (Foucault 1977/1979, 31).[5]

Derrida (1993, 16) "suggest[s] that a sort of nonpassive endurance of the aporia [is] the condition of responsibility and of decision." He further remarks upon "the necessity of *experience* itself, the experience of the aporia . . . as endurance or as passion, as interminable resistance or remainder," even as he notes that "*the aporia can never simply be endured as such. The ultimate aporia is the impossibility of the aporia as such*" (19, 78). The indeterminacy inherent in structural aporias points not only to a temporal unpredictability, but also to an inability to determine its parameters from within. What is at stake in aporias is precisely "the 'not knowing where to go'" (12). Because structural aporias operate in part at the level of social meanings— upon and within our very conceptualization of our social world—their operation necessarily remains at least partially opaque to those in the midst of aporetic tremors. And yet the experience of the aporia must be "interminable [and] remain such if one wants to think, to make come or to let come any event of decision or of responsibility" (16). Precisely by analyzing the space of structural aporias, sociologists, cultural critics, and political economists might take ethical responsibility toward the past and future. In other words, the indeterminacy of when and how political rupture might occur creates the space for careful, responsible analysis of the systems of social meanings and institutions at work in a society's structural aporias, as well as of how various societal and historical pressures have affected them and might yet affect them.

SOCIAL CONTRACT, LANGUAGE, AND HISTORY: THE PROMISE

Just as grammar systematically and logically produces the text without allusion to referential meaning, Western law systematically and logically produces a legal system without regard for specificity of application. Further, Western political theory produces explicit generative textual moments "since the political model . . . cannot pretend to ignore the referential moment entirely" (de Man 1979, 270). In fact, de Man claims that it is "in the description of the structure of political society [that] the 'definition' of a text as the contradictory interference of the grammatical with the figural field emerges in its most systematic form" (270). And he posits Rousseau's *Social Contract* as exemplary here: "The tension between figural and grammatical language as duplicated in the differentiation between the State as a defined entity (Etat) and the State as a principle of action (Souverain) or, in linguistic terms, between the constative and the performative function of language. . . . The text [of the *Social Contract*] can be considered as the theoretical description of the State considered as a contractual and legal model but also as the disintegration of this same model as soon as it is put in motion" (270–71). That is, Rousseau's *Social Contract* operates as a generative and deconstructive social text, an aporetic text. And how its aporias actually function can be analyzed, de Man tells us, "by asking what it is the *Social Contract* performs, what it keeps doing despite the fact that it has established that it could not be done" (275). The answer, he concludes, is that it promises, and in doing so continues "to perform the very illocutionary speech act which it has discredited and to perform it in all its textual ambiguity" (275–76).

Rousseau's text embeds the function of promising at several levels. The *Social Contract* promises a certain future that it can never provide, that perhaps can never be reached, in its elaboration of necessary forms and principles of political legislation. In this sense, all laws and contractual forms are structured as future-looking promises. De Man elaborates: "Considered performatively, the speech act of the contractual text never refers to a situation that exists in the present but signals toward a hypothetical future.... All laws are future-oriented and prospective; their illocutionary mode is that of the *promise*. On the other hand, every promise assumes a date at which the promise is made and without which it would have no validity; laws are promissory notes in which the present of the promise is always a past with regard to its realization" (273). Derrida marks this underlying temporal aporia of the promise, of contracts, of law, as fundamental to Western democracy. And he extends the ethical duty to experience the aporia invoked earlier to a Westerner's ethical duty to experience the aporetic promise of democracy: "The *same duty* dictates assuming the European, and *uniquely* European, heritage of an idea of democracy, while also recognizing that this idea . . . is never simply given . . . but rather [is] something that remains to be thought and *to come* [*à venir*]: not something that is certain to happen tomorrow, not the democracy (national or international, state or trans-state) of the *future*, but a democracy that must have the structure of a promise—*and thus the memory of that which carries the future, the to come, here and now*" (1993, 18–19). Democratic political subjects live in this aporetic space of the promise that suffuses Western democracy—this space from which a democratic, just, and egalitarian future is promised, and yet which is never present—this space that is now always both a promise for the future and a memory of the promise from the past: Derrida's "à venir," or *to come,* and Drucilla Cornell's (1991) "futur antérior." Precisely in this aporetic space of the promise, the *Social Contract* morphs from a constative theory of politics into a performative history (de Man 1979, 271). But the movement through this aporetic space is necessarily covered by an elision, by what de Man terms "an act of deceit" (269). By definition, aporetic spaces are unbridgeable, impassable. Any apparent movement across or through them that leaves undisturbed the linguistic, political, institutional, or discursive structure in which they are embedded must, in actuality, elide some other movement. The promise of justice lives in this moment of elision, where the structures of language and political theory mimic and elucidate each other:

No law is a law unless it also applies to particular individuals. . . . Only by thus referring it back to particular praxis can the *justice* of the law be tested, exactly as the *justesse* of any statement can only be tested by referential verifiability, or by deviation from this verification. For how is justice to be determined if not by particular reference? . . . What remains hidden in the everyday use of language, the fundamental incompatibility between grammar and meaning, becomes explicit when the linguistic structures are stated, as is the case [in the *Social Contract*], in political terms . . . [in which it becomes] clear that the incompatibility between the elaboration of the law and its application (or justice) can only be bridged by an act of deceit. (269)

The legal scholar Reva B. Siegel provides a concrete example of how the present-day U.S. legal system operates in exactly this manner in her discussion of Justice Sandra Day O'Connor's decision in a case centered on the legality of gender-based peremptory challenges in jury selection, *J. E. B. v. Alabama ex rel. T. B.* Justice O'Connor opined:

We know that like race, gender matters. A plethora of studies make clear that in rape cases, for example, female jurors are somewhat more likely to vote to convict than male jurors. . . . One need not be a sexist to share the intuition that in certain cases a person's gender and resulting life experience will be relevant to his or her view of the case. . . . Today's decision severely limits a litigant's ability to act on this intuition, for the import of our holding is that any correlation between a juror's gender and attitudes is irrelevant as a matter of constitutional law. But to say that gender makes no difference as a matter of law is not to say that gender makes no difference as a matter of fact. I previously have said with regard to *Batson*: *"That the Court will not tolerate prosecutors' racially discriminatory use of the peremptory challenge, in effect, is a special rule of relevance, a statement about what this Nation stands for, rather than a statement of fact."* (cited in Siegel 1996, 231)

Siegel ponders the everyday American experience of the elision that constitutes the heart of the democratic legal system's functioning, its continuing promise *in all its textual ambiguity*, "despite the fact that it has established that" it cannot make this promise. She asks:

How does this ritualized renunciation of social knowledge create a do-
main of symbolic meaning in which we believe ourselves capable of tran-
scending the gap between what this nation *is* and what it *stands for*? And
why does this turn from social experience of American life—even as
we recognize that it is law *in just this symbolic sense* that legitimates the
distributive inequities it is always summoning us to transcend? In the figure of color blindness [or gender blindness], or blind justice, the aspira-
tion and legitimating functions of law fuse in maddening consort. It is
on this figural terrain—where we fight some of the major social conflicts
of our time—that we must reckon with the authority of legal discourse,
both as it is expressed in the judicial opinion and as it circulates in everyday conversation of the sort conventionally referred to as "outside" law.
(1996, 231)

These considerations grapple with the fundamental aporetic form of West-
ern democracy, and with Derrida's *duty to experience it* as both *interminatable resistance* and as *the memory of that which carries the future, the to come,
here and now*. They begin to point to how democratic structural aporias are
daily lived and are often discomfiting.

In de Man's analysis, the *Social Contract*'s very use of language performs
this fundamental elision, plays in this promissory aporia: "*Die Sprache ver-
spricht (sich)* [language promises];[6] to the extent that is necessarily mislead-
ing, language just as necessarily conveys the promise of its own truth" (1979,
277). Language itself cannot be trusted to provide a solid grounding; the
very moment in which it is believed to be a clear and transparent medium,
a firm footing, brings it into the realm of the promise, the aporia, and a
generative relation to history. Language's promise is not simply "an inconsistency, a weakness in the text of the *Social Contract* that could have been
avoided. . . . This model is a fact of language over which Rousseau himself
has no control" (276–77). The aporetic space of promise is structured into
the *Social Contract* at multiple levels: (a) linguistically, (b) in legal referents,
and (c) in the structure of Western democracy—the latter two both situated
in the structure of the *Social Contract*'s abstract political theory. Certain of
the *acts of deceit* used to elide this abyss, to seem to negotiate it, turn out
to be foundational moments of American gendered history. In fact, the social contract and its inherent aporias arguably held greatest sway precisely

in the antebellum United States. Many in the new United States had experienced the American Revolution and the resulting construction of a new nation as an actualization of the concept itself, as "a voluntary association created by citizens equal under the law, a compact guaranteeing inalienable individual rights as well as the private contract relations arising from those rights" (Stanley 1998, 7). And "well into the nineteenth century American political thinkers" referred to the social contract simply as fact, "particularly during constitutional crises" (12).

(HETERO)SEXUAL-SOCIAL CONTRACT AND MARRIAGE

If Rousseau's *Social Contract,* Western democracy, contract law, and codified law generally are all structured as aporias through their promissory form, what have they promised? Or, more specifically, what have they promised women and what have they promised men? And the "individual"? In actuality, democratic societies of English[7] heritage contain gendered aporias that stem in part from social contract origin myths. When read aporetically, Carole Pateman's significant work of feminist political theory, *The Sexual Contract,* provides a guide of sorts to some of these gendered impasses. Pateman provocatively argues that social contract theories actually consist of a "sexual-social pact," in a double sense. First, in the very definition of their subjecthood, men are afforded control over women. Second, men's guaranteed sexual access to women is inscribed in the social contract, despite the apparent promise of equal entry to democratic society for all individuals (1988, 1–2). In fact, Pateman persuasively analyzes the logical structure of social contract theories—in which she includes those of Hobbes, Locke, Rousseau, and even Freud—as the precise site of the theoretical genesis of modern patriarchal right. An analysis of democratic society's structural aporias might usefully begin by examining the structures of these founding myths for their fundamental impasses.

The language employed by Hobbes, Locke, Rousseau, and Freud seemingly nominates all people as "individuals." Yet, Pateman argues, at the same time all but Hobbes "claim that women naturally lack the attributes and capacities of 'individuals'. Sexual difference is political difference; sexual difference is the difference between freedom and subjection" (6). For all four theorists, only "individuals" can be party to the social contract. Only "individuals" are able to rationally participate in contractual relations. In other words, by definition, women cannot participate in contractual relations. Curiously, the bar on contract participation by women does not extend to the marriage contract in either the state of nature or civil society.[8] Rousseau, Locke, and Freud include the marriage contract as an integral part of the state of nature, and all four theorists "insist that, in civil society, women not only can but must enter into the marriage contract" (6). This gendered elision 'structures-in' a site of instability at the very core of social contract theories.

In simpler terms, these theories bar women from entering contractual relations, the very form of interaction that the same theories define as rational and civilized, and on which they claim civilization is built. But, in an aporetic moment, they require women to enter into one specific contract at the precise moment that women become members of civil society. And the particulars of this contract define women as subject to men by revoking all bases of their now aporetic individuality in civil society. In making the marriage contract, women are required to revoke the individuality they hold— and yet, because they already lack it, they are not fit to contractually accept or revoke anything. A logical impasse indeed!

Specifically, Pateman argues that the marriage contract serves as the site of women's subjection to men in the state of nature and simultaneously operates as the site of displacement of patriarchal subjection in the mythical move from a natural state to a civilized state. Freud's tale of parricide and fraternal contract explicitly narrates the sexual aspect of the social contract in its double meaning. Pateman (1989, 42–43) elucidates:

> The motive for the brothers' collective act is not merely to claim their natural liberty and right of self-government, but *to gain access to women.* In the classic theorists' state of nature the "family" already exists and men's conjugal right is deemed a natural right. Freud's primal father, his *patria potestas,* keeps all the women of the horde for himself. The parricide eliminates the father's political right, and also his *exclusive* sexual right. The brothers inherit his patriarchal, masculine right and share the women among themselves. No man can be a primal father ever again, but by setting up rules that give all men equal access to women (compare their equality before the laws of the state) they exercise the "original" political right of dominion over women that was once the prerogative of the father.

In this way, social contract origin myths distinguish the patriarchy of modern democratic societies from earlier forms of patriarchy. In these origin myths, a fraternal patriarchy composed of two spheres arises in the mythical transition from the state of nature to civil society. The public sphere constitutes civil society proper in which men are equal before the law. The private sphere exists as a subordinate realm, as a sphere "that both is and is not in civil society" (Pateman 1988, 11) and through which women enter civil society as subordinate to men via their required participation in the marriage contract.[9] "Women are not incorporated as 'individuals' but as women, which, in the story of the original contract, means as natural subordinates" (181). Critically, the "sexual contract" is a contract of "(hetero)sexual relations and [focuses on] women as embodied [hetero]sexual beings" (17). Furthermore, Pateman notes that the one social contract theory explicit about sexual relations—Freud's—depicts the move to civil society as concomitant "with the establishment of orderly, universal heterosexual relations" (109).

In a blatant demonstration of the actual operation of the (hetero)sexual-social contract, postbellum white society and the U.S. government explicitly featured both of its enfolded aspects as the crux of their education and legal regulation of newly freed African Americans in a broad campaign that was supposed to turn freedpeople into proper citizens. In 1864, the American Tract Society published its first entry in the "Freedman's Library," *John Freeman and His Family,* which would be distributed in the South by Newman's civilization-workers. The freedwoman's elision as a member of the freedman's family was not incidental. In the story, John Freeman "embodied emancipation," and "his transition from bondage to freedom was told through three scenes of contract: a social contract, a labor contract, and a marriage contract" (Stanley 1998, 38). In these terms, his wife's new freedom only allowed her to engage in the marriage contract, which operated as a sexual contract with just one master. She could not participate in the social contract (and the question of her ability to make labor contracts was messy precisely because of the inherent contradiction between the country's dependence on her agricultural labor and the terms of the sexual-social contract that she was now required to enter). Stanley reports that as Congress struggled to shape the Civil Rights Act, it became "a forum for debating the meaning of antislavery contract principles for relations between the sexes" (57). While they never explicitly wrote the debates' substance into the law, it would intrinsically shape the legal framework:

> Limiting the scope of freedom, [Republican lawmakers] denied that [emancipation] altered either the marriage contract or the wife's status. . . .
>
> The congressional authors of emancipation thus elevated contract into a sovereign right of citizenship. Yet they simply extended free men's established contract rights to former bondsmen, leaving wives of both races to the protections offered by the marriage contract. Indeed, the subject of marriage arose only as a reduction ad absurdum. . . . [In the end,] at law, only freedmen fully made the exodus from slavery to contract. Emancipation turned the slaveholders' world upside down, but the bonds of marriage remained intact. (57, 59)

Similarly, in the 1887 Dawes Severalty Act, the federal government explicitly legislated the (hetero)sexual-social contract as a requirement for citizenship for Native Americans, employing it as a blunt tool of "civilization." Under the Dawes Act, which stood until 1924, Native American men could receive U.S. citizenship "only when they emerged as property-owning heads of households. . . . The federal government divided up tribal lands, dispersed them to Native American men, and granted citizenship to those who 'adopted the habits of civilized life.' Native American women could earn citizenship as well, but only through marriage to a male citizen" (Brandzel 2005, 175).

From such direct historical examples and an aporetic viewpoint, the (hetero)sexual-social contract's centrality to Western democracy raises a series of interesting questions regarding how democratic systems of social meaning have defined civil and political subjects. If participating in the required marriage contract revokes a woman's ability to be a legitimate actor in the public sphere, might women sidestep this abyssal existence by refusing to enter instituted heterosexual relations? Or would they then be positioned entirely outside of civil society?[10] While these questions are not further developed in this book, U.S. laws establishing married women's disabilities— the legal rights lost when married—made clear that single women were given the ability to participate in the market. In fact, the laws were written specifically to distinguish the rights of married women from those of feme soles. And, at times, married women were legally redefined as *feme soles* so that they could regain contractual and economic rights in order to support themselves and their children.[11] In Maine, Massachusetts, and Pennsylvania, a wife reverted to feme sole status if her husband permanently left the state, whether he was banished or had voluntarily abandoned her. Since the early 1700s, Pennsylvania had also allowed seafarers' wives to act as feme soles while their husbands were at sea, since the men were away for lengthy, undefined periods and very well might not return. South Carolina gave wives feme sole powers to run their own businesses, basing the practice on the rights given to women in London as urban businesswomen. This was a distinctly southern phenomenon, however; similar latitude was not provided in any of the northern states. The southern states had not fought against England and were more likely to adopt British law directly in form and content. The northern states in part distinguished themselves from the rulers they had recently overthrown by making their coverture laws even stricter than England's. Single women were not legitimate participants in civil existence themselves, though. In fact, they embodied the aporetic space I explore here.

Reading single women's history through a structural aporetic analytic clarifies their impossible social position. While unmarried women were allowed to make economic contracts, they had never legitimately entered civil society, for women could enter only through the marriage contract. Consequently, even as unmarried women bought and sold in the marketplace, they were not conceived as legitimate civil subjects, as legitimate participants in democratic society. An aporetic reading of Western democracies' origin myths, of social contract myths, provides an analytic base for understanding some of the apparent contradictions in single heterosexual women's and lesbians' historical positions. The fact that unmarried women, whatever their sexuality, were permitted to make economic contracts to support themselves suggests to the general reader that unmarried women were public actors and that their daily lives would therefore have left more historical traces than those of married women. A careful structural aporetic reading indicates, however, that only men and married women were subjects in civil society, and married women became subjects specifically by taking on their marital disabilities. Here, the structural aporetic analytic provides another approach to the question of whether every member of modern societies is subjectivated, or constituted as a social subject through discourse. It shows married women as subjects indeed, albeit silenced and delegitimated subjects, while single heterosexual women and lesbians remained external to civil subjecthood in Western democracies during this time.[12] In other words, definitions and parameters of subjecthood are defined and redefined in and through structural aporias. Which societal members experience subjectivation and which are kept outside of it is crucially defined by how interimplicated social meanings and institutions move in and through the particular society's aporetic crucibles. The process of subjectivation distributes societal members into particular subject positions, or excludes them from subject positions. How these subject positions are defined, both internally and in relation to each other and to larger social structures such as the economy, is also the result of how discourse travels through structural aporetic spaces. The process and parameters of subjectivation are interimplicated with the movement of discourse, with *the effects of power peculiar to the play of statements.* And the structural aporetic space is their site of imbrication. The relations between a society's structures and the impassable and impossible gaps that underlie and define it determine who can be a subject and what kind of subject they can be. A structural aporetic analytic enables sociologists, cultural critics, political activists, and political economists to effectively interrogate historical moments when the "who" and "what" of subjecthood is transformed.

STRUCTURAL APORIAS CONSIDERED: GENDERED LAW, MARRIAGE, AND WOMANHOOD

The gendered aporias located at the core of social contract theories hold striking parallels to the unique historical structure of the marriage contract under British and U.S. law. Matrimonial consent contract doctrine, which results in a marital rape exemption (husbands cannot be prosecuted for raping their wives because raping one's wife is a definitional impossibility), serves as a kernel of three hundred years of case law regarding marriage. Based on eighteenth-century jurisprude Sir Matthew Hale's assertion that "the husband cannot be guilty of rape committed by himself upon his lawful wife, for by their mutual matrimonial consent and contract, the wife hath given up herself in this kind unto her husband which she cannot retract" (cited in Freeman 1981–82, 10), it explicitly defines the moment of legal marriage by the two aspects of the (hetero)sexual-social contract that Pateman (1988, 164) describes elsewhere—that is, the marital vows and the sexual act of consummation. According to matrimonial consent contract doctrine, the performance of these two acts results simultaneously in women being legally considered parties to a contract which they themselves historically could not revoke, which historically only a court of law could revoke,[13] and in women's removal from the realm of legal contract. For over two hundred years, common law courts treated matrimonial consent contract doctrine as clear precedent, leaving it unchallenged until 1977.[14] In England and the Anglo-based United States, from the 1700s to the present day, matrimonial consent contract doctrine has remained a centerpiece of women's relation to contract.

In addition, the marriage contract institutionalized in Anglo-based law over these past several centuries has been unlike other legal contracts in myriad ways (see Barry 1980, 1088; Weitzman 1981, xv, xix). First, the parties to the contract have not been historically assumed to be free and equal participants—a status that is usually defined as the basis of a fair contract. Second, neither party could demand legal damages from the other party for failure to honor the contract's provisions, which has been the usual legal remedy for an unfulfilled contract. Third, under the law, one party, the husband, could physically force the other party, his wife, to adhere to the contract. In contradistinction, usually under contract law neither party can resort to physical force; instead, either can seek damages only in civil court, or, if physical force is used, criminal charges can usually be successfully brought against the aggressor.[15] Fourth, unhappy parties could not agree between themselves to revise or nullify either the contract's provisions or its entirety; only the state could legally revise or nullify a marriage contract. These unique characteristics of the marriage contract mirror with shocking precision the gendered structural aporia embedded in social contract theories, understood here as democratic origin myths.

Beyond the strange nature of the historical marriage contract itself, the larger eighteenth- and nineteenth-century history of women's rights and marriage in England, as imported to the United States, also bears striking parallels to this gendered structural aporia. Its logical impasses and core instabilities actually replicate themselves at two levels in the details of legal, political, and economic history. On the one hand, they are apparent at the level of daily institutional practice, or the historical institutional level: in legal oversight of marriage contracts and marketplace contract; in legal regulation of men's and women's functioning in economic markets as consumers, businesspeople, and financial agents; and in the period's overwhelming gendered division of labor and paths of social influence, divided between a domesticated private sphere and a politico-economic public sphere. On the other hand, these same logical impasses and core instabilities are apparent at the level of daily linguistic use that constitutes a communal understanding of social structures and human relations within them. They are apparent at the level of daily linguistic use that conceptualizes the very meanings and parameters of existence in the social world, or the historical social meanings level: in the systems of meanings constituting and interimplicating Womanhood, contract, morality, the economy, and the nation.

The Historical Institutional Level: A First Aporetic Reading

Over the past two and a half centuries, feminist scholars and activists as well as those who purvey the law have addressed the marriage contract's peculiarity, its difference from all other contracts. Perhaps the most powerful legal authority in the nineteenth century, Sir William Blackstone (1803/1969, 433), begins his considerations "of husband and wife" by defining the marriage contract as a quintessentially normal contract: "The law treats [marriage] as it does all other contracts: allowing it to be good and valid in all cases, where the parties at the time of making it were, in the first place, *willing* to contract; secondly, *able* to contract; and, lastly, actually *did* contract, in the proper forms and solemnities required by law." But only ten pages later, he delineates the marriage contract's unique powers, in an oft-quoted passage:

> By marriage, the husband and wife are one person in law: that is, the very being or legal existence of the woman is suspended during the marriage, or at least is incorporated and consolidated into that of the husband: under whose wing, protection and *cover,* she performs every thing; and is therefore called in our law-french a *feme-covert, foemina viro co-operta;* is said to be *covert baron,* or under the protection and influence of her husband, her *baron,* or lord; and her condition during her marriage is called her *coverture.* Upon this principle, of an union of person in husband

and wife, depend almost all the legal rights, duties, and disabilities, that either of them acquire by the marriage. (442)

Blackstone's description of the marriage contract uncannily resembles Pateman's description of the sexual contract. In nineteenth-century Britain and the United States, the marriage contract was the one contract socially expected of women and, at the same time, served as the legal basis of women's legal, economic, civil, political, and social subjugation. Women's very participation in this singular contract legally stripped them of the ability to participate contractually or economically in a social order based precisely in contract, property, and market relations. In other words, women's very participation in the actual historical marriage contract legally stripped them of their ability to take part in democratic society as free and equal citizens.

In Pateman's terminology, social contract theory posits that all citizens "contract in" as free and equal individuals. At the same time, it posits that women are incapable of all contract behavior other than at the moment of the required marriage contract, in which modern patriarchal right originates. In other words, not only can't women "contract in" to civil society freely and equally, but they are herein defined as patriarchal subjects. In the United States, the democratic ideal of equal participation and standing of all citizens is grounded in its founding documents. And the antebellum woman's rights movement drew on these documents, juxtaposing the documents' assertions of citizens' rights against women's legal disabilities. An 1858 pro–women's suffrage pamphlet attempted to turn democracy's systems of social meanings against themselves by highlighting this gendered gap located in both social contract origin myths and historical practice. In his included statement supporting women's claims to rights of participation in the polity, William Lloyd Garrison placed women's actual legal subjection in stark contrast to a famous passage from Thomas Jefferson's Declaration of Independence: "Women have the whole ground conceded to them at the beginning. 'All government arises from the consent of the governed.' Our fathers [held][16] that doctrine as self-evident, and [by doing so] the men of this country have conceded the whole ground" (Garrison 1858, 2). Here Garrison historically grounded the popular and mythical conception of the modern democratic social order, of social contract theories, of citizens freely and equally "contracting in" to a joint government in the founding fathers' claim to independence. And he pointed to the conflict between the mythical understanding and the concomitant historical reality—a conflict embedded in both contemporary institutions and social meanings, wherein women were not afforded rights of participation. Garrison specifically addressed the question of suffrage, but his argument pertained equally to the realms of contract and property rights. In fact, history read asunder demonstrates that the narrowly political contradiction addressed by the suffrage campaign could not have been resolved until American society had struggled through transformations in the very real aporias underlying Womanhood, contract, and property rights. As discussed in chapter 1, the details of these distinctly gendered and legally codified property relations were critical components of the historical institutional level of Anglo-based democracy's gendered structural aporias.

What does a structural aporetic analytic suggest when confronted with the fact that gendered distinctions regarding contract and property rights no longer exist in today's marriage law in Anglo-based democracies? What can it tell us about this distinct societal difference between 150 years ago and the present? So far, reading aporetically has revealed that gendered contractual rights constitute an unstable core of modern democratic social orders. It has further revealed that gendered contractual rights took on a specific historical institutional form in the daily social practices surrounding married women's economic and property rights. This aporetic reading of social contract origin myths against the historical institution of the marriage contract implies that women could have gained economic and property rights and contractual rights more broadly only through a radical transformation in their position in civil society—through a transformation that fundamentally changed the roots of civil society, in fact. Such a transformation in the relations between societal structures and a foundational impasse, an unstable core, a structural aporia constitutes a fundamental shift, by definition. And fundamental shifts in social orders do not occur sui generis; they require pressure on a structural aporetic site, usually by a social movement in combination with other socio-environmental pressures.

As Gayatri Chakravorty Spivak (1988b, 4) eloquently wrote, "A functional change in a sign system is a violent event. Even when it is perceived as 'gradual,' or 'failed', or yet 'reversing itself', the change itself can only be operated by the force of a crisis. Yet, if the space for a change (necessarily also an addition) had not been there in the prior function of the sign-system, the crisis could not have made the change happen." Since gendered distinctions regarding contractual rights do not exist today in the United States, in marriage law or otherwise, a structural aporetic analytic implies that effective disruptive movement for social change must have put pressure precisely on the institutions and social meanings of women's economic and property rights, on *the space for a change [already] . . . there in the prior function of the sign-system.* It implies that we should examine these social locations for disruptive sociohistoric and social movements sometime between the early nineteenth century and the present, for *the force of a crisis,* for movements that resulted in radical social transformations.

In other words, the sighting of this structural aporia locates a potential site of social order transformation. If, in fact, historical change occurred at this site, a structural aporetic analytic argues for a careful genealogy of the historical process of change, with a focus on discursive transformation within the aporetic site. For if a structural aporia indeed locates interimplicated fundamental instabilities in a society's systems of social meanings and institutions, historical changes generated in and from this aporetic space must of necessity engage instabilities of both social meanings and institutions. In the same stroke, they must engage both the historical social meanings level as well as the historical institutional level of the particular structural aporia, resulting in fully discursive historical shifts and ruptures. Reading history asunder, or reading aporetically, does not reshape the facts of historical change itself, but renarrates them by discovering anew and analytically detailing the complex process of historically transformative rupture. In the case of U.S. women's economic and property rights, discursive transformation necessarily engaged (a) the historical institutions of marriage law and contract law and (b) the historical social meanings of Womanhood, contract, property, and the economy, which opened onto larger historical social meanings of labor, morality, and the nation.

The Historical Social Meanings Level: A First Aporetic Reading

Over the 1850s, the woman's movement successfully refigured True Womanhood, rewriting what had been an increasingly hegemonic understanding of Womanhood since the 1820s. As discussed earlier, the popular conception of True Womanhood anchored a sense of stability—a stable sense of the nation—for a society experiencing dramatic and rapid social, political, and economic changes. In other words, True Womanhood was entwined in a web of social meanings—including, in particular, meanings of the economy, labor, morality, and the nation—whose interrelations were crucial to citizens' sense of social stability and growing national identity. An attempt to shift or rewrite any aspect of this web of social meanings truly threatened the popular sense of a stable social order. Refiguring True Womanhood would require disruptive social transformation. By applying pressure to the aporetic site of Woman, contract, and subjecthood, the antebellum woman's movement rewrote the social meanings put into play by True Womanhood. Jill Elaine Hasday (2000, 1413–14, 1420) documents the antebellum woman's rights movement's battle for a woman's "right to her own person . . . a woman's right of self-possession," or against the marital rape exemption and for control over her own reproductive capabilities, as the kernel of all other rights of civil subjecthood. While these demands engaged the kernel of the (hetero)sexual-social contract, or matrimonial consent contract doctrine, they were one part of a broader struggle to rewrite women's relation to contract and, thereby, their civil subjecthood. Of particular interest here, the antebellum woman's movement redefined True Womanhood's entanglements, or lack of entanglements, with the burgeoning and continually reordered capitalist economy. An aporetic reading of women's contractual and economic relations in the antebellum United States focuses attention, in part, on the changes in webs of social meanings that were preconditions of a popular conceptualization of a True Woman who was equally "at home" in the economic sphere and in the domestic sphere—preconditions of its very legibility.[17] Significantly, this holds true whatever definition of the economic sphere would eventually be agreed upon. That is, it is equally true whether the economic sphere would be understood to consist solely of market relations or would include women's nonmarket labors and industry, rights in which were among the antebellum woman's movement's most radical economic claims according to Siegel (1994, 1112, 1127).

In January 1854, the monthly woman's rights periodical *The Una* published an article titled "Go to Work for the Sake of Women" that displayed one such attempt to rewrite the meanings and relations of respectable Womanhood:

> We call upon the women who are at liberty to take these forward steps, for the relief of their sex and for their own honor and benefit. Now you are occupying your waste time and idle talents in the wretched charities, that poor houses and hospitals can perform better and cheaper, than your voluntary associations are able to do, and you are diverted from the service which would prevent wretchedness, pauperism and dissoluteness by idle and vain attempts to relieve these evils by almsgiving, after they have become incurable. . . . Your condition is every day growing worse; the earnest woman-hood of the time is bestirring itself and the contrast will expose and disgrace you. Our earnest word to you is, drop your trivialities, your perpetual pursuit of amusement, and charities, that do but make paupers, and go to work for the world and for your own sake. (quoted in Russo and Kramarae 1991, 100–101)

This article remonstrates "women who are at liberty," or the new middling and upper classes, to stop their non-market-oriented pursuits external to the home; but, rather than demanding that they return to the sanctified site of the home, it calls on them to take their Womanhood forth into economic labor. According to the author, only women's direct engagement with the increasingly market-driven aspects of the world will prove truly useful in uplifting either themselves or others. Specifically juxtaposing economic labor to charity work, she argues that Woman's volunteer labors within the social realm—the acts of benevolence that provided the True Woman a respectable avenue via which to venture outside the home and display her "earnestness"—were not how *the earnest womanhood of the time* should be and was newly engaged. Only work, not individual or associational charity, was capable of raising Woman, her social position, and the nation as a whole. And here, the True Woman is refigured precisely as *going to work for the world and her own sake.*

By comparison, Butts's 1871 pamphlet, analyzed in the introduction, simply declared, "There is no cause which can take precedence of the material independence of woman" (1). The work of refiguring Womanhood and woman's relation to the economy was no longer necessary to make such a claim legible. The very possibility of this utterance making sense to a contemporary audience was contingent on an already partially successful rewriting of the antebellum web of social meanings imbricating Womanhood, contract, the economy, and the nation. His pamphlet *Material Independence of Woman* differs from antebellum woman's rights pamphlets in that it takes its audience's understanding of this rewritten system of meanings for granted. Butts assumes that he can write about Woman's integral relation to capitalism's economic realm without reference, analogy, or argument against the prior figuration of Woman and the economy, in which respectable Womanhood only existed external to economic concerns. "Thus the most vital of all questions to be settled by thinking women is that of their true relations to a material order of society," he claims. "From this standpoint of observation it is obvious that woman's relation to the production and distribution of wealth is as much more important than man's as her material resources are more circumscribed, and her social condition more dependent than his" (10–11). These declarations stand alone; they assume that women might have *true relations* to the economy, *to a material order of society*, with no need to address that assumption. While the 1854 *Una* article provides an example of the 1850s woman's movement's attempts to rewrite the historical social meanings of Womanhood, the cultural legibility of Butts's 1871 pamphlet demonstrates that at least a partial refiguring of Womanhood had occurred by the time of its publication.

HISTORICAL MOVEMENT: MARRIED WOMEN'S
PROPERTY ACTS AND THE 1850S WOMAN'S
RIGHTS MOVEMENT

The difference between the 1854 *Una* article and Butts's 1871 pamphlet makes visible a shift in the social meanings interimplicating Womanhood and the economy, serving as one exemplar of the relative success of a fully discursive antebellum woman's rights movement. The difference between the 1848 and 1860 New York State Married Women's Property Acts makes visible a shift in institutional practices interimplicating Womanhood and the economy, serving as another exemplar. At first glance, the act of 1848 gave married women the right to ownership of real property (for instance, land) brought to the marriage or received during it, but it was only with the act of 1860 that married women received the right to both own and control their personal property, which crucially included their earnings. By itself, this difference does not necessarily imply the type of disruptive societal reorganization that a structural aporetic analytic suggests must have occurred in order to shift the meanings of and relations between Womanhood, women, social and marital contract, and the contractual relations underlying the economy.

To review: the discursive underpinnings of modern democracy are intricately interwoven with notions of legal contract, notions that are inherent to the market economies that define modern democracies. A structural aporia analogous to the one apparent in social contract origin myths of modern democracy underlies the social meanings and institutions of early U.S. democracy. A society that claimed to have been established with freedom and equality of contractual participation for all members actually stood starkly opposed to women's ability to participate in any contracts other than the marriage contract. And, at its core, it was defined by this self-negating juxtaposition. The marriage contract operates as woman's required entry point into society, eliding its legal engendering of her patriarchal subjugation. This structural aporetic form is now apparent at both its mythical level—the heterosexual-social contract—and its historical levels, which replicated the aporetic moment in both systems of practices, or institutions, and systems of social meanings. Consequently, an aporetic analytic implies that the difference between the 1848 and 1860 Married Women's Property Acts should be reconsidered with a focus on contemporary institutions and social meanings of Womanhood and contract. Reading this history asunder demonstrates that women's movement into the economic realm as legitimate actors was by no means achieved through a gradual progression of liberty.

New York State's Married Women's Property Act of 1848, along with similar acts in other states, served two purposes: It protected the property holdings of an extended family lineage (E. C. Stanton et al. 1889/1970, 63–64); and, in an unstable economy, it protected married women's property from being demanded by creditors as payment for family debts (Rabkin 1980; Thurman 1966; Warbasse 1987). The act of 1848 allowed women to retain legal ownership (in their own name) of real property brought to the marriage (land, buildings, productive equipment), as well as any real property inherited or given to them during the marriage. In this way, wealthy fathers, such as the landed Dutch who helped to push the New York State act through the legislature, could ensure that profligate or simply unfortunate sons-in-law would not waste their family property or lose it to creditors. Nor, in the case of a son-in-law's death, would their family property devolve to his immediate family, leaving only a fraction to the daughter, when the original purpose of giving or willing the property was to sustain her throughout life (E. C. Stanton et al. 1889/1970). This set of motives had been particularly apparent in what was by far the earliest married women's property act legislated: Mississippi's act of 1839. Four of its five provisions concentrated on the transfer of property in slaves; the act ensured that neither the acreage nor the human labor necessary to run a successful plantation would be diluted through the son-in-law's and his family's claims on a daughter's inheritance, or on the share of her family's fortune given to her by gift before or after marriage (Warbasse 1987, 142–43). In addition, "these four sections on slave property were more carefully drafted and contained fewer loose ends than the first section which allowed a married woman to own property," suggesting their relative importance to the legislators (143).

Reading history asunder, it is particularly telling that women were generally not given the right to contract in these early acts, or in what can be seen as the entire first spate of acts, which continued into the 1870s. In fact, once these acts were passed, married women's lack of a right to contract created a critical legal problematic. Married women now owned parcels of land—productive property. Yet they could not make any legally enforceable contracts regarding them on their own; they could not sell them, rent them, or buy other parcels in their own name. Previously, they could make contracts regarding this property with their husbands' permission. This was no longer possible, though, since husbands no longer had any legal rights in these pieces of property. In effect, by giving women ownership in real property and not allowing women the right of contract, parcels of land suddenly existed over which no one could contract. In other words, no legal contracts could be made regarding landed property owned by women (Thurman 1966, 39), effectively removing a certain amount of productive property from the reach of the market just at the time that industrial capitalism's growth created a push for greater fungibility (Horwitz 1977; Rabkin 1975, 1980). Legal historians have commented that "the refusal of most judges to read into the early statutes the power to contract regarding the property exempted from liability for the husband's debts seems anomalous, in view of the general nineteenth century bias toward freedom of contract in the interests of an expanded market" (Thurman 1966, 46). An aporetic reading of history renders their refusal no longer anomalous by pointing out that the early married women's property acts failed to address modern democracy's gendered structural aporetic site: the social meanings and institutions interimplicating Womanhood and contract. They shored up some troublesome issues of debtor-creditor relations for nuclear families, and of family lineages in property holdings for extended families, by implementing minor changes in women's legal abilities. But they did not approach the foundational impasse of women's contractual relations, which constituted the core instabilities of women's position in Anglo-based democracies.

The critical legal problematic that arose from this lack of address—the inability of anyone to make contracts regarding property women now owned—would have effects of its own. The need to rectify it would force legislators and the public to confront women's troublesome discursive relations to the economy. The first major step toward its resolution can be seen in the passage of a second spate of married women's property acts, beginning with New York State's act of 1860. The 1860 act was also known as an earnings act, for it secured a married woman the ownership of her earnings, whether from "her trade, business, labor or services" (*Laws of the State of New-York*, 1860, chap. 90, § 1). Equally important, and generally not remarked upon, was women's concomitant gaining of the right to contract not only regarding how they procured their earnings but also regarding their personal and real property (chapter 90, §§ 2–3). The gendered structural aporia delimiting the rift between Womanhood and the economy was first legally addressed here, eleven years before the appearance of Bryan J. Butts's 1871 pamphlet declaring women's material independence as thinking women's utmost concern. What enabled such a movement on the part of the male political elite in U.S. legislatures, when the same legislators had vociferously attacked women's earnings and contractual rights from the 1840s through the late 1850s? Between the passage of New York State's Married Women's Property Acts of 1848 and 1860, or, more generally, between the passage of the first spate of property acts throughout the country and the second spate, a partial transformation must have occurred in how the social meanings of Womanhood, contract, and the economy were imbricated.

Otherwise, legislators and the public could not have even conceived of the relations between Womanhood and contract inscribed in the 1860 Earnings Act. But how did such a transformation occur? What various historical forces, *forces of a crisis,* effected this transformation? And what does such a dramatic historical shift in the social meanings and institutions interimplicating Womanhood, contract, and the economy imply for an understanding of the 1850s woman's rights movement and social movements in general?

Certainly, an aporetic analytic implies that a movement disrupting the social order's very conceptions of Womanhood and contract—their interimplicated systems of social meanings—was a precondition of women's gaining of any viable position within the economic sphere, gaining contractual rights. Only if the very meaning of Womanhood through which people conceived of the social world changed could women begin to enter the social contract, thereby beginning to become "free and equal citizens." Further, this analytic framework implies that women could not have gained political rights such as suffrage unless a transformative disruption of social meanings and institutions of Womanhood, contract, the economy, and the nation had already occurred. The 1850s woman's movement was not the sole cause of this disruption in meaning, though, or of the consequent passage of the Earnings Act of 1860 in New York State or later similar acts elsewhere throughout the United States. Rather, the woman's movement participated in and put pressure on a social rupture occurring at the site of one of modern democracy's foundational impasses. For "a change in a sign system . . . can only be operated by the force of a crisis. Yet, if the space for a change . . . had not been there in the prior function of the sign-system, the crisis could not have made the change happen." The antebellum woman's movement combined with the simultaneously changing and disordered political economy and legal battles of the time to enable this discursive shift. Interimplicated change at both the historical institutional level and the historical social meanings level was a precondition for women gaining contractual and economic rights. But, while each was necessary, neither a fully discursive social movement nor a changing political economy nor a legal reform movement alone, nor even their combination, would have been sufficient to change women's social position in relation to the economy. Their historical combination was successful only because they operated on the site of a structural aporia—*the space for a change*—enabling a disruptive change in the gendered social order.

To be absolutely clear: When and how such a rupture occurred is not immediately apparent simply by noting the presence of the structural aporia. Given women's position in relation to the economy in today's democracies, it can be inferred that such a rupture must have occurred. But only a careful genealogy of the structural aporia can determine when and how the discursive shift or shifts took place—an intricate tracing of the historical details of the social meanings and institutions of early industrial capitalism and gender. Renarrating history through an aporetic analytic performs a genealogy of the present. It presents us with an understanding of how the discursive relations we live within were formed, and, in fact, how they interact today. A structural aporetic analytic recognizes history's and society's detail as "an unstable assemblage of faults, fissures, and heterogeneous layers that threaten the fragile inheritor from within or from underneath" (Foucault 1988/1977, 146). And it calls on the sociologist, cultural critic, political economist, and activist to trace the details of the *unstable assemblage of faults, fissures, and heterogeneous layers* that comprise our present discursive order in an analysis that invokes our *fragility* as the site of the *à-venir, the promise of what is to come.* The rest of this book reads the traces of the *faults, fissures, and heterogeneous layers* of a specific gendered structural aporia in Anglo-based modern democracies—that of Woman and contract—as they shifted, held firm, and disrupted the northeastern U.S. social order from the early 1800s to 1860, with a particular focus on New York State. The following historical details shape the narrative: a changing system of social meanings intertwining Womanhood, property, and contract; the economic tumult experienced with the rise of industrial capitalism; political economic ordering and disordering of gender's relation to the economy; changing legal regulation of both gender and the economy; the early to mid-1800s legal codification movement; and the 1850s woman's movement's efforts at rewriting Woman into history. All played significant roles in the outcome of contemporary struggle within this particular structural aporia. They comprise the specific *accidents of history,* constituting the *politics of the event* that generated its particular movements through this aporetic space.

PART II

OVER THE COURSE OF THE NINETEENTH CENTURY, ECO-
nomic and legal structures in the United States underwent vast
and wrenching transformations, as did their social meanings.
People's daily material lives and social relations were perhaps
more continually disordered between 1820 and 1860 than at any
time in recently preceding centuries. Chapters 3 and 4 renarrate the era's socioeconomic and legal upheavals, with an eye to
the consequences for contemporary social meanings and institutional practices related to Womanhood. They trace these
changing social meanings and institutional practices in the concomitant and interimplicated effects of demographic, occupational, and class changes; the growth of a market economy; the
rise of separate spheres; the gendered division of labor; changing
popular understandings of Womanhood and the True Woman;
changing legal understandings of contract and property; changing legislation on marriage, property, and contract; and legislative debates over the appropriate relation between women,
property, and the economy. A politics of daily power moved
through these varied aspects of antebellum society, playing in
and through democracy's gendered aporetic spaces.

Reading asunder the history of antebellum Womanhood illu-
minates the 1850s woman's movement from distinctly new an-
gles. What at first glance seems to be a well-worn history of

industrial growth, the gendered division of labor, and the rise of separate spheres exposes radical shifts in the underlying social order when read aporetically. Chapters 3 and 4 follow the movements of societal *faults, fissures, and heterogeneous layers* in their dramatic and mundane details by tracing how Womanhood, contract, property, the economy, and the nation moved in and through this aporetic space—in other words, by performing a careful genealogy of Womanhood, contract, and property.

Chapter 3 explores how antebellum demographic, economic, and moral changes flowed through the aporetic figure of Woman. Between 1820 and 1860, changes in the very meaning of Womanhood, as embedded within a complex web of social meanings, elevated the respectable Woman into a sphere of high moral status apart from all others. As Womanhood became suffused with the nation's morality, it grounded an orderly national narrative on an aporetic site, allowing the general populace to maintain a sense of social order during an ungrounded, disorderly time. Chapter 4 traces changes in antebellum legal institutions, legal meanings, and laws— centered as they were in the aporetic abyss of property and contract and intertwined with the economy's dislocation. From the 1820s to 1860, changes in New York State's property laws and legal structures and in the very system of social meanings embedding property and contract combined with the far-reaching changes documented in chapter 3 to enable the success of the antebellum woman's movement. The gendered aporia of marital contract and marital property was made suddenly visible, demanding address. Its pressing cultural presence in turn allowed the antebellum woman's rights movement to move in and through the aporetic space—a space through which Womanhood's fundamental discursive transformation was possible.

Chapter 5 traces how the 1850s woman's rights movement transformed the nation's discursive order—its interimplicated systems of social meanings and institutional practices—by applying pressure to the contemporary structural aporetic space of Womanhood and contract. While the antebellum woman's rights movement was absolutely crucial to changing marriage, property, and contract law and to transforming the social meanings suffusing Womanhood, success at that particular historical moment was possible only because of the complicated interrelations between nineteenth-century economic, moral, and legal institutions and systems of meanings. Several distinct social forces interacted to provide the necessary conditions of possibility: (a) changes in the social meanings and institutions of Woman-hood, contract, and property in the legal system; (b) changes in the social meanings and institutions of Womanhood, contract, and property in the economic system; and (c) a fully discursive antebellum woman's rights movement. None was sufficient, alone or combined. Without these social forces occurring concomitantly—without the specific *politics of the event*—the dramatic changes effected by the antebellum woman's rights movement could not have succeeded. And, just as important, the woman's movement's successful reform was possible only because these social forces unintentionally moved through one of modernity's gendered structural aporias, to which the woman's rights movement applied pressure.

Chapter 3

GENDERED ECONOMIES

The Social Meanings of Womanhood

> What was radically new [in the nineteenth century] was the great acceleration in the rate of economic progress, so great that instead of buttressing the material foundations of American society, it shook apart the institutions of the old social order.
>
> —ROWLAND BERTHOFF, *AN UNSETTLED PEOPLE*

> By the 1850s, gender difference was distinct and public enough to figure prominently in the most vitriolic local conflicts. . . . By 1860, gender had appeared on the public stage as something far more complicated than the simple representation of the female sex.
>
> —MARY P. RYAN, *WOMEN IN PUBLIC*

SOCIOECONOMIC DISORDER

The period from 1820 to 1860 witnessed the beginning of rapid industrialization in New England. During this time, central and western New York quickly changed from an agricultural frontier land to a moderately industrialized and urbanized setting with a remaining agricultural base. The antebellum woman's movement traces its beginnings and base to central and western New York, and this remained its center of operations from 1848 to 1860. In addition, or as a consequence, a dramatic change in the married woman's property acts occurred significantly more quickly here than elsewhere in the country, also framed by the years 1848 and 1860. These two contemporary facts arose contingent upon central and western New York's experiencing what Mary P. Ryan (1981, 59) described as the telescoping of "a significant demographic transition into a span of family time that enclosed fewer than two full generations. This vertiginous social atmosphere attained the velocity of a hurricane in the 1820s, roughly as the second generation came of age." The pressure of such rapid change meant that the region experienced an even greater sense and reality of becoming detached from stable societal structures in its urbanizing and industrializing process than the rest of the country did. Multitudinous changes took place in how life was experienced by the general public, manifesting in major shifts in the occupational structure, the forms of daily social relations, the patterns of residential and familial life, the place of religion in private and public life, the relation to a national commodities market and a burgeoning capital-based cash economy, and the lived meanings given to all of these intertwined human relations. Every single one of these shifts was critically gendered. And their composite depicts the extreme social flux generally experienced throughout the formation of a new social order. The vast number and impact of new links made between central and western New Yorkers and nonlocal sectors of the country and economy literally unmoored people from their previously stable practices and social relations.

As has often been described, transportation innovations took hold in the region, connecting central and western New York to the eastern seaboard and the far west. The Erie Canal, built from 1817 to 1825, connected New York City to Buffalo and beyond, by way of Albany, Utica, Syracuse, and Rochester. Its heavy use promoted rapid settlement around these ports. While its path from New York City to midstate was already populated by at least six people per square mile prior to the beginning of construction, the region from midstate to Buffalo reached an equivalent level by approximately 1830 as a direct result of population convergence on Erie Canal ports (Berthoff 1971, 132–33). This "relatively stable agrarian maturity," which would remain in place until the 1850s, resulted from population growth during the 1820s that was "more rapid here than in any other part of the country. Albany gained 96 percent, Utica 183, Syracuse 282, Buffalo 314, and Rochester 512. The entire five counties surrounding the western half of the canal increased 135 percent in the decade" (Cross 1950, 56). Rail would overtake and close down the building of canals by 1840 (Berthoff 1971, 163), but this would not diminish the effects the Erie Canal had upon the life, culture, and economies of its ports for some decades.

The Erie Canal reached Utica, for instance, in 1820, resulting in the tripling of the town's population and its growth from a "frontier trading post into a small city of twenty-two thousand people with a variegated urban economy" by the 1850s (Ryan 1981, 5). By contrast, in the early 1830s, at the time of the city's first charter, approximately nine thousand people had resided there (8). These changes were representative of urbanization throughout the region. This region, designated the East North Central area in U.S. Census Bureau data, had only 0.9 percent of its total population living in urban areas in 1810. By 1830 urban population had tripled to 2.5 percent of the total, and by 1850 it had increased tenfold to 9 percent of the total, while the population of the New England and Middle Atlantic areas had only doubled (North 1961, 258).

The economic and gendered transformations experienced by the port city of Utica provide an exemplar of the growth and composition of cities along the canal route:

> The city's social and economic structure was very much like the other middle-sized cities of the era . . . [that] shared Utica's basic economic organization, wherein a few large steam-powered factories coexisted with many small craftsmen and shopkeepers and a growing number of salaried white-collar workers. Like Utica, these cities were characterized by rapid population growth, a high level of transience, voluminous social mobility (in upward, downward, and horizontal directions), and a massive influx of immigrants from abroad. Much of the fluid social and economic life of nineteenth-century America was caught up in the constant movement in, around, and out of cities like these. (Ryan 1981, 5)

The continuous internal migration, along with the tremendous and steady growth in immigration from 1820 to 1854, meant that even small to midsize urban communities and social networks were much more unstable during this period than today's popular representations intimate.

Changes in U.S. immigration levels represent the intensity of the changes undergone by these newly urban populations. In 1820, only 8,385 people immigrated to the United States. By 1830, this figure had tripled to 23,322; in 1840, it had more than tripled again to 84,066. The next ten years saw another 440 percent jump, to 369,980 in 1850; and, by 1854, national immigration had reached 427,833. After 1854, it decreased dramatically but remained over 120,000 annually through 1860—still more than fourteen times the 1820 figure and more than five times the figure for 1830 (North 1961, 245). Additionally, over half of any given locale's residents relocated between each decade's census, moving between communities of various sizes and economic makeup throughout the country (Berthoff 1971, 224). This suddenly mobile populace stood in direct contrast to what not too much earlier had been a static and stable agricultural society based on the patriarchal household. Along with the new immigrants, single young men were also moving into urban centers, commonly residing in boardinghouses. Their influx forced a dramatic dislocation of previous familial living arrangements in both urban and rural areas.

Religious revivalism served as a partial outlet for the societal dislocation experienced as a result of the rapid demographic transitions and rapidly growing economy. The Second Great Awakening, a religious movement, swept through central and western New York in the early 1800s, gaining the region the name "Burned-Over District." Stable gendered and family relations were temporarily consolidated in the fires of the Second Great Awakening, subsequently enabling transformations in daily gendered systems of meaning and related institutional practices. These transitional gendered and family relations also enabled the rise of numerous historically important charitable and reform movements, such as temperance and abolition (Epstein 1981; Hewitt 1984; Ryan 1981). Oneida County—the location of Utica's precursor, Whitestown—presented a picture of this dramatic dislocation and temporary restabilizing of gendered and familial systems of meaning and institutional practices through religious movement. Ryan (1981, 59, 65) describes the social terrain:

> Before 1820 the first settlers had succeeded in re-creating a New England social organization that included the reincarnation of such seventeenth-

century institutions as the corporate family economy, a patriarchal household structure, and the covenanted religious community. These throwbacks to the days of the Puritans, however, coexisted with the culture, economics, and society of the eighteenth century—with habits of trade, industry, and benevolence that had been acquired east of the frontier, especially in Connecticut. [In the 1820s,] the residents of Whitestown adapted these old and new social forms in the course of a rapid transition from the primitive home economy to a specialized trade network. . . .

It was the generational ties of the home economy that seemed most fragile, most vulnerable to the corrosive power of commerce. The men and women of Oneida County were not unaware of this fact. They did not express their family concerns in economistic terms, however, but rather in the language and central ideological structure of their time, that is, in an essentially religious mode of thought.

In other words, the rapid and destabilizing changes experienced in productive relations, family relations, gender relations, trade relations, and demographic proximity were not expressed in economic metaphors and idioms. They were not expressed in the language of the messily nascent democratic capitalist economy. Rather, the local populace conceived of these dislocating changes in the metaphors and idioms through which they had framed the just prior traditional and stable social order, including those of "the corporate family economy, a patriarchal household structure, and the covenanted religious community" (Ryan 1981, 59). People experiencing great social dislocations turned to an old language of social stability to conceptualize their most fragile and vulnerable relations, thereby maintaining a sense of stability and continuity in the social meanings they lived by, if not in their daily practices. A religious revival movement provided this language, tenuously mooring an increasingly unstable social order in the system of social meanings that structured people's daily and institutional relations in the prior social order. Rapid socioeconomic transition had primed central and western New York State for the fires of the Second Great Awakening, which brought communities together to insist on a central set of social meanings and relations, even as the very ones they insisted upon were being destroyed.

The canal cities were centers of the complex dynamic between economic and social change and evangelism. For instance, Rochester "was a burgeoning

commercial center at the hub of an increasingly specialized agricultural hinterland and the fastest-growing boom town in the nation between 1825 and
1835. . . . At the heart of the Burned-Over District, the town was illuminated
(or ravaged, depending on one's perspective) by the fires of religious and reform enthusiasms in each of the decades from 1830 to 1870" (Hewitt 1984,
21). A particular set of gendered, familial, and public relations were forged
in this religious crucible. They lay a base for the resonance of both True
Womanhood's domestic, pious, and public figure and a seemingly contrary
figure of Womanhood, that of the True Woman who actively uses her morality to shape her community by, in this case, working through religious
institutions and associations. By the end of the Second Great Awakening,
neither Rochester nor Oneida County "could [any] longer be character-
ized as a community whose central constituting element was the patriarchal
household. . . . Within families, furthermore, it was the mothers rather than
patriarchs who exerted increasing control over the religious allegiances
of the young. In other words, a more decidedly privatized and feminized
form of religious and social reproduction was beginning to take shape
around the relationship between evangelical mothers and converted children" (Ryan 1981, 104).[1] Reading history asunder, the Second Great Awakening strengthened True Womanhood's societal importance while founding its societal operation on definitionally inchoate terrain.

    At the same time, activist women and their public-directed works did not
form a single, unifying force. For instance, in Rochester, New York, three
distinct groups of female activists emerged from the early 1820s on: benevolent women, religious activists focusing on moral causes, and radical activists (Hewitt 1984). Each group most strongly allied themselves with the
men in "their own economic, social, and family circles and in opposition to
women and men of competing circles" (22). Just as a True Woman primarily
mapped her path in relation to her husband and sons, these connections
powerfully shaped each activist group. Additionally, each emerged at a distinct moment in the urban, capitalist economy's dislocating birth. Clearly,
women's class position—or the class position of their husbands, fathers,
and sons—defined each group's entry into activism. While aspects of True
Womanhood suffused each group's good works, the form their activism
took and the issues they focused on were distinctly shaped by their class's
moment of entry into the canal cities' trajectory of capitalist formation and

concomitant socioeconomic dislocation. Each group's activism necessarily engaged the systems of social meanings embedded in True Womanhood, a web of social meanings that made daily life cohere by intricately interweaving Womanhood, contract, property, labor, the economy, and the nation. How they each traversed these webs of meaning was in part defined by their moment of entry into urban capitalism. So this moment is worth a bit more detail.

A brief overview of their patterns of emergence in Rochester reflects the general patterns of female activism in central and western New York from 1820 to 1860. Female benevolent associations were first formed prior to the arrival of revivalism and coincident with the arrival of the cash economy and specialized trade networks via the Erie Canal (Hewitt 1984, 22). These benevolent women were the first to become detached from the traditional family economy as the gradual progress of urbanization, mercantilism, and industrialization got underway. They were merchants' wives who organized an associational base for the new city, placing them solidly at the center of the new socioeconomy. A second group of woman activists, perfectionists, "sought to eradicate rather than ameliorate social ills" (40). These women came from the middling classes as the city grew—the very classes that were experiencing the greatest occupational growth and consequent reorganization of gendered and family life in urban living. They brought their activist fire from the flames of evangelism and its moral dictates of community engagement. The Second Great Awakening reshaped popular conceptions of Woman's domesticity and morality such that women could and should focus it outward, specifically in order to purify society. Just as the middling classes themselves were in an increasingly central and yet precarious position, perfectionist women, who hailed from these classes, "introduced new issues and new forms of public activity to the community but were never able to reproduce the social acceptability and stability of female benevolent societies" (40).

Interestingly, when compared with benevolent women and perfectionists, ultraist women activists were "clearly marginal to the ranks of fashionable society" (Hewitt 1984, 62). But, viewed with an aporetic eye, they can actually be seen to be positioned at the very center of the transformative and dislocating mid-1800s socioeconomy and would form the core of the antebellum woman's movement from the late 1840s through the 1850s.

Hewitt's description of ultraists' arrival in Rochester mirrors descriptions of the most dislocating aspects of the transition from agrarian family economy to small township to urban center. Generally Hicksite Quakers, ultraist women "were predominantly from New York farming villages rather than New York or New England commercial centers. They were younger, on the average, than women who entered benevolent ranks, and they arrived in Rochester later than either benevolent or perfectionist leaders: at least thirty of the fifty ultraist women active in the 1840s did not arrive in the city until 1835 or later. When ultraist women did arrive, they lived on the outskirts of the city or in its less affluent wards" (61–62). Of the three groups, ultraists personally experienced the most extreme socioeconomic dislocation and transformation. In the same way that central and western New York telescoped a process that took much longer in most other regions of the United States, ultraists experienced the same process in a more telescoped form than others in the region, and therefore with greater impact and resulting dislocation. These women moved quickly from a stable agrarian home economy to the most precarious positions in the new socioeconomy and felt the full effect of societal transformations.

At the same time, ultraists used perfectionism's gendered networks of moral activism and reform sensibilities to build support for their radical causes. They also understood themselves in terms of True Womanhood's tenets, but would actively refigure the meaning of True Woman's domesticity. For instance, in Utica, one of the leaders of the woman's movement well into the late 1800s, Paulina Wright, began by "pump[ing] that [Presbyterian women's] network for every reforming supporter she could find. She went the familiar women's route from door to door, promoting moral reform, distributing temperance tracts, promulgating abolitionism, and in 1837 she circulated a petition in support of the Married Women's Property Act" (Ryan 1981, 124). Ultraism arose from the economic, social, religious, and demographic dislocations experienced in the birth and growth of the canal cities, such as Utica and Rochester; yet, these same forces further consolidated the web of social meanings embedding True Womanhood rather than shaking it apart. The Erie Canal brought ultraists the possibility of travel and access to larger circles of reformers. It also brought pamphlets and women's magazines promulgating the national importance of True Womanhood and its ideal of domesticity to women of the middling classes, who avidly read these new cultural materials.[2] Consequently, an increasingly popular-ized and seemingly stable understanding of True Womanhood and its radi-cal renarration by the ultraists straddled the tumultuous formation of a new socioeconomic order.

Contrary to familiar historical narratives, then, the rise of True Wom-anhood was doubly aporetic. First, as discussed in chapter 2, True Wom-anhood's social meanings were interimplicated with the social meanings of contract, property, the economy, and the nation in a precise parallel to the aporetic social meanings of social contract mythology. Second, True Wom-anhood rested on definitional and socioeconomic foundations that were a swirl of dislocation. In fact, the True Woman was perhaps more a distract-ing cover over an abyssal space than a figure on a firm pedestal. The follow-ing section examines contemporary data of socioeconomic dislocation and macrolevel proxies for a society in tumult, locating some of the specific are-nas in which the "vertiginous social atmosphere" shaped gendered labor and gendered meanings—in other words, shaped the social meanings and practices of True Womanhood in nineteenth-century New York State.

MACRO VARIABLES VARYING

Economic Growth and Integration: An Overview

New York canal cities still relied on their agricultural hinterland as a produc-tive base between 1820 and 1860. But, rather than continuing to subsist on lo-cal products, the cities joined the newly forming national and international product and capital markets, shipping their raw materials east over the ca-nal and shipping in finished products. While this connection furthered the growth of canal cities' craft, mercantile, and financial sectors, it simultane-ously exposed the entire region to the frequent, harsh fluctuations common to markets-in-formation. Central and western New York State truly entered the cash economy around 1820, coincident with the beginning of the Erie Canal's socioeconomic effects on the region. By 1850, a new interstate econ-omy had permanently impacted the local and regional economies.

Again, Utica provides an exemplar for the canal cities' changes as they moved from agricultural regions to mercantile cities to manufacturing bases: "The approximate date of 1820 demark[s] that point when diversified agricul-tural production lost hegemony to the small-scale merchandisers and man-ufacturers. . . . By around 1850, the dominance of artisans and shopkeepers was challenged, in turn, by the more massive mercantile and manufacturing firms of an embryonic industrial era" (Ryan 1981, 11). When its first city charter was written in 1832, Utica consisted of an agricultural region and one township (8). Its original nine thousand residents more than doubled to twenty-two thousand over the next fifteen years. Like other Erie Canal port cities, Utica grew first as a mercantile center. In the 1840s, "a typical edition of the *Utica Observer* . . . advertised wares of more than a hundred different specialty shops, hawking everything from fine-ground flour to colorful ginghams and shimmering looking glasses. The financial apparatus necessary to this expanded commerce—banks, insurance companies, law offices—grew apace" (8). The manufacturing sector grew concomitantly, as the growing mercantile sector supported skilled craftsmanship. During the 1840s, "the largest single mode of employment, accounting for 45% of the occupations listed in the city directories, was provided by the skilled crafts" (8). Industrial production remained minimal at this time, though. In fact, "as late as 1850, 3 out of 4 firms [still] employed fewer than ten workers. The modal shop counted only two or three workers, who relied on their own skill and muscle rather than horse, water, or steam power" (8).

Such rapid demographic, productive, and financial transformations, defined by great geographic and socioeconomic mobility, could not possibly occur smoothly. The very links that the Erie Canal provided to the national commodities market and national and international capital markets—the links enabling growth of the canal cities' mercantile, manufacturing, and financial sectors—also provided a direct conduit to the region for national economic shocks. As always happens in the shift to a new socioeconomic order, a period of severe socioeconomic disruption ensued. As central and western New York delinked from stable local economies based in domestic production, it became just one sector of a volatile, emergent national economy. The same links enabling local integration into modern capitalism also dislocated and unsettled people's daily lives, making their economic stability tenuous. Such a period of disruption, disorder, and extreme socioeconomic fragility accompanying the birth of industrial capitalism is of course a commonplace to economic historians and political economists. This is as true for seventeenth- and eighteenth-century Britain as for the nineteenth-century United States and for mid- to late-twentieth-century third world nations. Creating a stable economic, political, and social infrastructure for a newly emerging politico-economic system is a tall historical order. Reading history asunder specifically implies that how social meanings and institutions shift and reconsolidate in these moments of disruption is critical to a *history of the present*. An aporetic analytic implies that the sociologist, cultural critic, and activist should pay precise attention to the details of these disruptive moments in order to better understand a given society's present constitution and impasses.

Mid-1800s socioeconomic fragility was extreme by today's standards. General depressions occurred in every decade from the 1830s through the 1850s and particularly severe financial panics took hold in 1837 and 1857, resulting in rapid and painful changes in class or socioeconomic standing for many individuals and families. Dramatic numbers of small merchants abruptly failed and threw their laborers out of work, "hasten[ing] the transition from the merchant employer to the factory owner" in good Marxist fashion (McGrane 1924, 111). Importantly, canal cities were not linked to already established, stable product and financial markets; rather, they attached themselves to an industrial capitalist economy in the process of emerging. The national financial sector and today's commonplace financial instruments were just being tested and put into place. More accurately, a multitude of interconnected regional financial sectors existed rather than a coherent national financial sector. The U.S. government gamely attempted to create a central bank, but the Second Bank of the United States failed in 1841 after having suspended payments for two years as a result of the depression that followed in the wake of the Panic of 1837 (Temin 1969, 154–55). Local banks offered their own paper notes, which could then be traded for goods, returned to another bank for specie (actual coin) by the producer, and then returned to the original bank for specie by the receiving bank. But with no central control over the practices of the various individual banks, merchants and financiers had no assurance that any one bank would always honor another bank's notes. And banks themselves could not trust that other banks would honor their own notes.

Precisely these mechanisms broke down in the Panic of 1837 and the Panic of 1857: banks suspended specie payments for notes or refused to honor the notes at face value, whether from their own bank or others, at the same time calling in loans from their most stable borrowers and attempting to force other banks to make good on their notes (McGrane 1924; Temin 1969; Van

Vleck 1967). This left merchants, financiers, industrial and agricultural producers, and any of the general populace who used banks holding pieces of paper that could no longer be traded for actual coin. In other words, the paper money they held was now just paper or devalued paper. Individual merchants and large financial and exchange houses could not meet their obligations as they came due, leading to merchant failures as well as the closing of large financial and exchange houses. According to the *Journal of Commerce*, by April 8, 1837, failures had already included:

> 5 foreign and exchange brokers, with capital of $15 million,
>
> 30 dry good jobbers, with capital of $15 million,
>
> 16 commission shoe and clothing houses, with $7 million capital,
>
> 28 real estate speculators, with $20 million capital,
>
> 8 stock brokers, with $1 million capital, and
>
> 6 miscellaneous houses, with capital of $2.5 million. (cited in Temin 1969, 142–43)

Additionally, industrial and agricultural producers could not repay loans advanced earlier to purchase raw materials and to be repaid postproduction, and neither could they afford new raw materials, both of which led to more production failures.

It would be some time before the economic innovations of these decades—banks, money markets, stock markets—functioned nearly as smoothly or predictably as they do today (even when compared to today's financial market crises). An impressionistic description of the Panic of 1837 provides a view of the sort of socioeconomic fragility experienced by the general populace. By May 1837, generalized panic had created a "pressure [that] was too great for the banks to bear. . . . The banks in New York City suspended payment on May 10, but the suspension soon became national. Banks in Albany, Hartford, New Hampshire, Philadelphia, Providence, and Baltimore suspended on May 11; banks in Mobile and Boston, on May 12; banks in New Orleans, on May 13; and so on" (Temin 1969, 113). What began as a financial crisis quickly spread well beyond any confined financial sector and set off seven years of depression, almost sending New York State into bankruptcy in 1842 when the state was unable to repay $1 million in debt to the Erie Canal contractors (McGrane 1924, 104). Laborers throughout the Northeast were extremely hard hit, and the unemployment levels point to a drastic decline in production as well: "Fifty thousand workers were reported idle in New York sometime in 1837, 2,000 unemployed were reported in Lynn (Massachusetts), and cotton mills in Boston and Lowell were idle" (Temin 1969, 120). These numbers represented a significant portion of the labor force; county censuses recorded New York City's entire population, of which the labor force was only a portion, as 268,089 in 1835 and 312,710 in 1850 (New York State, Secretary's Office 1867, xxiv–xxv).

> In New York City, alone, in 1837, it was said that "six thousand masons and carpenters and other workmen connected with building had been discharged." *Niles'* [*Weekly Register;* Philadelphia] records that by September, 1837, nine-tenths of the factories in the eastern states had closed, and that the same proportion of employees had been discharged. From Dover, Massachusetts, came word that a mill there closed its doors throwing "two hundred females and forty males" out of work. "The streets of Bedford," said one report, "are now thronged with seamen out of employment. Forty whale ships are lying at the wharves, but nothing doing to fit them out for sea." Haverford, Massachusetts, announced "the almost entire failure of the shoe business in this vicinity"; while similar accounts came from the manufacturers of Lynn and Salem. Many of the dry-goods jobbing houses of New York were in a state of bankruptcy by the close of 1837. . . . One-half to two-thirds of the clerks and salesmen in large commercial houses in Philadelphia were without work by June, 1837. (McGrane 1924, 130–31)

Economic data for the following years depict the Panic of 1837's long-term impact. Tons of merchandise shipped west over the Erie Canal—from the East Coast and canal cities—dropped by a third in 1837, partially recovering along with the rest of the economy in 1838 and 1839 and then again dropping by a third in 1840. These quantities would not return to pre-1837 levels until 1843 (North 1961, 254). Similarly, the number of businesses incorporated in New York State reached a high in 1836 at 136, almost double the previous high from 1832.[3] Sixty-three of these new incorporations were in railroads and turnpikes; twenty-six were in finance, divided evenly between banks and insurance. In 1837, new incorporations dropped by over half to sixty-one, and would continue to fall through 1843, which saw only six new incorporations. From 1829 to 1836, seventy-one new banks were chartered in New York State. From 1837 to 1844, only four new banks were chartered. New manufacturing charters fell from thirty-three in 1836 to three in 1842. Long-wave data, compiled as moving averages of New York State incorporations over five years, depict these trends without the particular years' idiosyncrasies affecting the view. Turnpike incorporations held fairly even from 1820 to 1836, with a minor peak from 1834 to 1836, and then dropped through 1844, the last year for which data are available (Evans 1948, 22). Manufacturing incorporations grew steadily from 1820 to 1836, with a slight dip from 1828 to 1832 and a strong peak from 1834 to 1836, and then dropped precipitously (23). Railroad incorporations peaked dramatically in 1836 and then dropped even more precipitously (25). Overall, business incorporations' rapid decline would not end until 1844, when incorporation levels stabilized at 22 percent of their 1836 numbers.

While the Panic of 1857's long-term effects were not as dire, it came to a similar head when banks suspended specie payment for two months, from October 14 to December 14, "literally paralyz[ing trade] from Bangor to New Orleans. . . . With people obliged to restrict their purchases to articles of primed necessity, all business was at a standstill" (Van Vleck 1967, 74). Again, massive unemployment ensued, reaching into the hundreds of thousands, with estimates of 100,000 unemployed in New York City alone, "of which nearly 20,000 were thrown out of work in a single fortnight" (75). And again, the unemployed represented a significant portion of the labor force, given that county censuses recorded New York City's total population as 629,810 in 1855 and 813,669 in 1860 (New York State, Secretary's Office 1867, xxiv–xxv). In 1858, tonnage of merchandise shipped to western states via the Erie Canal also dropped again, this time by just over a quarter, and climbed back to its prior level in 1860 (North 1961, 254). The Panics of 1837 and 1857 were but two crisis moments in a period of vast market fluctuations and repeated generalized depressions.

Tenuous Transitional Economies, 1837–1865

Economic histories generally claim that the Panic of 1837 and the ensuing depression fell heaviest on western speculators and eastern laborers (McGrane 1924, 133) or that the effects were felt primarily in "a few major urban centers" (Temin 1969, 20). Both claims are based in part on a supposition that the national financial market was not important for farmers until the

1850s, when they became interested in capital investment (Brownlee 1988, 210). But economic data show that the cities of central and western New York were heavily affected despite their minimal industrialization. The canal cities still specialized in subsistence products: "Rochester, specializing in flour, Syracuse in salt, and Utica in cloth" (Cross 1950, 56). Economists generally expect that demand for primary goods or subsistence products is income-inelastic; that is, people will continue to demand approximately the same amount of basic foodstuffs, such as salt and flour, despite fluctuation in their income because there are no equivalent goods that can easily be substituted for them. Salt is required to preserve foods; flour is required for the working class's most basic of foods: bread.

If the assumption of income inelasticity held true during the Panic of 1837 and the ensuing years of depression, canal cities' shipping of primary goods should have held steady. In this case, a financial market crisis would have affected farmers only once they were acting as medium- to large-scale investors or businesses—once they were participating in the financial markets themselves in order to make capital investments to further their production. But, in fact, tonnage shipped on the Erie Canal from central and western New York State ports to the tidewater was highly volatile from 1836 to 1860, responding sharply to economic shocks. It dropped dramatically from 1837 through 1842, regaining its pre-1837 level only in 1843 (North 1961, 251).[4] Tonnage dropped again by 17 percent from 1848 through 1852, increased by 20 percent from 1852 through 1854, and then dropped by 50 percent or more from 1855 through 1858. In more detail, beginning at 364,906 in 1836, tonnage from within New York State to the tidewater dropped by 9 percent in 1837 to 331,251 tons. It then dropped another 9 percent to average just above three hundred thousand tons from 1838 through 1841, for approximately a 20 percent decrease from 1836. In 1842, it again dropped precipitously, to 258,672 tons from 1841's level of 308,344 tons—another decline of 16 percent, for a total decline of 29 percent from 1837 on. Finally, in 1843, tonnage increased by 47 percent, recouping business to a pre-1837 level of 378,969 tons.

Over the next fifteen years, shipments east from central and western New York State continued to display such volatility. From 1843 through 1845, tonnage doubled again; then it dropped 24 percent by 1849. Certain years were especially volatile. For instance, shipments increased 29 percent from

1852 to 1853, from 492,726 tons to 637,648 tons, and then decreased by 46 percent from 1854 to 1855, from 602,167 tons to 327,839 tons. During the same time period, tonnage shipped over the Erie Canal from western states to the tidewater grew steadily, other than a brief dip in 1847 and 1848. In 1853, western states shipped twenty times their 1836 tonnage, and kept shipping at this level until another 75 percent increase in 1860. The extreme and frequent fluctuations in shipping tonnage from within New York State to the tidewater meant that central and western New York producers could not and did not rely on a steady cash income. And it suggests that in difficult years they probably still regularly substituted clothing and foodstuffs that were domestically produced rather than relying on commercially produced clothing and food, which would have been imported regionally in exchange for their flour, salt, and cloth.

In fact, both market and family economies were in a transitional stage during this period. While domestic production declined from the 1820s on, the 1855 and 1865 censuses indicate that women still produced at home, even if at a diminished rate, and their products had entered the public commodities market. Census tables listing a wide array of domestic manufactures with market valuations show the absolute quantity and value of home-produced goods offered in the public market increasing between 1855 and 1865; the proliferating census categories for domestic manufactures signaled that the types of goods commonly bought and sold in the public market also increased. The 1855 census listing covered two pages and included only the following: baskets, bedspreads, blankets, brooms, carpeting, cloth, coverlids, currant wine, dried fruit, gloves, hats, mats, mittens, oil of peppermint, plaids, socks, and yarn (New York State, Secretary's Office 1857, 41–42). By 1865, the census listing of "Miscellaneous Domestic Manufactures" had expanded to cover four pages. More important, prior categories required subcategorizing; numerous domestic manufactures newly entered the public market; and some domestic manufactures exploded onto the market as a basis for new forms of transportation and newly industrialized construction and production. For instance, currant wine expanded to wine—blackberry, currant, elderberry, rhubarb, and unspecified; mittens expanded to mittens—buckskin and wool; cloth expanded to cloth—fulled, flannel, and linen. Many items not previously marketed in large quantities defined new categories in 1865, such as bark, boots and shoes, cider, shawls, and sorghum molasses. Certain newly marketed domestic manufactures signaled regional economies' entry into the industrialized era, especially: railroad ties in Broome County; stakes and bolts in Broome, Erie, and Monroe Counties; saw logs in Allegany, Oswego, and Washington Counties; shingles in Broome, Fulton, and Montgomery Counties; wood in almost all counties, particularly Madison and Suffolk; and dried apples in Chautauqua, Erie, and Niagara Counties (New York State, Secretary's Office 1867, 411–14).[5] Clearly, in 1865, home production played a significant role in both providing necessities for families and creating goods for market. Basic production and consumption did not yet move entirely through the market, and home-produced goods were still substituted for manufactured goods in years of low cash income. In other words, demand was not yet income-inelastic in these primary goods markets because subsistence goods were still being produced domestically, even if some portion of them were headed to market. Consequently, the producers in these midsize port cities in central and western New York were able to respond to shocks transmitted through their new and tenuous connections to national product and financial markets by shifting their consumption and production back toward the home economy. Additionally, though, the decreased regional export of goods to East Coast markets meant sharp financial losses to those farmers who had invested in their crops and relied on outside markets to recoup their investments. As a result, from 1840 to 1860, financial panics and depressions frequently and dramatically affected trade patterns from and to these cities.

The effects on canal cities of their erratic export levels would also have been exacerbated by the extreme flexibility of prices in the 1840s (Temin 1969, 171).[6] As the prices of canal cities' primary products decreased, the cash income brought in by the same amount of exports would have decreased in turn, allowing canal city producers to invest less money in their next season's production. Based on the tonnage data above, it appears that financial crises had a direct effect on the amount of goods exported from this region, which would then have been compounded by the effects of flexible prices. Decreased exports would bring in further decreased cash income, leading to lessened consumption of manufactured imports and lessened investment in future production. Fewer products were shipped, and therefore less money could be invested in the next year's crop. Prices fell from early 1837, rising unsteadily again from the end of 1837 through the spring of 1839;

then, beginning in late 1839, "prices fell by almost one half in the next four years," in the same years that tonnage decreased precipitously from within New York to the tidewater (148). These price and tonnage decreases demonstrate how economic shocks traveled over the Erie Canal from the newly linked commodities, financial, and capital markets.

Bad years for agricultural production do not generally coincide only with market forces; rather, they tend to be affected by seasonal changes, especially when a connection with the market is still tenuous. But these data demonstrate that the Erie Canal transmitted economic dislocations from the east that overwhelmed any seasonal effects for these regions in the midst of the transition from frontier land to industrialized urban centers. In eastern urban centers, the price drop was good news for unemployed laborers because it dampened the decrease in their real incomes by making necessities such as cloth and flour more affordable. By the same token, however, the price drop meant a greater decrease in real income for agricultural producers, for the residents of the canal cities who had begun to rely on commodities brought in from the east and who owed creditors for the money borrowed to produce the subsistence goods they sold. Along the Erie Canal, the very links that provided the basis for a newly emerging social order also acted as the means of further unsettling people's daily lives by creating a sense of socioeconomic flux that could be experienced only as disorder.

Economic Growth, Land Use, and Changing Social Meanings of Contract

Rapid legal transformations created further dislocation, as the social understandings that would support capitalist industry emerged. From 1820 to 1860, the legal conception of property and contract and their regulation changed critically. Common law rules of property, which conceived of land as a static and nonproductive good in a feudal agrarian society, were challenged in hundreds of court cases that asked whether these rules were appropriate to an economy newly based in speculation and production (Horwitz 1977, 54). Wildly fluctuating land prices and new uses for attributes of private property such as rights to water use, with which mills could now be powered, forced a fundamental reconceptualization of the very meanings and legal understandings of property that formed one of the bases of a new political economy. The social meanings and legal understandings of contract also changed over this period, providing another base of the new so- .

cioeconomic order. With the formation of national commodities markets around 1815, goods became understood as easily soluble for financial capital in response to market movements. And "the function of contracts correspondingly shifted from that of simply transferring title to a specific item to that of ensuring an expected return" (161).[7] Now, if a contract went unfulfilled, the contractor could seek and receive legal recompense for (a) the value of the item that should have been transferred, as before, as well as (b) damages that covered any further value that the contractor expected to gain by using the item for production, investment, or arbitrage and was therefore lost when the contract was not fulfilled.

Growth in the new economy relied in part on the rise of expectation damages as the new object of contracts, since contracts were now frequently used to speculate on changes in commodity prices rather than to establish possession rights over particular items (Horwitz 1977, 164). In fact, the rise of futures agreements marked a necessary change in the social meanings and legal understandings of contracts. Regulating the exchange of one specific piece of property for another specific piece of property in the immediate present became just one of the functions of contracts. Contracts had previously been legally understood through the title theory of contract, which held that the "inherent justice or fairness of [such] an exchange" could be judged. By contrast, futures agreements are primarily speculative contracts with no guarantee of the value of the return to the contracting parties (160). The rise of speculation on national commodities markets meant a rise in futures agreements, in which "the source of the obligation of contract [became] the convergence of the wills of the contracting parties. . . . The entire conceptual apparatus of modern contract doctrine—rules dealing with offer and acceptance, the evidentiary function of consideration, and especially canons of interpretation—arose to express this will theory of contract" (160–61). Futures agreements essentially constitute promises based in the contracting parties' expectations. Judgment of the contract's fulfillment then becomes judgment of the initial wills of the parties, the extent to which their intent has been fulfilled, and the extent to which expectation damages have been incurred. Notably, "the moment at which courts focus on expectation damages rather than restitution or specific performance to give a remedy for nondelivery is precisely the time at which contract law begins to separate itself from property" (174). From 1820 to 1860, contract law loosened its moorings from the concrete—from property itself—and became abstract, based in the codification of promises.

The historical details of New York State's legislative reform movement reveal aspects of this critical process of reconceptualizing contract and property. Begun at the time of the Revolution, legislative reform sought to remove aristocratic tendencies from a legal system inherited from Britain. Its main goals were to distinguish the new nation's law from English common law, to lessen the perceived tyranny of judge-made law, and to defeudalize relations legally structured by the common law (Cook 1981; Rabkin 1980). Legislative reform unquestionably had its greatest impact in New York State, where it became a serious public concern from the 1820s through the 1840s and resulted in the passage of the 1828 and 1836 Revised Statutes and the Field Code of legal procedure in 1848. Legal relations structuring inheritance, such as primogeniture, were the first to be renegotiated. In the 1820s, a commission was directed "to revamp the law of future interests, or those interests in property other than present rights of possession" (Rabkin 1980, 61). As the most concretely moored legal form of future interests, inheritance law provided reformers an entry into reconceiving property law based on new practices of contract. This commission's work led directly to the passage of the 1828 Revised Statutes for New York State—the first tangible evidence of what would be profound changes in contract law and property law.

Thus, through the growth of national markets and futures agreements, we return to promising and the heart of modernity's contract, witnessing the consolidation of a legal institution of contract specific to Anglo-based democratic capitalism. A new institution of contract coincided with and was born from the economic disorder experienced during the birth of a new political economic order[8]—from the rapid market fluctuations, the movement toward national commodity and money markets resulting in extreme socioeconomic fluctuations at the community, family, and individual levels. Contract was unbound from the solidity of property and came to inhabit the less tangible realm of promise, in a precise analogy to the form contract takes in social contract theories. Here, in the historical realms of both social meanings and institutions, legal contracts came to be based in promising—an aporetic form. And this new center of the socioeconomic order—the promissory operations of contract—was founded precisely on the socioeconomic disorder of the 1820s to 1860.[9]

> The impact of work on the social position of the worker has never been
> determined by the importance of that work to the economy; rather,
> work's social meaning is determined by the constellation of social rela-
> tionships within which work takes place.
>
> —Julie A. Matthaei, *An Economic History of Women in America*

Not surprisingly, the vast transformations in early nineteenth-century economic, productive, and demographic realms led directly to changes in the
occupational structure. As Matthaei notes, the economic role of a laborer's
product does not define what it means to be a laborer. Taken rather more
broadly than I suspect she intended, Matthaei's comment implies that, in
order to understand the social meaning of labor, the laborer's position in
relation to demographic and institutional changes as well as to concomitant changes in webs of social meanings must be taken into account. From
the 1820s to 1860 in the northeastern United States, "the constellation of social relationships within which work took place" were powerfully affected
by urbanization and industrialization as well as the webs of social meanings interimplicating Womanhood, contract, property, labor, the economy,
and the nation. In fact, changes in the occupational structure broadly construed were intertwined both with changes in the gendered division of labor and with changes in the very meanings of Womanhood, contract, and
property.

A standardized New York State census was first taken in 1855 and repeated in 1865.[10] Consequently, my discussion here relies on comparative
data depicting changes from 1855 to 1865.[11] Although they do not give a view
of the overwhelming changes that occurred from the 1820s on, the data
provide clear evidence of the transformations New York experienced as it
entered the manufacturing era; remember, only in the 1850s did the midsize port cities of central and western New York grow from stable agrarian
maturity into industrialized urban centers. Cultural acceptance of True
Womanhood as the social meaning of reputable Womanhood itself—with
its combined attributes of morality, piety, purity, and submissiveness—also
peaked during the 1850s among the native-born middling classes. These
comparative data provide insight into the socioeconomic dislocation experienced in what was a critical decade for New York State—dislocation that

went beyond the Panic of 1857 and the more generalized instability of financial, labor, and commodities markets.

Changes in Public and Family Economies: Occupations and Production

Since the New York State censuses of 1855 and 1865 caught the demographic transition from agrarian and domestic economy to market economy mid-stride, they reflect individuals' and families' uncertainty as to their place in the agrarian and market economies and an inconsistency in the sense of macrocategories such as the labor force. Consequently, "the occupations of only 994,829 persons, or 28.70 per cent of the total population, were reported in 1855 . . . [and] in 1865 the number thus reported was 1,117,181, or 29.18 per cent of the total" (New York State, Secretary's Office 1867, lxxv). Although common economic measures such as "share of labor force" cannot be calculated and the accuracy of the absolute numbers reported in each occupation cannot be thoroughly relied on, the data available manifest significant trends in class formation and resultant changes in people's daily lives. For instance, while the New York census data show the reported number of farmers remaining fairly steady from 1855 to 1865, they also report the number of unskilled laborers increasing by approximately 23 percent, from 115,800 to 142,261.[12]

Increases in two distinct groupings depict growth of the middling classes in these data: first, occupations that were at the heart of the new middling classes themselves; second, occupations that served its consumption needs and demands (see table 1). Demonstrating the former case—growth of the middling classes themselves—the reported numbers of clerks, copyists, and accountants rose by 41 percent, salesmen by 67 percent, and students by 20 percent. Demonstrating the latter case—growth in conspicuous consumption—the reported numbers of toy and fancy goods makers rose by 538 percent and of furriers by 243 percent. As the new middling classes decreased their domestic manufacture and began to purchase more goods, the reported numbers of wine and liquor dealers also increased, from 749 in 1855 to 2,524 in 1865, or by 237 percent. Significantly, these jumps in numbers did not reflect a similar increase in population.[13] Rather, these data literally depict class formation in process.

Growth in the middling classes and in opportunities for entry into them unsettled family life in several ways, demonstrating once again the dislocation of people's daily lives and practices inherent in new social order formation. First, young men left rural areas for urban areas, thereby reordering the population demographics of both the rural and urban areas along with the family structures in rural areas. Second, in urban areas, young women began to work outside the home until marriage, contributing their income to the family to help support their brothers, who remained at home longer to pursue more years of schooling in an attempt to move into the middling classes (Ryan 1981). Third, the young men who flooded the urban landscape resided in homes that had been turned into boardinghouses, restructuring both urban family life and the scale and relations of urban women's domestic labor. Women whose families took in boarders were suddenly producing market labor from previously purely family-centered tasks by cooking, cleaning, and laundering for many men. In 1855 and 1865, 20 percent of Utica housewives had boarders and by today's standards could be construed as running inns and laundries (201). Measures of urbanization manifested changes resulting from the combined increase in population and in single young men as percent of population (see table 2). Absolute numbers of policemen and firemen increased by almost 60 percent. And the growing cities were well stocked with alcohol and alcohol-centered meeting grounds for men, providing plenty of grist for what would soon become a strong temperance movement; reported numbers of saloon keepers and barkeepers rose by 351 percent and 101 percent, respectively.

A tremendous rise in manufacturing was clear throughout the reported changes in the occupational structure (see table 3). By 1865, brass workers had increased their 1855 numbers by an incredible 1,214 percent, no doubt a consequence of the manufacture of gun cartridges for use in the Civil War. Other manufacturing occupations also demonstrated strong, albeit less dramatic, increases: Reported numbers of iron workers jumped by 68 percent, factory operatives by 69 percent, and unspecified manufacturers by 137 percent. Guard labor also proved necessary to the efficient organization of manufacturing, as demonstrated by growth in certain new occupations of the middling classes.[14] Overseers and superintendents provided a solution to what is known as the labor extraction problem: Workers may be gathered in a setting for production, but it is in their interest to expend as little productive effort as possible to gain their wages, and it is

TABLES 1–5. *Implications of Changes in the Occupational Structure*

Source: Data are culled from the comparative report on occupations presented in the preface of the *Census of the State of New York, for 1865* (New York State, Secretary's Office 1867, lxxv–lxxvi), which included all occupations reported to either the 1855 or 1865 census by more than 500 respondents each. The total number of people reporting occupations increased by approximately 12 percent from 1855 to 1865 (lxxv), while the total measured population increased by approximately 10 percent (xliii). In my data, I have included only occupational changes that were significantly greater than the population change when increasing, or at least as great when decreasing.

TABLE 1. *Formation of Middling Classes*

Occupation	1855	1865	% Change
Salesmen[a]	723	1,208	+67
Clerks, copyists, and accountants[a]	30,259	42,593	+41
Overseers and superintendents[a]	475	1,177	+148
Apothecaries and druggists[a]	1,438	1,809	+26
Dentists[a]	761	1,084	+42
Students[a]	4,184	5,000	+20
Toy and fancy good makers[b]	164	1,046	+538
Furriers[b]	227	779	+243
Music teachers[b]	621	901	+45
Photographers[b]	389	955	+146
Wine and liquor dealers[b]	749	2,524	+237
Servants[b]	58,441	108,351	+85

[a] These occupational categories represent members of the middling class itself.
[b] These occupational categories represent both conspicuous consumption and the commodification of goods previously produced domestically and serve as broad proxies for the relative size of the middling class.

TABLE 2. *Urbanization*

Occupation	1855	1865	% Change
Policemen	1,513	2,378	+57
Firemen	416	660	+59
Saloon keepers	871	3,925	+351
Barkeepers	987	1,984	+101
Apothecaries and druggists	1,438	1,809	+26
Dentists	761	1,084	+42

TABLE 3. *Manufacturing Expansion and Industrialization*

Occupation	1855	1865	% Change
Brass workers[a]	756	9,933	+1,214
Factory operatives	2,477	4,197	+69
Iron workers	990	1,659	+68
Machinists	6,309	10,090	+60
Overseers and superintendents	475	1,177	+148
Manufacturers— not specified	1,448	3,425	+137
Boot and shoe makers	24,804	21,899	–12
Tailors	29,236	21,847	–25
Weavers	3,141	2,052	–35

[a] The great increase in brass workers can be directly connected with the Civil War since gun cartridges were made from brass. But the shift of workers into this job still represents a move into manufacturing—simply one that was war-driven.

TABLE 4. *Changing Technologies*

Occupation	1855	1865	% Change
Boiler makers	708	1,721	+143
Coal dealers	138	706	+412
Furnacemen	1,807	993	–45
Plumbers	958	1,700	+76
Railroad men	4,006	6,300	+57
Telegraph operators	258	842	+226

TABLE 5. *Financial and Capital Market Formation*

Occupation	1855	1865	% Change
Bankers	432	1,053	+144
Bank officers	539	729	+35
Brokers	1,223	2,524	+106
Speculators[a]	487	944	+94
Insurance officers	319	672	+111

[a] Individuals who speculated on the difference in prices between regional commodities markets.

in capital's interest to extract as much labor as possible for the same wages paid. Consequently, changes in the occupational category of guard labor play double duty as proxies for both the rise of the middling classes and the rise of manufacturing. In this ten-year period, reported numbers of guard labor increased by 148 percent.

Finally, occupational categories indicating involvement in the consolidation of interregional and national financial sectors also rose dramatically: Reported numbers of bankers increased by 144 percent, brokers by 106 percent, and those who named their sole occupation as speculators by 94 percent (see table 5 above). Since speculators made their fortune by pitting prices in regional commodities markets against each other[15]—that is, in classic arbitrage—their existence in approximately the same numbers as bankers indicates that an integrated national commodities market did not yet exist. Tables 6 and 7 show pieces of the national market's steady consolidation out of three major regional markets—New York, Cincinnati, and New Orleans—between 1816 and 1860. While there was still money to be made by selling wholesale commodities between regions in 1855 to 1860, average regional price differences were only 10 to 35 percent of what they had been in 1816 to 1820. Of course, financial markets and transportation had also steadily consolidated over this period, making speculation much less risky. By showing the decreasing regional differences in prices, these data depict the intertwined consolidation of national financial and commodities markets, which both linked Erie Canal port cities to the newly forming national socioeconomic order and transmitted financial shocks from other regional and national markets back into the port cities, destabilizing their populace's daily lives.

Not surprisingly, as national financial and commodities markets consolidated, reported numbers of skilled craftsmen decreased dramatically: for instance, tailors by 25 percent and weavers by 35 percent. In earlier decades, these skilled craftsmen had held a central place in the middling classes (Ryan 1981). Their decrease, concomitant with a rise in manufacturing, speaks to an occupational dislocation that was only exacerbated by frequent financial panics and depressions. Young men with education entered the middling classes as clerks, accountants, and bankers, while skilled craftsmen exited the middling classes to become laborers and factory operatives whose jobs were highly insecure. An 1855 cotton mill superintendent noted laborers' tenuous location in the new economy with a clarity worthy of Marx's

TABLES 6–7. *National Commodities Market Consolidation*

Source: North (1961, 261).

TABLE 6. *Wholesale Commodity Prices: Average Absolute Differences between Cincinnati and New York by Five-Year Periods*

Year	Lard ($/lb.)	Mess Pork ($/Bbl.)	Flour ($/Bbl.)	Corn ($/bu.)
1816–20	.048	9.53	2.48	.48
1821–25	.031	4.46	2.81	.39
1826–30	.026	4.18	1.78	.36
1831–35	.025	3.48	1.43	.38
1836–40	.020	3.11	2.02	.42
1841–45	.011	2.25	1.37	.30
1846–50	.010	1.06	1.68	.36
1851–55	.007	1.56	1.36	.31
1856–60	.004	1.18	.28	.27

TABLE 7. *Wholesale Commodity Prices: Average Absolute Differences between Cincinnati and New Orleans by Five-Year Periods*

Year	Lard ($/lb.)	Mess Pork ($/Bbl.)	Flour ($/Bbl.)	Corn ($/bu.)
1816–20	.051	7.57	2.16	—
1821–25	.027	2.81	2.37	.59
1826–30	.024	2.41	1.75	.59
1831–35	.017	2.03	1.29	.64
1836–40	.014	2.67	1.66	.49
1841–45	.006	1.66	.61	.14
1846–50	.005	1.31	.60	.20
1851–55	.006	1.24	.59	.16
1856–60	.007	1.27	.63	.21

Capital: "I regard my work-people just as I regard my machinery. So long as they can do my work for what I choose to pay them, I keep them, getting out of them all I can. What they do or how they fare outside my walls I don't know, nor do I consider it my business to know. They must look out for themselves as I do for myself. When my machines get old and useless, I reject them and get new, and these people are part of my machinery" (cited in Berthoff 1971, 201–2). In these times, people's possible life trajectories changed quickly and sharply. Skilled craftsmen's daily lives came suddenly ungrounded, no longer linked to a prior life built upon apprenticeships and work for themselves or in small establishments. Almost no occupational position was secure, resulting in a constant sense of impending and actual dislocation. The voluminous pamphlet press included many tracts expostulating on appropriate creditor-debtor public policy for the times, attesting to the commonplace experience of quick changes in economic fortune.[16] One such 1850 pamphlet, *Debtor and Creditor*, argued, "How far the relation of debtor and creditor should be treated as one of political interest, whether it should receive protection or tolerance from government, and to what extent a creditor should be permitted to control the property and the person of his debtor: these are questions which have been deemed worthy of consideration in ages past, and questions to which the engrossing pursuit of this age attaches a strange and fearful importance" (Anon. 1850b, 1).

In fact, it is likely that the very earliest married women's property acts were passed in response to these questions' "strange and fearful importance." As debtor relief acts, they made some family property unseizable by creditors who were trying to recoup the husband's debts by allowing wives to be the legal holders of real property (Rabkin 1980; Thurman 1966; Warbasse 1987). In its argument, *Debtor and Creditor* invokes both the family's subsistence resources and the married woman's personal property as assets that should be protected from creditors by government legislation (by the state of Ohio, in this case):

> No principle of political or social wisdom, no rule of humanity or justice, can ever require that the family of the debtor shall be doomed to starvation, more than to servitude. The earnings by which the wife and the children are supported, from day to day, should not be diverted to any other object; lest the debtor, becoming desperate, be tempted to crime or dishonest practices, or abandon all efforts to keep want from his door. . . .
>
> But, beside imprisonment of the body, the common law allowed all personal property to be sold. The very vagueness of a writ of execution, as even now used, is pregnant with the thought of distress and sacrifice. . . . The personal property of the wife, even to her apparel, went to pay the husband's debt. (Anon. 1850b, 13, 9)

Antebellum legislators could and would choose to pass legislation, such as the earliest married women's property acts, to protect some extent of individual debtors' land, housing, and productive assets from creditors. But contemporary conceptions of personal and financial property, as embedded in contract and property law, meant that no legal form could protect monetary assets in this early cash economy.

Changes in Social Meanings of Property

Popular conceptions and legal understandings of property divided it into two types:[17] real and personal. Real property existed with some permanence beyond the individual; until the nineteenth century, it primarily consisted of land, forests, and buildings. Its ability to be passed down through familial generations comprised its social value. Personal property was more transient in nature and mainly held value for a living individual; it primarily consisted of clothing, furniture, tools and utensils, crops from land once they had been harvested for use, animal products, and what small bits of cash might exist. Contemporary social meanings of property placed little importance on personal property, and money was a small and equally unimportant portion of personal property. Property, in general, held functional value rather than market value. Personal property was valued for its use in daily life; people wore it, ate it, and ate off of it. Real property was valued for its long-term life-sustaining capabilities and was further understood as sustaining social relations over time; people lived on it, cultivated it, lived in it, and passed their social position on to their children through its bequest. It was not partitioned for sale or inheritance, since that would dilute a family's stature. Neither real nor personal property was conceived of in terms of fungibility. From the late 1700s through the 1800s, legal battles over appropriate use of and definitions of rights in real property reshaped the legal understandings of property and contract. Suddenly, an owner's perpetual rights of use and undisturbed enjoyment guaranteed by his right to absolute dominion over his land had to be weighed against its use as a productive asset and as a contributor to economic growth. At the same time, as small businesses, the middling classes, and market consumption all grew, monetary assets became an increasingly important part of personal property. Familial and individual relations to both real and personal property had to be reconceived on a societal level, both legally and popularly.

Two theories of property rights, the natural use of land and priority of development, had meant that owners held rights to maintain their property in its "natural" state against any encumbrances placed on them by neighboring landowners.[18] These legal tenets had dovetailed in practice since the 1700s; the first use of land, and therefore the use that held priority, had always been considered that of land in its natural state. In legal understandings of real property in the early to mid-1800s, natural use and priority combined with the English common law concept of waste, which was immediately problematic in the American context. Any changes tenants made in the state of the land that they occupied constituted waste, based on the agrarian priority of land in its original state. Landowners were legally protected against waste by holding tenants liable for the property in its original state. In other words, this understanding of property could not conceive of capital investments. What today seems a commonsense legal distinction between tenants' liability for damage to property and their right to recompense for capital investments in property did not then exist or make cultural sense.

During this period of transitional public and home economies, the social meaning of property was caught in a struggle among jurists, farmers, small businessmen, and others. The ways that property had been understood for centuries had become impediments to economic development. For example, any landowner could prevent a mill from setting up on a stream that bordered his land because its use of the water for power would change the natural flow of the stream, possibly diminishing his access to water for any crops and husbandry and even for leisurely enjoyment, or possibly flooding his land. Alternatively, if the first mill owner on a stream was recognized as holding priority rights, he could prevent any other mill from using the stream for water power since it would affect his already established use of the stream. Finally, if tenants deforested a parcel of land for farming or built agricultural buildings on that land, they had no rights to their investment when the owner removed them from the land. They could actually be held liable for waste, leaving tenants with no incentive to develop the land economically; in effect, tenants were punished for productive development.

Although American courts never fully accepted the legal doctrine of waste, they spent the first half of the nineteenth century adjudicating it. Not surprisingly, its problems were most apparent in cases of marital property—in particular, in cases of widows' dower. When a husband died, his widow had a right to the use of one-third of the land held during the marriage under common law. Her right to dower terminated and the land reverted to the husband's children or brothers, however, if she remarried or when she died. The widow had only use rights, which meant that she could not develop the land or she would be liable to the heir for waste. It also meant that she could not sell the land during her tenancy, and no one else could sell it out from under her. Either way, large parcels of land were effectively removed from productive capacity and the market for long periods of time, impeding both production and market growth. Since land values were no longer static, further questions arose as to whether a widow had rights to one-third of the original value of lands held or one-third of their profits (value based on changing land prices and development of the land). Additionally, as long as dower remained a legal right, anyone who purchased land from a married man had no incentive to improve it or put it to productive use since its use might revert to the widow when the seller died. This early appearance of logically impassable moments in the law and societal understandings of real property and marital property presaged the coming public and legislative conflagration as this aporetic space became increasingly and unavoidably visible in the 1850s.

MORAL ECONOMIES

> By midcentury women commanded through their charitable activities a vital post outside the home, one of crucial importance to the social order of the city. They had not, however, entered the formal public sphere nor the realm of capital. Their benevolence was still conducted under private auspices, not in an authoritative, legally sanctioned public arena. However much they saved capitalists, they never soiled their own hands with profits.
>
> —Mary P. Ryan, *Cradle of the Middle Class*

> The silent, resistless influence of home and the affections,—this is woman's true glory.
>
> —Mrs. Louisa C. Tuthill, *The Young Lady's Home*, 1848

Women's rise in moral status from 1820 to 1860 drew on the emergence of the modern family structure, composed of a companionate marriage and a new focus on childhood rather than a patriarchal household (Degler 1980a, 1980b), and on a thread of gendered meanings that came into being just after the Revolution. The Erie Canal's construction promoted its rise by allowing the geographic spread of a new moral economy and culture. Just as it brought rapid population growth and connections to a growing national cash economy to central and western New York State, it also enabled the creation and expansion of a national printed media culture by carrying advice literature, journals, newspapers, magazines, and novels throughout New York and on into the West. In one fell swoop, the 1820s through the 1850s saw the rise of what could be said to be the first national value system for the new middling classes and opened the door to a broader geographic organization of social movements. Printed material and lecturers embarked on extensive lecture circuits, making their way up and down the Erie Canal and prevailing upon previously inaccessible populations. The great majority of women's literature participated in shaping a figure of True Womanhood out of an earlier image of the Republican Mother.[19] A True Woman focused her energies on the home and domesticity, but the figure was pliable enough that a duty to be active in religious and benevolent associations outside the home became one of its central aspects over the decades. However, a True Woman was always required to remain untouched by the economic sphere, locating True Womanhood in juxtaposition to the contemporary disorder of political economic life.[20]

During the Revolutionary War, both women and men had necessarily taken on political activity. Once the war ended, though, women had to legitimate any continued political action. At this time, a small number of women wrote tracts declaring that women should receive a longer education and have a public role in the nation's life. But these ideas were ridiculed by the majority; only the idea of patriotic motherhood passed muster—a role in which women could fulfill a civic duty to the nation through their very domesticity. The Republican Mother held sole responsibility for the education and morality of her sons; and, through them, women were responsible for the morality of a nation built upon the common man. This image of Womanhood held the country's imagination into the 1850s; True Womanhood both grew out of and merged happily with it. In 1856, praise of women as Republican Mothers could still be found in a pamphlet entitled *Woman's Mission*:[21]

> 'Tis hers to watch our childhood's budding powers
> And with sweet smiles first light our baby face . . .
> Her duty 'tis to call our reason forth,

By questions apt, set forth in simple guise,
And just comparison of nature's laws:
Make clear, by words of light, all things obscure:
Teach us our thoughts to scan, and actions weigh,
And strive to poise the balance of the soul;
Point out the path that leads to human weal,
And in it strive to guide our youthful steps;
Where knowledge, skill, and industry combined,
With saving, sober, honest virtues crowned,
Lead men to homes with cheerful plenty filled,
Make of unfavoured spots a fruitful land,
And build a nation up in freedom strong.
(Lovett 1856, 5–6)

Earlier works, from the 1830s and 1840s, read as undiluted odes to the figure of the Republican Mother and its submergence into True Womanhood. They emphasized the importance of motherhood as political activity and the evils of women's extradomestic politics. Lydia H. Sigourney, the author of numerous popular advice books, trumpeted Republican Motherhood in her 1838 *Letters to Mothers:*

> A barrier to the torrent of corruption, and a guard over the strong holds of knowledge and of virtue, may be placed by the mother, as she watches over her cradled son. Let her come forth with vigour and vigilance, at the call of her country, not like Boadicea in her chariot, but like the mother of Washington, feeling that the first lesson to every incipient ruler should be, "*how to obey.*" The degree of her diligence in preparing her children to be good subjects of a just government, will be the true measure of her patriotism. . . . This then, is the patriotism of woman, not to thunder in senates, or to usurp dominion, or to seek the clarion-blast of fame, but faithfully to teach by precept and example, that wisdom, integrity and peace, which are the glory of a nation. (15–16)

At the same time, in her *Letters to Young Ladies,* Sigourney joined the many who were significantly extending the Republican Mother's power over her sons' ways and virtues to her entire household by relying on the concept of Woman's Influence—the active force by which the True Woman's piety, purity, submissiveness, and domesticity ordered not only the social world immediately surrounding her but the entire society. In its sixth edition by 1841, *Letters to Young Ladies* stressed the critical importance of Republican Motherhood/True Womanhood to democracy, invoking the social order and stability they would impart:

> Does not the influence of woman rest upon every member of her household, like the dew upon the tender herb, or the sunbeam silently educating the young flower? . . . This influence is most visible and operative in a republick. The intelligence and virtue of its every citizen have a heightened relative value.—Its safety may be interwoven with the destiny of those whose birthplace is in obscurity. The springs of its vitality are liable to be touched, or the chords of its harmony to be troubled, by the rudest hands. Teachers under such a form of government should be held in the highest honour. They are the allies of legislators. They have agency in the prevention of crime. They aid in regulating the atmosphere, whose incessant action and pressure causes the life-blood to circulate, and return pure and healthful to the heart of the nation. (12–13)

In her two popular books, then, Sigourney employed the related meanings of True Womanhood and democracy in a specific formation. A just democracy, in which her children will be "good subjects of a just government" (Sigourney 1838), depended upon the *newly feminine civic values* (Ryan 1990) that lent social order to an otherwise distinctly disordered socioeconomy. The nation depended on the True Woman's Influence to regulate social order and provide social stability in these transitional and transformative times. Or, actually, the nation depended on the social meanings of True Womanhood to provide the sense of a stable social order, with its links to traditional values and its remove from the disturbingly new and unsettled socioeconomy.

Sigourney's was the prevalent understanding of how the social meanings of Womanhood and the nation were systematically related; similar pronouncements could be found throughout the advice literature, whether written by men or women. William A. Alcott's *Letters to a Sister; or Woman's Mission* (1850) left no doubt that the Republican Mother/True Woman was vital to the state of the democratic nation:

> In these days, the people are the rulers of the nations, and not those who have been generally denominated the princes. . . . To educate the princes

and rulers of modern days, therefore, woman must be, emphatically, an educator of the people. But to educate the people—I do not say to *instruct* them merely—a right influence in each family is most efficient; and above all, a right female influence. Doubt no longer, then, my dear sister, whether or not woman's mission is important. . . . Believe and obey. Believe that by the constitution of society, as God has established it, in his providence, you have your feet on the necks of all the kings or potentates of future ages; and that, under God, whom you will you can put down, and whom you will you can set up. And believing this, make haste to govern yourself accordingly. (97–98)

As can be surmised from Alcott's salutations to sisters, the move from Republican Motherhood into True Womanhood encompassed all who could be deemed Woman and their immediate social relations in its terms, not just wives and mothers.

A glorious example of True Womanhood's expanded horizons of power beyond those of Republican Motherhood appeared in Mrs. Louisa C. Tuthill's 1848 advice book for young women, *The Young Lady's Home.* The chapter "A Sister's Influence" tells a long parable of a ne'er-do-well, aristocratically styled son returning home to western New York after a number of years in Europe, during which he had lived off his father's money while supposedly studying medicine. At first, he favors one sister, Julia, who like him has "refined" tastes, while looking with distaste upon another, Clara, who wants only to be the True American Woman. The introduction, "Leaving School," presages Clara's views on Womanhood when she elaborates upon her future and her position in the world to two school chums: "I expect to continue my studies, that I may more perfectly understand them. I hope to be useful to my mother, who has kindly promised to teach me domestic economy; so long as life lasts, there will be knowledge to which I have not attained, virtues to be perfected, and good to be done; 'vulgar' as it sounds, my highest aim is to be a good, *thorough-going* American woman" (9). By contrast, her brother George considers her "a mere household drudge, like most Yankee women" (130).

During a couple of weeks' stay at the popular spa at Saratoga, to which she had accompanied George and Julia, Clara captures the attention of all present, leading George to consider that perhaps there is more to her than he thought. But he remains uncertain as to what this "more" might be and continues his ne'er-do-well ways: first, by spending all of his sisters' money at the gambling tables after having dispensed with his own and having not yet provided for any bills; then by suggesting that Clara, as the apple of her father's eye, write home and get more money since George and Julia wish to stay on at Saratoga despite the fact that they are now living well beyond their means. At this point, George unexpectedly falls severely ill, as does his father back home, and they must all rush home to care for both. But just prior to her leaving, a U.S. senator proposes to Clara. She returns home nonetheless and indefatigably tends to her father in one room by day and to her brother in another by night, while her refined sister, Julia, proves incapable and incompetent in this situation. On his deathbed, her father gives permission for Clara's marriage. And, through Clara's nursing and attentions, George finally comes to recognize not only her worth, but his position as "a prodigal son," and he asks her to minister personally to his soul. She begins to read him the Bible regularly as he slowly recovers to turn around his life (120–48). Tuthill's trenchant tale of one woman's influence upon all of the welcoming social relations in her family and at Saratoga, and, most strikingly, upon her absolutely unwelcoming brother, coincided with the beginning of True Womanhood's peak as a nationally hegemonic conception of Womanhood. The 1850s saw the height of its long trajectory, just as they witnessed its critical and substantive refiguring by the woman's rights movement and the continued rise of alternatives such as Real Womanhood. However, the importance of Woman's Influence—by sisters, wives, mothers, friends, and benefactresses—continued to be heralded into the late 1800s.

From the beginnings of women's public participation in antebellum social movements, with the Grimke sisters' antislavery lectures in the 1830s, opponents argued that Woman's Influence on the nation was the very reason they must not participate. As Womanhood's social meanings shifted their center from the figure of the Republican Mother, who performed her crucial civic duties by educating her sons, to that of the True Woman, whose influence might affect all those she came into contact with if properly used, traditionalists argued that women's movement into the public sphere would besmirch precisely those qualities that defined her and enabled her to act effectively. They argued that, by definition, Woman's Influence could be used only domestically; once a woman used her Influence outside of her proper domestic realm, she was no longer a True Woman, and therefore no longer held Influence. The momentous "Pastoral letter of the General Association of Massachusetts to the churches under their care" (1837) decreed that Woman had no proper place in political debate precisely by invoking women's private and yet powerful duties through which they "form the character of individuals and of the nation." It inveighed against "the intimate acquaintance and promiscuous conversation of females with regard to things, 'which ought not to be named'; by which that modesty and delicacy which is the charm of domestic life, and which constitutes the true influence of woman in society is consumed, and the way opened, as we apprehend, for degeneracy and ruin" (reprinted in *The Liberator*, August 11, 1837, in Anthony [n.p.]).

Throughout the mid- to late 1830s, the U.S. Congress was overwhelmed by antislavery petitions, and many members found particularly galling the great numbers that were signed by women as well as those that were the direct result of women's organizing efforts. On June 14, 1838, Benjamin Howard, a representative from Maryland, articulated this sentiment for the record. His "regret" that women had engaged in abolition work stemmed from the simple fact that their appropriate activities should have remained confined to using their Influence within the domestic realm, "shedding over it the mild radiance of the social virtues." By moving beyond this realm, Howard claimed, the females who had signed petitions were "discreditable, not only to their own particular section of the country, but also to the national character" (cited in Zaeske 2003, 126). Such exhortations increasingly circulated throughout popular literature as well, marking the consolidation of True Womanhood as the hegemonic understanding of reputable Womanhood. Woman's piety, purity, submissiveness, and domesticity became her essential attributes. Without them, she could not effect a positive presence on the public world:

> Woman, at present, is the regulating power of the great social machine, retaining, through the very exclusion complained of, the power to judge of questions by the abstract rules of right and wrong—a power seldom possessed by those whose spirits are chafed by opposition, and heated by personal contest. . . .
>
> [Women] have, and ought to have much to do with politics. But in what way? It has been maintained, that their public participation in them

would be fatal to the best interests of society. How, then, are women to interfere in politics? As moral agents; as representatives of the moral principle; as champions of the right in preference to the expedient; by their endeavours to instil into their relatives of the other sex the uncompromising sense of duty and self-devotion, which ought to be *their* ruling principles! The immense influence which women possess will be most beneficial, if allowed to flow in its natural channels, viz.: domestic ones,— because it is of the utmost importance to the existence of influence, that purity of motive be unquestioned. (Anon. 1840, 45–46, 50–51)

In turn, women active in reform movements tried to turn True Womanhood's web of social meanings against itself in order to force a popular reconceptualization of Womanhood and even of Humanity. In 1843, in one such attempt among many, female abolitionists attending Rochester's moral reform meetings "condemned slavery as an institutionalized violation of women's virtue" (Hewitt 1984, 126).[22] But the color-coded and class-based delimitations of the very figure of the True Woman[23] buttress Hortense Spillers's (1987) claim that gender—constituted through the combined matrix of the separation of spheres and a maternal link to kinship—could not exist for African Americans during the Middle Passage and under slavery. Consequently, abolitionists' suggestion that a female slave might hold the attributes of a True Woman in any sense would have required white Americans to consider a paradigmatic conceptual change in the life status of Negro slaves in order to make sense of the claim. It was a radical suggestion indeed in a nation whose scientists and social scientists, in the 1870s and 1880s, would still weave their theories of civilization around the same raced and gendered web of social meanings: "The more advanced mental functions— imagination and reason—were presumed to be characteristic of the more highly evolved brains of civilized men. . . . 'Woman' was used to mean an Anglo-Protestant woman; 'lower races' or 'primitives' were used without reference to gender because [they] presupposed that there were no significant sexual differences among primitives" (Newman 1999, 31).[24] If female slaves were to be understood as possessing a virtue, domesticity, piety, and purity that could be besmirched, their position would first have to shift in the contemporary web of social meanings operating in and through Humanity; they would first have to move into the realm of Womanhood in all its interimplicated social meanings. And, clearly, a True Woman was Human. In fact, she embodied the epitome of human morality. If the white nation could be made to conceive of female slaves as residing in the space of True Womanhood, that same nation would by definition have reconceptualized African Americans as solidly existing in the space of the Human.

Anna Julia Cooper's 1886 remonstration to African American men regarding the power of African American women must be read through this understanding—an understanding of the political centrality of negotiations of systems of social meanings, in particular, between and across True Womanhood, the Negro race, and Humanity. Cooper (1886/1998b, 63) famously proclaimed, "Only the BLACK WOMAN can say 'when and where I enter, in the quiet, undisputed dignity of my womanhood, without violence and without suing or special patronage, then and there the whole *Negro race enters with me.'*" Indeed, "one might say today that she was intent upon inventing the discursive space of the black woman" (Lemert 1998, 19).[25] Less famously, Cooper (1886/1998b, 69–70) definitively restated her understanding when she called on the church to recognize Negro women's societal power and actively nurture Negro Womanhood: "That the race cannot be effectually lifted up till its women are truly elevated we take as proven. . . . Will not the aid of the Church be given to prepare our girls in head, heart, and hand for the duties and responsibilities that await the intelligent wife, the Christian mother, the earnest, virtuous, helpful woman, at once both the lever and the fulcrum for uplifting the race." Writing at the end of the nineteenth century, Cooper (1892/1998a, 116–17) reflected further on Negro women's unique position, invoking their discursive residence in True Womanhood—specifically in its Moral influence:

The woman of to-day finds herself in the presence of responsibilities which ramify through the profoundest and most varied interests of her country and race. Not one of the issues of this plodding, toiling, sinning, repenting, falling, aspiring humanity can afford to shut her out, or can deny the reality of her influence. . . . [And] no woman can possibly put herself or her sex outside any of the interests that affect humanity. All departments in the new era are to be hers, in the sense that her interests are in all and through all; and it is incumbent on her to keep intelligently and sympathetically *en rapport* with all the great movements of her time, that she may know on which side to throw the weight of her influence. . . . What a responsibility then to have the sole management of the primal lights and shadows! Such is the colored woman's office. She must stamp weal or woe on the coming history of this people. May she see her opportunity and vindicate her high prerogative.

In her writings and lifework, Cooper pinpointed a raced structural aporia of the time as a crucial site of Negro activism—one that was significantly shaped in relation to the structural aporia on which this book focuses and vice versa. Not surprisingly, activists struggled over the best way to approach that structural aporia, revealing all the incongruities and opacities of discursive activism. For "the dominant [white] abolitionist position was that slave emancipation would convert freedmen alone into sovereign self-owning individuals. Property in women would simply be conveyed from slaveholders to husbands" (Stanley 1998, 28–29). Abolitionist and woman's rights activist William Lloyd Garrison defined the freedman's position as "master of his own person, of his wife" (cited in Stanley 1998, 29). While his is certainly not Cooper's use of True Womanhood—she never married and spent her life in teaching, public speaking, community-building work, and parenting adopted and foster children—other black female activists centrally situated their rights to self-ownership and sovereignty. In one well-known example, Harriet Jacobs's slave narrative, *Incidents in the Life of a Slave Girl, Written by Herself,* "directly confronted the problem of sexual property in women. For Jacobs, freedom entailed self ownership of a clearly sexual character" (Stanley 1998, 31). The complexities and "correctness" of these varied deployments of Black Womanhood are still being contested today,[26] "but in disrupting any simple connection between emancipation and marriage—in affirming a slave woman's right to herself—black female thinkers transformed the meaning of contract freedom" (33–34). Reading gendered history asunder opens up other intertwined aporetic sites; here it points out that the operations of race—in particular, blackness—and Womanhood through the present day must be usefully analyzed and deployed aporetically in the United States, whether by cultural historians or activists. In other words, a detailed historical study of the U.S. democratic aporias of blackness and Womanhood would speak volumes to *a history of their conjoined present.*

The pamphlet frenzy of the 1840s and 1850s mobilized further twists and folds of True Womanhood in numerous political battles. In her 1858 *Appeal to the Women of America,* for instance, Desdemona Marke penned a patriotic call to women to defend the economic liberty of the United States by politicking for a protective tariff against England. Her call to arms deployed all the rhetoric of Republican Motherhood and True Womanhood:

> Descend, my sisters, from the commanding eminence of liberty; the passing clouds fill the air with an English fragrance. Haste to action; influence and breathe your inspiration upon the heart of man. Perform thy work, O my sisters! for your immediate posterity will be renovated, your latest descendants will know no death, and the universe in admiration, will hasten in its planetary course. . . .
>
> MY SISTERS, Our mothers of the Revolution sacrificed themselves, to bequeath to us a Godlike inheritance. Shall we exert our influence to preserve it? May the Ruler of nations, and the Upholder of truth and justice fill you with His power, and enable you to act. (3, 8)

The figure of True Womanhood also resonated with and was redeployed in one form or another by a great majority of women's groups and associations, as well as in the service of the many "motives of the often divergent devotees of maternity" (Douglas 1977, 74). In a study documenting the differences between distinct groups of women activists in the Erie Canal port city of Rochester, New York, between 1822 and 1872, Nancy Hewitt (1984, 66) concluded that all three groups—women in benevolent associations, women in social and moral reform movements, and women in legal and political reform movements—founded their activism and their activist tactics in part on domesticity's hegemonic meanings. In other words, different societal sectors publicly figured True Womanhood variously, simultaneously accepting and contesting its hegemonic social meanings while promoting their own constructions.

Regardless of the variety of deployments available, the tenacity with which a Woman sustained her True Womanhood was commonly understood to determine the power of her Influence. True Womanhood and Woman's moral influence stood and fell with one another. Minister Joseph Richardson (1833, 15) clearly articulated this popular view in his 1832 sermon "on the Duty and Dignity of Woman," distributed in pamphlet form: "The world expects of you stricter virtue and a nearer approach to perfection than it does of men. This expectation reflects on your character the highest honor, because it acknowledges your power to exert a happy influence upon the moral condition of society. It concedes to you the honor of exerting an influence, all but divine; but an influence you lose the power to exert, the moment you depart from the sphere and delicacy of your proper character." In its hegemonic form, the True Woman's *influence upon the moral condition of society* imparted a great sense of social order and stability—hence contemporary writers' and speakers' insistence that a True Woman's influence reached across all of society and down through the generations. As Reverend Nathan Beman noted in his 1850 pamphlet *Female Influence and Obligations,* addressed "TO EVERY MOTHER," "Females exert a vast moral influence upon *society at large*. . . . There is no department of human life, and no corner of the world, where your influence is not felt" (3–4).

At the same time, the figure of the True Woman was excluded from the public, political, and economic spheres, as were women themselves. And while her Influence provided her a form of access to the public and political realms, it distinctly did not reach into the economic realm. Woman's Influence seemingly had the very power to order society, but it specifically ordered only those societal realms external to the economic. Woman's proper sphere was implicitly, and sometimes explicitly, defined not just as domestic but as untouched by the new economy that was so quickly dislocating society. The True Woman was understood as providing her husband with a refuge from his labors, and, through this understanding and intertwined institutional practices, True Womanhood discursively provided society with a refuge from the daily disorder of urbanizing, industrializing life. Widely distributed pamphlets and private scrapbooks kept by women of the time made True Womanhood's proper place in the system of social meanings apparent. For instance, in an 1856 advice pamphlet on *Woman's Mission,* William Lovett told women:

> How much depends on woman's care and love,
> Whether man soars to excellence and use,
> His country to improve, his race to bless;
> Or sinks in vice, a stunted blighted trunk.
> If she her household mission wisely fill,
> Her home will be his refuge and his joy.
> On him the clouds of life may lowering fall;
> Adversity's chill blast or storms assail;

Her ever-welcome smile, and cheerful hearth,
Her voice of kindness, and her looks of love,
Dispel from off his heart all cloud and storm,
And spread calm, peace, and sunshine o'er his brow. (8)

A number of years earlier, Hester V. Phillips expressed corresponding sentiments in the poem she wrote into her personal diary on April 6, 1847, entitled "To Wives": "Endeavor to make your husband's habitation alluring and delightful to him. Let it be to him a sanctuary to which his heart may always turn from the calamities of life. Make it a repose from his cares, a shelter from the world, a home not for his person only, but for his heart. He may meet with pleasure in other houses, but let him find leasure in his own."

The women who wrote and edited the most popular women's magazines and advice books of the time produced similar commentary. Catherine Beecher, whose *Treatise on Domestic Economy* was reprinted almost annually from 1841 to 1856, explicitly purveyed women's noneconomic role as embodied in a female domesticity whose "far-reaching and immediately effective consequence . . . was to define an oasis of noncommercial values in an otherwise acquisitive society" (Sklar 1973, 161). And, Sarah Josepha Hale, the founder of the popular *Ladies Magazine,* which would become *Godey's Ladies Book,* publicly expressed horror at Lydia Maria Child's 1830 *The Frugal Housewife;* in her view, it suggested that women soil their purity and domesticity by playing a part in economic matters, even if only by being thrifty (Douglas 1977, 57).

TRUE WOMANHOOD'S APORIAS:
HISTORICAL SOCIAL MEANINGS

In the nineteenth century United States, True Womanhood was doubly aporetic. While providing a sense of social order and stability for all, it rested on foundations of disorder, on a wildly dislocated socioeconomy that founded a disruptively emerging social order. As the prevalent understanding of the reputable Woman's position in society, it replicated her expulsion from the new society's very terms of civic individuality, of legitimate subjecthood: the ability to participate in legal and economic contract. True Womanhood's location within a contemporary system of social meanings critically interimplicated it with popular understandings of contract, property, the economy, and the nation. In the antebellum United States, social meanings of

Womanhood replicated the gendered structural aporia embedded in Western democratic origin myths: the (hetero)sexual-social contract. These origin myths—social contract theories—defined Woman as unable to enter into contracts, the central participatory mechanism of the new social order. Simultaneously, the True Woman's position in the contemporary web of social meanings imbued her with a heightened purity and morality and the apparent ability to stabilize the social disorder inherent in the rise of the new market economy—the very realm based in the contractual behavior in which she could not participate. In other words, Woman had no civil existence in antebellum systems of social meaning. The figure of the True Woman embodied an aporetic space defined precisely by a lack of civil existence; it was a stable figure that elided historical expressions of one of Western democracies' gendered structural aporias, hiding it from contemporary view. From this aporetic space, the True Woman performed her *fearful obligation and solemn responsibility . . .—to uphold the pillars of the [national] temple* (Welter 1966, 152).

Chapter 4

GENDERED LAW

*Antebellum Institutions Regulating Women,
Property, and Contract*

> In these six decades [from 1800 to 1861], married
> women's status in the eyes of the common law
> changed more than in the preceding three hun-
> dred years or the succeeding one hundred years.
> From the legal nonentity, with few rights as to her
> property or earnings, to her children or to a di-
> vorce, the wife became an individual recognized
> by law, with definite prerogatives in each of these
> areas. Such statutes were and are more basic to the
> happiness of most women than even the right to
> vote.
>
> —ELIZABETH BOWLES WARBASSE, *THE CHANG-
> ING LEGAL RIGHTS OF MARRIED WOMEN,
> 1800–1861*

CHAPTER 3 INVESTIGATED HOW THE ANTEBELLUM SO-
cial meanings of Womanhood defined an aporetic space. This
chapter analyzes how interimplicated antebellum institutions defined this aporetic space of Womanhood, specifically
through Anglo-based legal structures that created distinctly
gendered realms of property and contract law. Women's legal

status in the contractual economy was removed at common law upon their socially expected entry into the marriage contract, contrary to the claims of equality for all made by the founding documents of U.S. democracy. That is, once women engaged in the marriage contract, they were relieved of all further ability to engage in contract, which was the centerpiece of the new political economic order. Interestingly, this institutional elision constituted a precise analogue to the elision found in Western democracies' origin myths, in social contract theories.

Modern capitalist democracy's growth forced dislocations and changes in the antebellum foundations of property and contract law, as well as in popular understandings of property and contract. Most of these legal transformations did not displace the aporetic gap in social meanings of and institutions regulating Womanhood, property, and contract; they merely reinstated, and even exacerbated, the aporia. With the market's growing dominance came a new understanding of contracts as promises to be executed in the future, and often across geography, rather than simpler exchanges of rights of possession in the immediate present. The new conception of contracts in turn dovetailed with the rise of futures markets and economic speculation. At the same time, lawyers and legislators worked to remove the remnants of feudal relations from the legal edifice, relations that they understood as embedded in the history of English common law and its laws regulating real property. To this end, the codification movement pursued legal reform meant to democratize the law from the 1820s through the 1840s, working to make it accessible to all by codifying the common law. This work to defeudalize common law also focused on making property more easily alienable, or more easily exchanged through market contracts. For centuries, much of the property law embedded in English common law had developed around the singular purpose of preventing the division of feudal lands in order to protect feudal power relations, which rested in great part on extremely unequal ownership of arable land. For the Revisers, who were charged with codifying New York State's statutory law, restructuring these laws would not only remove traces of an inegalitarian feudal history, but would also shape property law to the needs of a new form of economy. Increased fungibility of property would invigorate the new economy, which was based in part in the constant economic development of property and its market.

Ironically, the very legislation meant to defeudalize the system of real property law—meant to open up market relations to all citizens by leveling what had been legally institutionalized, ascribed status relations under feudalism—led directly to a further distancing of married women from the market. In other words, the defeudalization and democratization of property and contract law—the systems of law that lay at the center of the new socioeconomy, at the center of modern Western capitalism—directly resulted in a move toward greater legally institutionalized feudalization of married women's relations to the economy and to their husbands. Married women did not live under feudalism while men lived in modernity; in practice, they entered a society based in market and contract relations only through an institutional elision in property law's movement from feudal to capitalist relations. The site of this institutional elision, married women's equitable settlements, appeared as a throwback to feudalism in the midst of modernity's legal structures. Because the gendered structural aporia in antebellum legal institutions remained unacknowledged, the immediate results of the codification movement were devastating for women. The process of defeudalizing the legal status of real property by making it easily accessible to market transactions entirely effaced married women's rights to property. Their only claims to civil existence in a market economy had been through legal "work-arounds," eliding their nonexistence under common law. The legal institutions of Equity Courts, Chancery, and passive trusts had provided a space through which married women could negotiate their relations to property and contract. At the same time, Equity Courts, Chancery, and passive trusts appeared to be irrational vestiges of feudalism, as they took circuitous detours around common law's rational logic. Of course, these detours provided married women's only path to civil existence by eliding the aporetic abyss of Womanhood and contract defined at common law. But the New York Revisers' linear understanding of the legal systems of common law and equity inherited from England directed their changes in, or defeudalization of, real property law.

The codification movement held its greatest sway in New York State, where statutory law was codified in 1826 and 1838 and legal procedures were codified in 1848. New York's revised procedures, known as the Field Code, and revised statutory law, codified by a committee known as the Revisers, significantly affected the institutional aporia's history by forcing legislative address of the aporetic site binding married women and contract. Removing married women's equitable settlements from common law was one of the codifiers' many successful reform efforts. By removing the legal operation that provided married women their only entryway to legal subjecthood— the institutional site that elided married women's civic nonexistence—the New York State codifiers denied married women any means to own property or make contracts. This was not the codification movement's intent, but an unintended result; it was the necessary result of rewriting laws of property and contract in a way that suited the newly "egalitarian" market while ignoring the constitutive aporetic space of Womanhood. This site that did not seem to have a proper location in modernity served precisely as married women's only site of access to capitalism's burgeoning economy and democracy. Its removal thrust women even further out of the contractual market.

In yet another unintended consequence, Womanhood's aporetic form became suddenly and shockingly apparent within antebellum institutions and systems of social meanings. New York State's codification movement unwittingly forced the legislature to encounter the institutional aporia of Womanhood, property, and contract by so exacerbating the elision taking place that an open recognition of some of the aporia's terms became unavoidable. And when legislators confronted this gendered aporetic space, it appeared inexplicable. Consequently, New York State's earliest married women's property act refused direct address of the abyss. The 1848 property act did not allow married women legal existence as actors in a market economy. Instead, legislators tried to detour the elision by replicating the earlier effects of married women's equitable settlements. Only the rise of an organized woman's movement and a consequent struggle to refigure legitimized relations between True Womanhood and the economy would allow direct address of the underlying gendered aporia, resulting in an 1860 New York State Married Women's Property Act that actually grappled with the institutional and conceptual relations between Womanhood, property, contract, the economy, and the nation. The history of married women's property rights, beginning before New York State's earliest such act, is one of movement from protection of family property from creditors to a consideration of women's legitimate role in the economy and society. Whether the passage of the later acts resulted in immediate court recognition of the economic and contractual rights they were meant to inscribe upon Womanhood and the nation might not be as important as the national discursive refiguring of Womanhood that these acts signified. The passage of married women's property acts, such as the 1860 Earnings Act in New York State, marked a social rewriting, a re-vision, of who and what Woman might legitimately be.[1]

Once the New York codifiers removed the false cover provided by institutional work-arounds, the newly visible aporetic space—the impassable gendered space—demanded address. The structural aporia's uncovering released an ethical call to reside in its space in the name of democratic promise. In this chapter I explore a founding institutional aporia of Anglo-based democracy by tracing the webs of relations between married women, Womanhood, and antebellum legal institutions regulating property and contract. By rereading the antebellum New York State legislative debates surrounding married women and property law, I explore how the legislators were forced to experience the uncovered aporetic space *as endurance . . . as interminable resistance or remainder* (Derrida 1993, 19).

Note on Laws and Social Meanings

In any given society, continual societal integration and continual re-creation of each self as human members of that society's social order occur together through habitually enacted social practices, institutions, and understandings.[2] In turn, that society's symbolic structure re-presents society's integration or coherence and the individual human's belonging back to societal members. Legal forms and their changes might be read as momentary crystallizations of the social re-presentation process, crystallizations of their systems of self-understanding and social meaning. Laws might serve as proxies for these re-presentations of a society to itself. Within the immeasurable, ungraspable flux of any social order, "social reality [also] possesses the property of crystallising. . . . Apart from the individual acts to which they give rise, collective habits are expressed in definite forms such as legal or moral rules, popular sayings, or facts of social structure, etc. As these forms exist permanently and do not change with the various applications which are made of them, they constitute a fixed object, a constant standard which is always to hand for the observer" (Durkheim 1982, 82). In this way, legal rules such as the 1848 and 1860 New York State Married

Women's Property Acts can be read as collective re-presentations of society to itself, as concretizations of both contemporary processes of societal integration and the social belonging possible for individual members of society. Further, the concepts and their classifications used by each society—such as the antebellum system of social meanings that imbricated Womanhood, the economy, property, contract, and the nation—can be read as "collective representations [that] express . . . the way in which the group thinks of itself in its relationships with the objects which affect it. Now the group is constituted differently from the individual and the things which affect it are of another kind. . . . The symbols in which it thinks of itself alter according to what it is" (40). In other words, the passage of disparate legislation regarding the same system of concepts in a brief time period, and the social and legislative struggles surrounding their passage, can offer insight into the very ways a society understands both itself and its individual members. Specifically, the passage in a brief period of two property acts, each with dramatically different assumptions regarding Womanhood and implications for women, and the details of the battles surrounding their passage, offer potential insights into how the system of relations between Womanhood, property, and the economy integrated antebellum society and constituted civic membership. Their aporetic location means that such insights speak to the underlying faults and fissures of the antebellum social order.

AN INDECENT PROPOSAL: TO LET WOMEN CONTRACT
FOR THE GOOD OF THE NATION

Early- to mid-nineteenth-century Americans rethought themselves and their social order through precisely the concepts of Womanhood, property, contract, the economy, and the nation. In the earliest recorded legislative discussion of their intricate interrelations, the legislators grappled mightily with this aporetic space in response to the proposal of a married women's property act. In 1837, Thomas Herttell proposed to the New York Senate a "Bill to Restore to Married Women 'The Right of Property,' as Guaranteed by the Constitution of this State." The woman's rights movement would later publish his lengthy speech in support of the bill and widely distribute it as a woman's rights pamphlet.[3] In his speech, Senator Herttell argued a wide variety of reasons for passing a married women's property act; however, the links between his various lines of argumentation become coherent for today's reader only once she realizes that he was arguing from the edge of an aporetic abyss at the very beginnings of its irruption. Initially, his arguments seem to partake of logical confusion, despite the fact that he laid out each point clearly and systematically. Clean, steady argumentative bridges cannot be built across aporias. To contemporary listeners and readers, though, his argument would have made sense, even as most would have disagreed with him. In his plea for women's rights to property, Herttell unknowingly journeyed along the very detours that contemporary social meanings and legal institutions used to bypass an aporetic abyss. Rhetorically traversing the convoluted edges of this structural aporia led Herttell to two seemingly unsavory conclusions regarding contemporary law: (a) a centerpiece of common law—its treatment of property, contract, and married women—was actually unconstitutional under both the New York State and the U.S. constitutions, and (b) the regulation of property and contract in relation to married women under common law and the 1828 revisions undermined the very morality and stability that True Womanhood provided the socioeconomically dislocated nation, thereby "spread[ing] demoralization, crime and misery throughout the community" (1839, 52). The record of Herttell's speech documents one of the earliest attempts at a *nonpassive endurance of this aporia as the condition of responsibility* (Derrida 1993, 16). His proposed married women's property act was the first to include a married woman's right to "that property 'which she may acquire by her own industry and management' . . . includ[ing] 'rents, issues, or profits of real estate,'" making it the only proposition for decades to afford women a legitimate position in the economic realm (Rabkin 1980, 85). Further, his bill focused on the inability of families to retain financial property, as distinct from landed property or capital, by bequeathing it to their daughters, a new problem in a growing market economy based in cash transactions (88). His bill was, in fact, a bold approach to solving the institutional aporias that gaped evermore in light of the new socioeconomy's dislocation and recent legal adjustments; it would not be matched for over two decades.

Herttell (1839, 7–8) began by calling on the public to *endure the aporia,* asserting that "when public attention shall be duly directed to the subject, the true character of the law in question will be fully exposed—its incompatibility with the principles, spirit and object of the political government of this state, will be made manifest—its inconsistency with the express provisions of the Constitution, will be clearly developed; and its mischievous influence on the rights, morals, happiness, and well being of the community will be found so great and obvious as to incur public censure and insure merited condemnation." Here he inhabited the gendered abyss of married women's relation to property and contract by noting, albeit through a refusal to recognize, the strange relationship married women seemed to hold to contracts. That is, he argued that the common law had constructed a strange and illogical relationship. But Herttell did not recognize that the logics of democratic law and democratic capitalism rested on this abyssal relationship; it could not simply be legislated away because it in fact constituted society's underlay. Nonetheless, his address of the marriage contract's practical relation to property rights faithfully mapped the congruent aporetic spaces of democratic origin myths' (hetero)sexual-social contract and the marriage contract under common law:

> To speak in legal parlance . . . there is no affinity between the marriage covenant, properly so called, and a contract for the transfer of property. The marriage contract does not necessarily, or of itself, produce the transfer of the wife's property to her husband. It is the *law* to which we are objecting, which attaches to the connubial association, consequences extraneous of marriage stipulations, and alien to the object or purpose of the marriage institution; and which, but for the *law* in question, as I shall show, would not follow. Her *knowledge* of the existing law . . . by which her property would be taken from her and given to her husband, constitutes no just or tenable ground on which, in the absence of an actual assent, to *assume,* that she consented to be dispossessed of her property, on becoming a wife. The privation would be the same whether she assented to it or not. Then why require her assent; and why *assume* it? (36)

Herttell accurately navigated this space without understanding that *it is not just the law to which he objected* but the very structure of Anglo-based democracies.

He further commented on the irregularities of the marriage contract when compared to all other contracts by tracing the historical site of the elision of women as civic participants and contending that its operations were unconstitutional under federal law. He could make this claim only by ignoring women's historic and mythic inability to make contracts, even as he argued against this historic inability. Enduring the abyss wreaks havoc on logical coherence. He reasoned, "Does not the *acceptance* of property by a female given to her on the *conditions* contained in the *deed* or *will* through which her title to it is acquired, amount to a *contract* between the *giver* and *receiver* of such property? If so, then the wife's rights, in relation to such property, is secured by the Constitution of the United States, which interdicts the existence of any state law, '*impairing* the obligation of *contract*,' *&c.* If the state law interdicts or prevents the performance of the *conditions* on which such property is acquired, does not the property revert to the *estate* of the donor or testator?" (11 n.). Under this line of reasoning, any exchange of goods implied a contract. If a contract was legitimately made, it was protected by the Federal Constitution. Ergo, an exchange of goods with an individual who could not legitimately make a contract implied a federally protected contract. Second, the outcome of nonperformance of a legitimate contract was that the object of the contract reverted to the individual who owned it prior to the contract. If New York State common law prevented the performance of a legitimate and constitutionally protected contract, the property contracted should have reverted to the original owner. Therefore, if New York State law prevented performance of a contract with an individual who could not legitimately make a contract (i.e., a married woman) the property contracted (i.e., a gift or inheritance) should have reverted to the original owner rather than having been transferred to a third party (i.e., her husband). The logical problem was clear, and it resided in the abyss he encountered and addressed even as he could not name it. By enduring the abyss, Herttell was not able to produce the logic of legal reform, but instead produced a call to social movement, envisioning the unseen aporetic space as the *heritage of an idea of . . . a democracy that must have the structure of a promise—and thus the memory of that which carries the future, the to come, here and now* (Derrida 1993, 18–19).

At every point, Herttell's logic rested and foundered on his ignoring of women's and Womanhood's definitional lack of civic existence in Anglo-based democracy, on the successful operation of this elision. Even as he addressed these congruent aporetic spaces, he argued as if the ground was firm and logic could pass smoothly across the site. His argument always assumed that women and Womanhood existed solidly in the civil realm, rather than as phantoms. By participating in the elision even as he encountered the aporia, Herttell was able to maintain that the government had "as little constitutional authority . . . to adopt the *common law of England,* or of any other country, by which to divest married women of their property, and give it to their husbands, as it has to enact a statute law by which to divest *any other* citizen of their property, and vest it in another individual" (20). But the logical conundrum he occupied—his own *endurance of the aporia*—led him to question the legal treatment of women's civic existence and subjecthood. He reflected:

> The 1st sec. of the [7th] article [of the Constitution] just mentioned, provides, that "no member of this state shall be disfranchised or deprived of any of the rights and privileges secured to any citizen thereof, unless by the law of the land, or the judgment of his peers." Is not a female a "member of this state," as well as a male? Is not a married woman as important a member of this state, as an unmarried woman? And is not the phrase "no member of this state" as applicable to female as to male members of the state? and to married as well as unmarried women? And is it not equally applicable to all, each, and every, of the "members of this state?" and when the abovementioned words are immediately followed by, and in connexion with, the words "shall be disfranchised or deprived of the rights and privileges," does it not refer as well to the rights of females, as of males, and to the rights of the married, as well as the unmarried members of the state? (23)

Once the aporia was uncovered, rather than its elision accepted, other questions would follow: Did women legally exist as social subjects, as legitimate members of society? In the continual and habitual collective practices that integrate society and make it work, were women repeatedly constituted as belonging to society or not belonging? The long struggle for women's property and contract rights would have to address these questions directly in order to change the societal relations between Womanhood, property, contract, and the economy so that women could be understood as fundamental actors in democratic capitalist society.

Then, in one long summary, Herttell grappled succinctly with the social illogic of gendered aporias in both their meanings and institutions, leading him to the seemingly perverse conclusion that the social position of pious True Womanhood would result in a contaminated nation rather than a purified, moral, and protected one. He traced the practical effects of Womanhood's parameters in a hypothetical boundary case that would be frequently deployed by the antebellum woman's movement—a case that I term the "widow in extremis," in which a married woman is left to fend for herself and her children and yet the husband still draws on every bit of their real and personal property while she submits as a True Woman. Herttell argued:

> The wife's personal property is given to the husband, and *his,* (not *her*) heirs and assigns, absolutely and unconditionally; and also the income of her real estate to be possessed by him as his own,—to be used as his own, and wasted if he pleases without any responsibility to his wife, children or any one else; and though it be, as in many, if not in most cases it has been, spent, and wasted in every species of folly, extravagance, vice and dissipation;—though thereby the family be reduced to poverty and want, and the delinquent husband stretched on a bed of sickness, and incapacitated by bodily disease induced by his dissolute and profligate habits of life, to sustain his family;—still, as before remarked, her natural, maternal and moral obligations require and insure her utmost exertions to maintain her children; and female benevolence, if not her conjugal affections or covenants induce her, in a majority of cases, even to administer to the subsistence and comfort of a worthless husband to whom the *law* gives her property, reckless of his worthless character;—and by which forced requisition upon his wife's purse, facilities are granted and supplies furnished which contribute to the irregularities of a dissipated husband. Thus do *law, injustice* and profligacy, conspire to deprive married women of their rights and property,—to destroy all their pecuniary resources;—reduce them and their families to poverty and want; to leave them no practical and efficient means of protection from abuse or oppression by brutal husbands; and thus finally to spread demoralization, crime and misery throughout the community. (51–52)

Here Herttell sketched the effect of certain parameters of a True Woman's existence that countered what a True Woman's Influence was supposed to ensure: the morality and piety of the nation. The troubled relation at common law between Woman, property, and contract stood charged as the culprit. Despite accepting this founding aporia's elision, he here pointed directly at it and indicted it in base social ills. In his insistent address of married women's abysmal and abyssal legal position, Herttell called for an address of common law and indicated its importance as an aporetic institution.

COMMON LAW AND NOT SO COMMON EQUITY: LOCATING THE INSTITUTIONAL APORIA

> [Judge William Blackstone] created a legal model of the family. It was around this model . . . that nineteenth-century debate revolved, and it was this model that shaped and in fact warped the public perception of the common law. Most important, more than any other jurist Blackstone was responsible for separating the right to property, which republicans equated with individual liberty, from the legal status of married women.
>
> —Norma Basch, *In the Eyes of the Law*

In the newly formed United States, legal regulation of marriage relied heavily on Sir William Blackstone's legal theory of unity, promulgated in the 1700s and handed down through common law.[4] An entire contingent of economic disabilities resulted from the theory of unity, under which the wife's legal existence became one with her husband at the moment of marriage.[5] Under common law, the married woman's economic disabilities centered on all rights pertaining to what had been her realty and her personal property as a single woman—as well as to any inheritance, gifts, or earnings she might receive while married—and extended to such matters as child custody and responsibility for crimes committed. In summary, "She could no longer perform legal actions in her own name. Since her husband controlled her estate, she had nothing to use as security if she wanted to contract with others. Nor was the *feme covert* able to make a binding agreement with her husband. . . . This same theoretical unity disabled her from prosecuting or defending a suit. . . . She had to be joined with her husband in the [legal] action. . . . Likewise she was generally unable to make a will. . . . When a *feme sole* married, any previous will she might have made automatically was annulled" (Warbasse 1987, 13–14). Tables 8 and 9 succinctly outline the legal rights and duties of husbands and wives under common law in New York State prior to 1848.

Married women's economic disabilities under common law were similar throughout the United States until at least the mid-1800s. Once married,

TABLES 8–9. *Common Law Regulation of Marriage*

Source: Basch (1982, 54, 55).

TABLE 8. *Common Law Rights and Duties of Wife and Husband during Coverture*

Wife	Husband
Entitled to support.	May sue on behalf of his wife without her consent.
Cannot contract except for necessaries and as her husband's agent.	Owns wife's personalty outright.
Cannot sue or be sued in her own name.	Can reduce wife's choses in action to his possession.
Cannot make a will except with her husband's consent.	Controls management of wife's realty.
Cannot alienate her realty except with her husband's consent.	May charge wife's realty, but may not devise it.
	Responsible for wife's necessaries.
	Responsible for maintenance of children.
	Responsible for wife's debts incurred before marriage.
	Cannot alienate wife's dower without her consent (cannot alienate his own realty without her consent).

TABLE 9. *Common Law Rights of Dower (Surviving Wife) and Curtesy (Surviving Husband)*

Dower	Curtesy
Wife entitled to tenancy in one-third of husband's realty as long as she does not remarry.	Husband entitled to tenancy in all of wife's realty for as long as he lives.
Wife entitled to her paraphernalia.	At his death, wife's realty reverts to her family if there are no living children.
Wife may lose custody of children by husband's will.	Husband has custody of children.

ownership of all of a woman's personal property—or movable property such as clothing, housewares, jewelry, and cash—devolved to her husband. The husband also had the right to reduce to personal property any investments, contracts, and credit held by his wife prior to marriage, at which point they belonged to him; in other words, he could convert them to their monetary value or their value in movable property, after which they were defined as personal property, giving him legal title (Basch 1982, 54). When the husband died, his wife could not retrieve her personal property; rather, she received one-third of his personal property left after payment of debts (Warbasse 1987, 13). In a meager attempt to prevent undue hardship, the state guaranteed her a minimum of utilitarian and subsistence items, designated her "paraphernalia" and consisting mainly of bedding, some clothes and jewelry, and some cookware and place settings.

A wife retained legal title to her realty, or unmovable property such as land and buildings, but her husband assumed control over its management. However, he could not legally transfer her land without her permission, and if he did, "the wife or her representative could regain possession after his death" (Warbasse 1987, 9). All profits from realty were considered personal property, as they were now detached from the realty itself; crops were thus considered personal property once harvested. As such, all profits from the wife's realty legally belonged to her husband. The husband additionally held rights of curtesy, which meant he had lifetime rights to tenancy of her lands after her death, as long as there had been a live birth during the marriage. Her realty fell to her children only after his death; if there were no longer any living children, it reverted to her family. The wife's rights of dower were the legal counterpoint to her husband's curtesy. Dower entitled her to tenancy of a legally given fraction of his lands after his death, with the percentage varying by state. Of the original states, nine defined the wife's dower as one-third of any and all realty held by the husband during their marriage, and four defined dower as one-third of realty held at the time of his death (10). Because she held this right, her husband had to obtain her permission when transferring not only her realty, but his as well.

The wife's right of dower and to repossess lands transferred without her permission complicated all sales of land, as long as they held. A widow's right to tenancy of a proportion of lands held during her husband's lifetime placed all land buyers in jeopardy. Once the seller died, the purchased land might be among those to revert to his widow. Dower operated to protect families' generational status in an agrarian-based society by preventing dissolution of their property, precisely by making land sales risky and by retaining matrilineal rights to land. In a commercial economy, dower prevented capital investment and growth by doing the same thing—by making land sales and improvements on purchased land risky. The possibility that a seller did not have his wife's permission carried the same threat; the land, along with any capital investments made on it, might at any time revert to the prior owner's widow. Here, with concomitant changes in the economy and legal understandings, the web of institutional relations between Womanhood, property, contract, and considerations of what was good for the economy and the nation became further entangled around and through the site of marriage.

Exceptions to married women's legal disabilities did exist for the purposes of either increasing land's fungibility or protecting women's and children's subsistence or promoting the commercial economy by allowing married women limited rights to contract. In practice, wives were sometimes allowed to convey their own real estate, since they did retain the title. In Pennsylvania, Massachusetts, and Maine only, wives legally reverted to feme sole status if they were left to fend for themselves and their children because their husbands had been banished or permanently left the state. Pennsylvania, as a state with a major port city, also allowed married women feme sole powers when their husbands were at sea. And South Carolina based its interpretation of common law on changes made in London to promote urban business, allowing "any married woman running her own business . . . to have *feme sole* powers and liabilities with respect to [that business]" and that business only (Warbasse 1987, 20). All of the practical exceptions left the institutional aporetic site intact. Women's economic disabilities at common law were offset, however, by the existence and growth of the Chancery or Equity Court in England and subsequently in the United States. In the nineteenth-century United States, and particularly in New York State, equity constituted the institutional detour that bypassed married women's aporetic legal position in relation to property and contract.

Equity's History: Bypassing the Institutional Aporia

The Chancery Court arose as a distinct institution in thirteenth-century England to address and offset injustices under common law, generally in relation to matters of legal, social, and economic status.[6] While equity first emerged from "special petitions for relief to the king's chancellor, [it] grew into a whole system with its own forms, pleadings, and precedents and with its own jurisprudence" (Basch 1982, 20–21). Over time, equity came to focus on overseeing matters of married women's legal relations to property, but its proceedings and decisions always remained supplementary to common law. Common law regulation of land tenure was a centerpiece of the feudal social order, defining each person's relative social status and duties: "All land ultimately was the dominion of the king, but interests in the land . . . were delivered down the feudal social, political, and military hierarchy. In exchange for the right to use the land, each person holding an interest in the land promised to render loyalty and military services to the person above him" (Rabkin 1980, 65). Land holdings were the mechanism that determined each person's and family's position in a strict social hierarchy. In a society ruled by status, any change in land ownership directly affected the individual's or family's social and political position and duties owed. Chancery developed the legal mechanism of the use, or the trust, to enable landholders to transfer lands to others for use without weakening their own position in the social hierarchy. By allowing the original landholder to retain the legal title while others held all rights to use of the land, the use or trust provided a detour around feudalism's strict common law relation between possession of land, obligations of tribute and military service in the name of the nobles and king, and social and political status. Equity existed as a legal institution distinct from and subsidiary to common law, with the specific purpose of mitigating particular hardships wrought by common law. Individuals could appeal to the Chancery or Equity Court to rule on their case, usually in order to ameliorate some effect of common law. Importantly, though, even as equity functioned as a socioeconomic leveler of feudalism and the use or trust provided a critical tool with which people could beneficially navigate aspects of their feudal status and duties, it operated only within the larger frame of feudalism's status hierarchy upheld at common law.[7]

In the socioeconomic transformation to capitalism, the very meanings and utility of feudal property law were transformed. Under emergent capitalism in the nineteenth-century United States—in an economy and polity where people presumably owned their land without owing fealty—the utility of the use or trust was unclear and even confusing, since it made legal ownership of and rights in land indirectly related. From the fourteenth-century beginnings of Chancery's battle with feudal law in England, "the use or trust was developed in equity to facilitate conveyancing, but [in a commercial economy] it resulted in further complications, or as the [1828 New York State] Revisers termed it, 'impenetrable mystery'" (Rabkin 1980, 67). Ironically, in the new economy, where easy transfer of property ownership was increasingly prized as a means to economic growth, the legal trust actually hindered property's fungibility since, under a trust, the property's owner did not have legal rights of use. In fact, the New York State committee charged with codifying law in the 1820s, the New York State Revisers, saw the remnants of feudal property law as a curb to economic growth, free contract, and individual liberty—as a confining holdover from a bygone era. Increased alienability of property was one of their primary goals in their efforts toward defeudalization of the law.

For married women, however, the use or trust provided precisely the site of displacement or elision through which they might enter the modern capitalist socioeconomy, just as they entered the realm of civil society only through the elision of the marital contract. A legal instrument known as the separate equitable estate for married women served as the mechanism for this institutional elision, emerging gradually in England from the sixteenth to the eighteenth centuries under the jurisdiction of the *Equity Court* to mitigate married women's disabilities at common law. Always administered by trustees, such equitable estates were either the result of trusts drawn up by donors of property or of prenuptial agreements. By the eighteenth century, a married woman could keep her property entirely separate from her husband's in equity. And, from its beginnings, the operations of the separate equitable estate and its negotiations of married women's rights at common law pointed to aporetic relations between women, property, and contract. Legal logic that was illogic defined this impassable and impossible space. While all ability to contract and all contracts previously made were nullified at the moment of a woman's marriage, equity recognized a wife's rights to her separate property precisely when she had "so contract[ed] with her husband before marriage" (Warbasse 1987, 33). In addition, and in direct contradiction of the legal theory of unity, under equity wives could make contracts with their husbands in relation to their separate property as long as they had already defined it in a contract prior to marriage. Women's legal disabilities doubly folded in on themselves as equity operated to bypass the inoperable aporia. In the early U.S. evolution of imported English common law and equity, the separate equitable estate for married women became the precise institutional site of Woman's elided and elusive move into a legitimate civil existence. Through this institutional site, a father could give or will to his daughter portions of his estate, to be overseen by a trustee, and thereby ensure that all profits from and control of property, whether realty or personalty, would remain with her. If she married, she would retain ownership and control through her trustee; her husband would secure none of her property. Additionally, a woman could put her own land and personal property into a trust of her own accord prior to getting married, and in this way maintain control and title over it. Otherwise, under common law, all her personal and business property immediately transferred to her husband, as did control over landed property. The married women's separate equitable estate operated as an exception to common law while in full recognition of common law's institutional dominance. In its English beginnings, the equitable estate provided married women with a wide spectrum of contractual capabilities. But they were all limited to the property put in trust for her and to those allowed her by the terms of that trust: "She might defend and prosecute suits in the Chancery Court against her husband or others in order to maintain her rights. She was able to obligate her separate estate by contracts when they were made with that intention, and she could even dispose of her separate property or its income by deed or will unless her powers were circumscribed by the bequest or settlement from which her estate derived" (34). Under equity, as at common law, married women still had no general powers of contract with which they might legitimately participate in the economic and political arenas.

Equity in New York State

For the most part, Equity Courts did not exist in the northern states in the 1700s and early 1800s. Anti-aristocratic sentiment ran high in the northern states, which waged a revolution against the British during this period. Equity Courts had historically been overseen by an unelected chancellor, whose decisions did not have to refer to historical precedent. Consequently, the northern states viewed Chancery Courts as an unwanted vestige of the very British aristocracy and feudal system against which they fought. New York State was an exception, however, and was in the forefront of establishing both common law and equity in the early United States. Throughout the 1700s, the New York State governor sat as the New York chancellor for equity, by definition, presiding over an embattled Court of Chancery. During this time, the New York Assembly continually fought the Court of Chancery precisely because of its seemingly inherent antidemocratic structure (Warbasse 1987, 38). But from 1814 to 1823, New York Governor and Chancellor James Kent worked to consolidate the common law, since printed records of decisions were scarce, and to establish equity as a viable alternative to the common law. His work as Chancellor is commonly recognized as the source of equity's authority in the United States. By 1823, he had succeeded in aligning equity law in New York with current practices in England, including its oversight of married women's separate equitable settlements (41). Kent managed to instate, "first, the passive trust, which might give the wife extensive powers; second, the simple antenuptial agreement without a trust, which established a married woman's separate estate; and third . . . the principle that in relation to her separate estate a married woman was like a single woman as long as the deed that created that estate did not specifically restrict her" (Basch 1982, 78–79). Married women still held no general rights of contract, but held rights only in relation to their specific property settlements, as specified in those settlements. Common law prevailed over all other aspects of married women's lives, particularly in its focus on political and economic rights of contract. And equity did not reach women whose property had not been put in trust or who had no property to put in trust. Separate equitable estates did provide a modicum of economic existence for those women situated within the classes that could benefit from them. But a few short years after equity reached its full strength in 1823, legal reform undertaken by the 1828 New York State Revisers would make it difficult for even the most learned lawyer to create a separate equitable trust that could withstand scrutiny. Despite equity's original function as a leveler of feudal status hierarchies, the broad powers of judiciary discretion it vested in the state's political leader were seen as tyrannical and antidemocratic. For the next twenty years, the codification movement would attack the New York State Chancery Court's powers before abolishing it completely in 1846.

Even at its peak, equity never afforded married women any general rights of contract; they could contract only regarding the disposition of property already established in their separate equitable settlement. Equity certainly never allowed married women to participate legitimately or legally in a burgeoning economy and polity based on contracts through time—on futures contracts, investment, and speculation. Rather, separate equitable estates were precisely the site of elision that enabled this fundamental gendered aporia to continue functioning. The married women's property acts would emerge from this institutional aporia and would be shaped by how the prodemocracy, antifeudal legal reform movement moved through this space. In the next few years, equity's confusing position as a leveler of feudalism and yet a relic of feudalism would lead reformers to entirely remove the legal mechanisms of uses or trusts; in their attempt to defeudalize the law, the New York State Revisers would eliminate the only operable bypass of this aporetic institutional space. In so doing, they would force societal address of this institutional site of elision and of the aporia's troubled existence itself.

THE LEGAL MOVEMENT FOR CODIFICATION: MAKING THE APORIA VISIBLE

The legal reform movement for codification began in earnest in 1823 with William Sampson's "Anniversary Discourse" to the New York Historical Society (Cook 1981, 106).[8] The movement had its greatest success in New York State, where it lasted into the 1860s; elsewhere its strength dwindled in the 1840s after gaining partial general acceptance. Unlike most legal reform efforts, demands for codification brought together lawyers and the lay population, although they were motivated by somewhat different interests. Invoking the spirit of a democratic nation, lawyers and lay reformers called both for abolishing all vestiges of English feudal tyranny and for making the legal system's operations more accessible. In fact, the reformers' radical segment went so far as to argue that almost all English content should be stripped from the American legal system (84). On the other hand, the moderate reformers primarily hoped to achieve accessibility: first, by extracting all substantive law from its common law form and rewriting it more precisely; second, by organizing the quickly growing field of statutory law (81).

Lawyers sought a consistency and transparency in the law that would allow better and easier lawyering. Appointed judges made common law in their written decisions, relying primarily on previous judges' decisions, or on what was popularly perceived as judges' whimsy. This meant that, unlike statutory law, case outcomes were highly unpredictable. Additionally, elected legislators made statutory law, which seemed to promote democratic lawmaking, rather than "feudal," judge-based lawmaking inherited from England. Finally, the proliferation of a wide variety of both case law and legal statutes made proper legal argumentation very difficult. Codification promised much easier access to the multitude of legal materials necessary to represent clients in court. Lay reformers also sought greater legal accessibility in the name of the average citizen, hoping that statutory codification would make the law transparent (Cook 1981, 91). Again invoking democracy, lay reformers believed that legal transparency would remove some of the legal profession's power and allow people to protect their individual rights and to argue their own legal cases effectively. All reformers—moderate and radical, lawyers and laypersons—agreed that codification would benefit the nation by making the law both clear and accessible. Since such reforms would remove power from the judicial bench and bar, judges and some lawyers feared the result. But an emerging commercial society required that the legal system and its practices be more predictable to the lawyer and layperson alike, just as it required double-entry bookkeeping. Similarly, it demanded that property law be reconceived so that property's legal meanings and regulation fit a market newly based on futures agreements and productive development rather than on long-term, static leaseholds.

Successful substantive codification took place in two waves in New York State. In 1828 and 1836, committees dubbed the Revisers worked to "bourgeoisify" property law, with a stated goal of removing "all technical rules and distinctions, having no relationship to the essential nature of property and the means of its beneficial enjoyment, but which are derived from the feudal system" (cited in Cook 1981, 147). A further effort at procedural codification, in 1848, passed the legislature in the same session as New York State's first Married Women's Property Act. The 1828 and 1836 Revisers' focus on defeudalizing the legal system would long haunt married women's legal relation to property and contract, since they eliminated married women's equitable settlements in the process. Subsequently, delegates to the 1846 Constitutional Convention voted on procedural codification that eliminated the office of Chancellor that had overseen equity, designated common law courts as the new overseers of equity, and created a commission to streamline legal procedure headed by David Dudley Field. Three years later, in April 1849, the New

York State legislature implemented the Field Code of Procedure, finalizing equity's elimination. By dismantling equity, the Revisers, the Constitutional Convention delegates, and Field's commission had by 1849 unintentionally made visible the Anglo-based democratic aporetic site of Womanhood, contract, and the economy.

The New York State Revisers began their attack on uses and trusts with the 1828 Revised Statutes. Equity's oversight of uses and trusts was one of their prime targets since it complicated real property law, making land less fungible, and it vested power over that law in judges rather than the legislature. As they dismantled uses and trusts, the 1828 Revisers did not completely obliterate married women's equitable estates, but they created so many ambiguities that confusion resulted for any lawyer attempting to write a foolproof settlement. In fact, "by abolishing passive or formal trusts—trusts in which property was transferred to a third party to circumvent the wife's common law disabilities but in which the wife exerted control over the property—they seemed to destroy the prospective wife's best option" (Basch 1982, 80). The Revisers also effectively nullified many existing settlements by declaring that all passive or formal trusts were to become straightforward legal property. As a result, wives' property that had been held in trust for them reverted to their husbands' control in direct contradiction of their settlements' purpose.

The still existing Equity Court struggled to respect passive trusts nonetheless and sought ambiguities to allow will making, but these ambiguities made creating law and enforcing judgments extremely difficult (Basch 1982, 80–83). The one form of trust that still could be clearly utilized "if it were meticulously drafted" was the active trust or "classic caretaker trust" (82). Active trusts were designed to protect minors and those deemed incompetent to care for themselves rather than to afford contractual capabilities to individuals denied them at common law. But they were all that was left to married women after the 1828 Revised Statutes passed. In the 1836 Revised Statutes, the Revisers further expanded their dismantling of uses and trusts to any "application of the *trust*, whereby one person had an equitable ownership in property and another person had legal title to the property" (Rabkin 1980, 74). In other words, the 1836 Statutes abolished all forms of uses and trusts useful to married women—ones that allowed married women to use their property at equity while a trustee held the legal title—and again

nullified all such uses and trusts already in existence. These statutes immediately converted all married women's trusts into their legally held property,
no longer in trust; under common law, this property then immediately reverted to their husbands' control.

Once the 1828 and 1836 Revised Statutes had passed, the trust or use was
no longer a viable means to accord married women any property or contractual rights, a legitimate relation to the economy, or a legitimate civic
existence. Legal reforms meant to defeudalize legal regulation of property
and wealth and to make land more easily alienable, thereby making it more
accessible to "all," instead thrust married women entirely out of the economic realm. They eliminated the legal work-around that had allowed
married women to elude common law's economic disabilities and to elide
a civil nonexistence. The Equity Court's abolition by the 1846 Constitutional Convention and the Field Code's 1849 adoption by the New York
State legislature only finalized the process. In a sense, the legal codification movement had hollowed out one of modernity's knotholes and made
the knothole's structural makeup and societal importance painfully visible.
Consequently, from 1836 to 1848, New York State legislators repeatedly debated whether to restore the trust to its prior status or legislate an equivalent form of property for married women that would be accessible and
common to all. And for the first time their debates explicitly addressed the
question of Woman's proper relation to property, contract, the economy,
and the nation.

LEGISLATIVE DEBATES IN THE 1840S:
A FORCED ADDRESS

> The battle, which began in 1836 in a judiciary committee of the state
> assembly and ended in 1860 with the Earnings Act, was one of the few
> legislative issues before the Civil War to inject the debate over the ap-
> propriate roles for women into the maelstrom of American politics.
> —Norma Basch, *In the Eyes of the Law*

New York State Senator Thomas Herttell's 1837 bill was the first proposed
legislation giving married women the rights of contract. His lengthy speech
in support of the bill is the first recorded legislative discussion entwining
the questions of proper Womanhood and married women's property and

contractual rights, addressing both in relation to the state of the economy and the nation. The bill's legislative history demonstrates that the 1828 and 1836 Revised Statutes affected how these questions would be addressed over the next decades; the Revised Statutes affected the very shape their entwinement might take. Once Herttell had argued the legal and social issues, he still needed to gain legislative support for his bill. In order to do so, he refocused on the holes brought to light by the 1828 Revised Statutes, "chang[ing] the title of his original bill from 'An Act for the Protection and Preservation of the Rights and Property of Married Women . . .' to 'An Act to Amend the Revised Statutes Relative to Uses, Trusts, and Powers. . . .'" (Basch 1982, 117). Similarly, in the 1840s, the public and the legislature began to address the aporetic relations that the 1828 and 1836 Revised Statutes had made visible. Most strikingly, the public submitted petitions to the legislature demanding married women's property rights, and delegates to the 1846 New York State Constitutional Convention debated the attendant issues. For instance, petitioners to the New York Assembly in 1844 requested what would become the provisions of New York State's first married women's property act in 1848. The Committee on the Judiciary, having been charged with consideration of the petitions, offered a telling response. Their report located the moral order of society in the propriety of the marital relation. According to the committee, that propriety and social stability required "that, for some purposes and to some extent, the wife should lose her political and civil existence." Consequently, they refused to advocate a legitimate legal relation between married women and the economy. Instead, they proposed reinstating the married women's trust as it existed prior to the Revised Statutes (Assembly Doc., No. 96, 1844, 5), reporting that "the committee, while they would deprecate the radical change in the laws, contemplated by the petitioners and by the act introduced, believe that experience has shown that no evil can result from giving to the wife the benefit of property intended for her use through the intervention of a trust. . . . The committee, therefore, advise the House that the act for the more effectual protection of the right of property of married women, ought not to be passed into a law, and offer as a substitute the bill herewith submitted, entitled an act in relation to uses and trusts, and recommend its passage" (10–11).

These legal issues came to a head at the 1846 New York State Constitutional Convention. Heated debates over whether a married women's property rights provision should be added to the state constitution in the end only resulted in the renewal of the old constitutional provisions. But the debates were themselves clearly framed by the aporetic site interimplicating married women's property rights and Womanhood. Delegates debated numerous associated resolutions over the course of the convention. The first suggested provision, introduced by Mr. Harris, proposed legislating exactly what had been married women's capacities under equity, without requiring that an equitable settlement be made: "All property of the wife, owned by her at the time of her marriage, and that acquired by her afterwards, by gift, devise or descent, or otherwise than from her husband, shall be her separate property. Laws shall be passed providing for the registry of the wife's separate property, and more clearly defining the rights of the wife thereto; as well as to property held by her with her husband" (Bishop and Attree 1846, 1038).[9] While Mr. Harris's proposal did not give wives any rights of contract regarding their property, it did provide room for expansion in the laws as well as the implicit possibility of interpreting earnings as her separate property.

His proposal marked the first forced address of the aporetic space's centrality to contemporary legal and economic questions. But it did not further movement within the institutional aporia; it merely attempted to legislate a prior status quo that had facilitated the aporia's bypass. Mr. Harris made clear that legislating what had been removed by earlier reforms was his sole purpose. According to convention records, he explicitly stated that his proposal was simply intended to legislate equity: "The proposition pending, he urged, contemplated only doing that directly which by our laws could now be done indirectly, and which was always done when there was any considerable amount of property belonging to the woman before marriage. The proposition made that a general rule, and gave to the poor also, where the greatest amount of suffering was under the present state of things, the benefit of the same provision. He urged it, also, as a father, anxious to secure to his own the benefit of the little that he might have then" (Bishop and Attree 1846, 1060).[10] On October 2, 1846, Mr. Harris's provision was accepted as a revision to the New York State constitution by a vote of fifty-eight to forty-four (1042). But debate continued—the topic seemingly could not be contained—and three days later his moderate proposal was defeated (fifty to fifty-nine; 1060).

Mr. Harris's provision had initiated a round of proposed substitutions, including one clearly framed as debtor legislation—that is, as legislation meant solely to protect the wife's property from creditors so that a debtor family would not lose all of their possessions. This provision emerged as the primary competition for inclusion in the revised constitution: "The property of married women, real or personal, which belonged to her before marriage, or acquired afterwards by gift or devise other than from her husband, and the avails thereof, shall not be liable in any wise for the debts of the husband" (1041).[11] Offered by Mr. Brundrage, the successful proposal yielded fifty ayes to forty-eight noes. It vested absolutely no property rights in married women, whether in the property's management or alienation or in contracts regarding it. While such debtor legislation was common throughout the country at this time, it did not in any way address the aporia in which married women resided. On the other hand, Mr. Harris's original proposal had.

From October 2 to October 5, 1846, convention delegates debated over competing provisions. Their various arguments, particularly those opposed to the equity legislation, demonstrate the legislation's entanglement in the aporetic site of Womanhood, property, contract, and the economy and in the swirling eddies flowing through this aporetic space. For instance, in a lengthy diatribe against Mr. Harris's provision, Mr. O'Conor accepted only that settlements might sometimes be useful, but doubted their propriety overall. He expressed fear that reinstating settlements through new legislation would place that "fiend pecuniary self-interest" in women's souls, endangering their True Womanhood and in turn the national social and moral order (1058).[12] Mr. O'Conor argued:

> Woman, as wife, or as mother, had known no change of the law which fixed her domestic character, and guided her devoted love. She had as yet known no debasing pecuniary interest apart from the prosperity of her husband. His wealth had been her wealth; his prosperity her pride, her only source of power or distinction. Thus had society existed hitherto—did it need a change? Must the busy and impatient besom [straw broom] of reform obtrude, without invitation, its unwelcome officiousness within the charmed and charming circle of domestic life, and there too change the laws and habits of our people? He trusted not. He called

upon not only husbands, but brothers, sons—all who held the married state in respect, to pause and deliberate before they fixed permanently in the fundamental law, this new and dangerous principle. (1057)

While Mr. O'Conor was probably not an aporetic reader of contemporary times, he clearly recognized that True Womanhood and married women's property and contract rights were not two distinct "social problems" that could be solved through legal reform, but constituted the disordered underlay of the national social order. As such, he correctly feared that they might irrupt when pressure and historical accident coincided, disruptively reordering certain crucial aspects of the social order. He feared the potential social disruption as precisely *that unstable assemblage of faults, fissures, and heterogeneous layers that threaten the fragile inheritor from within or from underneath* (Foucault 1977/1988, 146).

Several opponents of Mr. Harris's equity provision tried a final tack, completing the structural aporia's emergence in these debates, as they logically argued from one of capitalist democracy's illogical founding sites. For today's reader, their arguments clearly demonstrate the contemporary social order's unconscious aporetic moorings. Specifically, these antagonists argued that a provision legislating equity's equivalent should not be passed because it would create a mass of nonfungible, nonalienable property during the length of any woman's marriage. Their argument relied on the unstated assumption that married women did not and could not have any legitimate relation to contract or the economy. Consequently, they argued that any land owned by married women would prevent economic growth, remaining static and undeveloped. If this was allowed to occur, the Revisers' efforts to defeudalize real property law would be reversed by the creation of a new form of ascribed-status holdings, with married women holding precious property off the market that could aid the economy's development.

In other words, and again, if married women did not remain in the realm of proper Womanhood, the economy and the nation were endangered. Why? Because even when contemplating the step beyond the bounds of Womanhood, the legislators could not conceive of this womanly step, for it was still a step *beyond*. Consequently, they imagined Woman at once beyond and unable to contract. Mr. Brown argued along these lines that "it was impolitic . . . thus to tie up, not merely the real, but the personal property of the wife, with all its accumulations during coverture" (1059).[13] Later on the same day, after Mr. Harris's provision had been rejected, Mr. Loomis spoke to the various provisions offered in the three days of debate, "urg[ing] that this was a subject that should be approached with great caution, and went on to say that some of the propositions offered here would change the whole face of society, independent of their moral effect directly on the parties—for it would result in all real property descending in the female line, and being tied up in families, secure from the reach of creditors, and from alienation" (1060–61; Croswell and Sutton 1846, 813).[14] His admonition rested on his inability to conceive of the right of alienation of property or contractual powers vesting in married women. In what, in retrospect, are confounding arguments, a social order's *unstable faults and fissures* can be sighted.

EARLY MARRIED WOMEN'S PROPERTY ACTS:
PROTECTING FAMILY PROPERTY

> The [1848 New York State] statute's primary effect was to create a new category of exempt assets for family use. The special sphere of married women was thus largely confirmed. Assets belonging to married women were to be set aside and insulated from the harsh realities of the commercial world.
> —Richard H. Chused, "Married Women's Property Law: 1800–1850"

Although Thomas Herttell first proposed married women's property acts in a form that included expansive contractual rights for women in 1837 New York, the southern states actually first passed them with a focus on debtor relief.[15] In the wake of the Panic of 1837, Mississippi passed the first married women's property act in 1839, but only one section of the statute addressed married women's rights to real or personal property they brought to or obtained during the marriage. Mississippi's economy was built on the aristocratic estate, and four of the five sections of the final statute addressed property in slaves. The law separated married women's title to their realty and slave property from their husbands' in order to remove it from creditors' reach, but it gave control of all of their property to the husbands. The careful composition of the four sections regulating property in slaves, when compared with the more sloppily written section on real and personal property, underscored legislators' focus on maintaining the integrity of the family estate as a productive unit and marker of social status (Warbasse 1987, 143). In an economy built on slave labor, this most important portion of the aristocratic estate would remain intact through bouts of economic misfortune. In Mississippi, as would be the case in New York in 1848, "the courts were left the definition of the extent of the wife's estate," and they could choose whether to include personal and financial property as well as wages (Thurman 1966, 40). A number of states copied the Mississippi act almost exactly. In 1846, Arkansas passed an identical act, except for a provision clarifying that slave property brought to the marriage by the wife would not be liable for the husband's debts (Warbasse 1987, 159). In 1848, Maryland also passed an identical act, save for changing the definition of property to which the wife retained title: from "real or personal" to "real or of slaves" (157). Again, the act focused on maintaining the slave estate. Southern states did not have the same antagonistic relation with Equity Courts as the northern states; they had not been party to the struggle against Britain and, consequently, took no part in the legal codification movement that had unsettled the aporetic site of Womanhood and contracts in the Northeast. Their legislatures aimed to relieve debt, paying no attention to the aporetic site.

The first spate of married women's property acts succeeded as debtor relief, providing a means to protect some portion of a family's wealth from creditors and, in turn, cushioning the effect of constant economic fluctuations. In the early and mid-nineteenth century, national bankruptcy law and regulation provided negligible protection for individual debtors. "The first federal bankruptcy law (Act of April 3, 1800, 2 Stat. 19 § 1) was applicable only to merchants or traders involuntarily taken into bankruptcy," leaving individuals and families unprotected from the dramatic economic flux of a newly forming economy (Thurman 1966, 15 n. 31). In response to the economic devastation wreaked by the 1837 and 1839 financial panics, the 1841 Federal Bankruptcy Act allowed individual debtors to petition for bankruptcy voluntarily and creditors to petition to take debtors into bankruptcy involuntarily. Under this short-lived and controversial act, well over thirty thousand debtors received legal discharges of all their financial obligations, but the act was repealed in March 1843. The next Bankruptcy Act would not pass until 1867, and only after the act of 1898 would a stable bankruptcy process come into existence that allowed for voluntary individual application (Balleisen 2001; Coleman 1974). In the meantime, the general populace and legislators sought ways to protect some portions of debtors' property from creditors.

In 1848, New York State's first married women's property act granted married women legal title to any real and personal property brought to the marriage or obtained thereafter "by gift, grant, devise or bequest" (*Laws of the State of New-York, 1848*, chap. 200, § 3). For years, many states would use the 1848 act as a template, making it "the most significant of the early married women's property acts" (Warbasse 1987, 205–6). Under the New York State act, married women retained title to their personal property, and accordingly they retained ownership of any profits and rents that accrued from their real property. But wives were given only legal title to their property without any broader rights of contract.

In fact, the 1848 act kept married women at such a distance from the market and property rights that it led directly into the aporetic space of Womanhood and contract. Under the 1848 act's terms, married women's property could no longer be bought, sold, or transferred at all. Wives had been given sole title to and control of their property but no rights of contract, while their husbands could not make contracts regarding property no longer vested in them. No longer able to detour around this aporetic site, the 1849 New York State legislature passed an amendment that gave married women additional rights to "convey and devise" their real and personal property (*Laws of the State of New-York, 1849*, chap. 375, § 1). The legal dilemma that had arisen from the aporetic space forced the New York State legislature to pass its first law that narrowly addressed women and contract. It forced them to recognize the aporia's existence, even if they did not confront it. As with the acts considered by the 1846 Constitutional Convention, the 1848 and 1849 acts did not provide married women with any general rights of contract or property. They only granted married women the right to contract regarding property that was given to them during the marriage and that they owned prior to the marriage. In other words, a married woman still could not start a business because she would have no legal rights to make contracts regarding any part of the business. Equally, wages a wife earned during her marriage did not fall under her protected property.

The goal of protecting family estates played an especially strong role in the New York State's 1848 and 1849 legislation. The Hudson River was one of the only locales where feudal land relations still reigned in the northern antebellum United States. Dutch patroonships had been granted there in the 1600s, and their lords continued to demand rent in perpetuity from tenant settlers, who had life leaseholds only—meaning that the tenant settlers held no rights to bequeath their land use to future family generations (Friedman 1985, 61–62). Because the Dutch lords wanted to ensure their own families' continued power and status, they played an important role in the passage of the 1848 act: "Among the Dutch aristocracy of the State there was a vast amount of dissipation; and as married women could hold neither property nor children under the common law, solid, thrifty Dutch fathers were daily confronted with the fact that the inheritance of their daughters, carefully accumulated, would at marriage pass into the hands of dissipated, impecunious husbands, reducing them and their children to poverty and dependence. Hence this influential class of citizens heartily seconded the efforts of reformers" (E. C. Stanton et al. 1889/1970, 63–64).

By and large, the early spate of married women's property acts succeeded at providing debtor relief and protecting family estates,[16] but they did not address the aporetic site containing Womanhood, property, and contract. The twenty-year codification movement in New York State, however, forced the New York legislature to recognize this aporia in its 1848 and 1849 acts. Even in their recognition, the legislature retained the prior aporetic status quo that had existed under equity and the practice of married women's settlements until 1846. The New York State legal codification movement's successes from 1828 to 1848 had forced an encounter between legal institutions and women's aporetic contractual and economic position, placing pressure on a particularly sensitive point in the social order's foundation. By doing so, they made possible the irruption of the antebellum woman's rights movement around this point.

NEW YORK'S 1848 MARRIED WOMEN'S PROPERTY ACT:
RECOGNIZING, AND TIPTOEING AROUND, THE APORIA

By 1848, property law's defeudalization had unintentionally displaced married women's relation to property, contract, and the economy, despite the Revisers' aim to democratize property relations and access to property. According to a New York State senator, Hon. George Geddes, legislators' encounter with the institutional aporia, crystallized in the laws regulating married women and contract, directly resulted in the passage of New York State's Married Women's Property Act of 1848. Elizabeth Cady Stanton wrote to Geddes in 1880, asking him to reminisce about the act's passage. In response, he described in detail how two key participants had previously been frustrated in their attempts to create satisfactory trusts once the Revised Statutes of 1828 and 1836 demolished most of uses and trusts' viability and the 1846 Constitutional Convention finalized their demise by merging law and equity. Geddes wrote that the bill's originator, Judge Fine, "gave me his reasons for introducing the bill. He said that he married a lady who had some property of her own, which he had, all his life, tried to keep distinct from his, that she might have the benefit of her own, in the event of any disaster happening to him in pecuniary matters. He had found much difficulty, growing out of the old laws, in this effort to protect his wife's interests" (cited in E. C. Stanton et al. 1889/1970, 64). Geddes then expounded on his own reasons for actively supporting the bill: "I had a young daughter, who, in the then condition of my health, was quite likely to be left in tender years without a father, and I very much desired to protect her in the little property I might be able to leave. I had an elaborate will drawn by my old law preceptor, Vice-Chancellor Lewis H. Sandford, creating a trust with all the care and learning he could bring to my aid. But when the elaborate paper was finished, neither he or I felt satisfied with it. When the law of 1848 was passed, all I had to do was to burn this will" (64–65).

Finally, Geddes left no doubt that the legislators recognized that they were addressing a site of aporetic proportion—*an unstable assemblage of faults, fissures, and heterogeneous layers* whose occasional irruptions would disrupt established societal social meanings, practices, and institutions, *threatening the fragile inheritor from within or from underneath* (Foucault 1977/1988, 146): "The measure was so radical, so extreme, that even its friends had doubts; but the moment any important amendment was offered, up rose the whole question of woman's proper place in society, in the family, and everywhere. We all felt that the laws regulating married women's, as well as married men's rights, demanded careful revision and adaptation to our times and to our civilization. But no such revision could be perfected then, nor has it been since. We meant to strike a hard blow, and if possible shake the old system of laws to their foundations, and leave it to other times and wiser councils to perfect a new system" (cited in E. C. Stanton et al. 1889/1970,

65). Thus, the proverbial pot was stirred. Varied historical forces' conflu- ence at the site of a structural aporia made possible, but not necessary, its transformation—the rearticulation and refiguration of the interimplicated societal relations residing within the aporetic site: in this case, of Woman- hood, property, contract, the economy, and the nation. Conditions of possi- bility were sufficient, however, to require that the site be addressed. In turn, a successful address of the aporetic site—an address that refigured the im- bricated institutional systems and webs of social meanings that lay within it—required the force of an active social movement as a necessary but by no means sufficient participant in the confluence of events. The 1850s woman's rights movement would provide this force.

Chapter 5

THE ANTEBELLUM WOMAN'S MOVEMENT

Reshaping the Interimplicated Relations
of Womanhood and Contract

> Women's reform work was neither halted nor
> postponed during the decade of the 1850s. Rather,
> it was engaged in one of the most profound and
> wrenching shifts of its history.
>
> —LORI D. GINZBERG, *WOMEN AND THE WORK*
> *OF BENEVOLENCE*

HISTORIANS USUALLY DATE THE ADVENT OF THE ANTE-
bellum woman's movement from the Seneca Falls Woman's
Rights Convention, held on July 19 and 20, 1848.[1] Just two weeks
later, in early August 1848, woman's rights activists held a second convention over a two-day period in Rochester, New York.
The movement quickly swelled throughout New York State
and New England, with vigorous activism continuing until the
Civil War broke out in 1861. In 1850, the first National Woman's Rights Convention was held in Worcester, Massachusetts,
followed annually by national conventions until 1861, with the
sole exception of 1857. In these years, activists also organized
myriad state conventions, county conventions, and city and
town conventions. Then, at the onset of the Civil War, activists set aside their woman's rights work and did not hold their

next national convention until 1866. Table 10 lists the largest and most note-worthy conventions held during this period and their published reports, as annotated by one of the most tireless woman's rights activists, Susan B. Anthony. At these well-attended conventions, proponents and opponents alike spoke their minds, and, beginning in 1853, activists distributed a printed series of Woman's Rights Tracts culled primarily from speeches given and letters read to the conventions. The Tracts' wide distribution via the Erie Canal greatly enlarged the movement's audience.

The woman's rights conventions and well-organized speaking circuits also served as a basis for petition drives. The form and content of the conventions, petitions, and memorials manifest the breadth of issues concerning the antebellum woman's movement and its focus on married women's legal disabilities—especially those relating to property, contract, and the economy—and suffrage as its most important targets. The suffrage movement would not truly come into its own until after the Civil War, when it became the woman's movement's primary focus for the rest of the century. During the 1850s, however, it was only one among many pressing issues placed before the public and the legislature by woman's rights activists, as they "strode in and out of legislative halls—places where, in theory, females were not welcome. There they lobbied for new laws, sought appropriations for their organizations, and argued for changes in their own status—in short, they worked hard to influence the leadership of local, state, and national governments" (Ginzberg 1990, 68–69). In New York State, for instance, the antebellum woman's rights movement submitted petitions with thousands of signatures to the legislature at its opening each year, beginning in 1854.

A petition call from late 1853 demonstrates at once the movement's exhortation of "the women's masses" in print and voice, their legislative activity, and their reliance on grassroots organizing:

> Our Petitions will be sent to every county in the State, and we hope that they will find at least ten righteous Women to circulate them. But should there be any county so benighted, that a petition cannot be circulated throughout its length and breath [sic], giving to every man and woman an opportunity to sign their names, then we pray, not that "God will send down fire and brimstone," upon it, but that the "Napoleons" of this movement, will flood it with Women's Rights Tracts and Missionaries. . . .
> Let the Petitions be returned as soon as possible, to Lydia Mott, Albany,

TABLE 10. *Susan B. Anthony's Annotated List of Woman's Rights Conventions, 1848–60, and Reports Produced from These Conventions*

Convention	Year
First Convention, Seneca Falls, N. Y. James Mott, President. Printed at office of Frederick Douglass, "The North Star."	1848
Second Convention, Rochester, N. Y., two weeks later. Abigail Bush, President, with Mrs. Stanton's Speech delivered at both Conventions.	1848
Third Convention, Salem, Ohio. Betsey M. Cowles, President. Speeches by J. Elizabeth Jones, Emily Robinson and others.	1850
Fourth Convention, assuming a more National Character, held at Worcester, Mass. Paulina Wright Davis, President.	1850
State Convention, Akron, Ohio, Francis Dane [sic] Gage, President.	1851
Second National Convention, Worcester Mass. Paulina Wright Davis, President.	1851
State Convention, West Chester, Pa. Mary Anne W. Johnson, President.	1852
Third National Convention, Syracuse, N. Y. Lucretia Mott, President.	1852
~~Fourth National~~ Convention, New York City. Lucretia Mott President, in conjunction with the World's and whole world's conventions. The only Woman Suffrage convention which was really mobbed.	1853
Fourth National Convention, Cleveland Ohio. Francis Dana Gage, President,	1853
Mrs. Stanton's Speech before Legislature. Report of Convention at Albany, N. Y.	1854
Some Newspaper Clippings, Albany Convention Philadelphia Convention. Ernestine L. Rose, President.	1854
Saratoga Springs Convention, Ernestine L. Rose, President.	1855
There were no Reports of the Philadelphia Convention in 1854, Cincinnati 1855, New York 1856 and 1858, (No Convention in 1857)	
Ninth National Convention, New York City Lucretia Mott, President. Speech of Wendell Phillips.	1859
State Convention, Mercantile Hall, Boston Mass. Caroline Severance, President.	1859
Tenth National Convention, Cooper Institute, New York City. Martha C. Wright, President Discussion on the Rights of Divorce.	1860

Source: Woman's Rights Convention. [n.p.] "Reports: 1848–1870." In Susan B. Anthony Collection, Rare Books and Special Collections Division, Library of Congress. Annotated by Susan B. Anthony.

N.Y., as we wish to present them early in the session and thereby give our Legislature due time for the consideration of this important question. (in Anthony [n.p.] 1837)[2]

Once collected, these petitions were sent to the 1854 Woman's Rights National Convention in Albany, New York, which the daily press covered, and were then sent to the New York State Legislature for consideration during its 1854 session. On February 15, 1854, the New York *Atlas* reported on the convention and the petition drive:

Mr. [William] CHANNING then addressed the Convention as to its aim and objects. He stated that the petition to be presented to the Legislature, contained 6000 signatures, all of which had been obtained by a few individuals in one month. Had they devoted more time to the collection of signatures, he had no doubt but that they would number hundreds of thousands. The Convention did not ask for the privileges they claimed prematurely. The proper time had already come to award them. It would ask of the Legislature, that a select committee be appointed in each House to consider the subject which would be presented to it. (in Anthony [n.p.] 1837)

Pressure for economic, property, and contractual rights was a centerpiece of the woman's movement agenda throughout the 1850s. As late as 1859, a memorial sent to state legislatures named economic and contractual rights among the main injustices suffered by women. The 1859 Memorial argued that a citizen cannot "be said to have a right to liberty, when the custody of her person belongs to another; when she has no civil or political rights—no right even to the wages she earns; when she can make no contracts—neither buy nor sell, sue or be sued—and yet can be taxed without representation.... A citizen cannot be said to have a right to happiness, when denied the right to person, property, children and home" (in Anthony [n.p.] 1837). The Memorial laid this claim in part by refiguring Republican Motherhood and its progeny, such that the daughters—and not just the sons—of the brave "mothers of the Revolution" held weight and should share equally in the new nation's success.

In the early and mid-1850s, activists simultaneously distributed two distinct petitions: one demanding economic, property, and contractual rights for women; and another demanding women's suffrage. By the end of the decade, the two sets of issues were often merged into one petition. The years of presenting separate petitions demonstrate an initial understanding of economic and contractual rights and suffrage as two sets of distinct demands, involving distinct sets of intertwined social meanings and institutions, or at least a sense that this was how the public understood them. The first petition, in 1853, titled "Petition for the Just and Equal Rights of Women," targeted economic and property rights from its opening sentence:

> The Legislature of the State of New York have, by the [Married Women's Property] Acts of 1848 and 1849, testified the purpose of the people of this State their intention to place Married Women on an equality with Married Men in regard to the holding, conveying, and devising of real and personal property. We, therefore, the undersigned Petitioners, inhabitants of the State of New York, male and female, having attained to the age of legal majority, believing that women, alike married and single, do still suffer under MANY AND GRIEVOUS LEGAL DISABILITIES, do earnestly request the Senate and Assembly of the State of New York, to appoint a Joint Committee of both houses, to revise the Statutes of New York, and to propose such amendments as will fully establish the LEGAL EQUALITY of Women and Men. (in Anthony [n.p.] 1837)

This petition explicitly defined the right to contract as an economic and civil actor, specifically in relation to property, as fundamental to equal legal rights. In comparison, the connected 1853 "Petition for Woman's Right to Suffrage" explicitly called on the Declaration of Independence's language of civil equality and implicitly on women's rights of contract as political actors by invoking women's inclusion in "the consent of the governed": "Whereas, according to the Declaration of our National Independence, Governments derive their just powers from the consent of the governed, we earnestly request the Legislature of New York to propose to the people of the State such amendments of the Constitution of the State, as will secure to Females an equal right to the Elective Franchise with Males" (in Anthony [n.p.] 1837). The connected petitions, with their calls printed in large type on a single broadsheet, relied on overlapping and yet distinct understandings of contract and its relation to Womanhood, in both contemporary institutions and popular social meanings. Neither of their demands could be met without tumultuously shifting and reshaping the aporetic site, the foundational impasse, in which the modern knot of Womanhood and contract resided. But the two petitions approached distinct but related entanglements of Womanhood and contract and, in their differing approaches, implicitly recognized that social meanings and institutions of both Womanhood and contract might shift differently to achieve each demand. By 1859, the petitions had been merged into one petition "for the Civil and Political Rights of Woman," and the authors no longer worked to refigure the troublesome knot of Womanhood and contract either explicitly or implicitly (in Anthony [n.p.] 1837). Rather, they simply demanded rights, recognizing that society had already significantly addressed the aporetic site and reconfigured the intricate sets of relations between Womanhood and contract. In other words, just as with Bryan J. Butts's 1871 pamphlet that began this book, the antebellum woman's rights activists no longer needed to appeal to the public and the legislature to confront this structural aporia. How the public and legislature would finally address the aporetic site was still under debate, but its need to address it was no longer in question. The 1859 merged petition read succinctly:

> To the Senate and Assembly of the State of New York.
> The undersigned, citizens of New York, respectfully ask that you will take measures to submit to the people an amendment of the Constitution, allowing Women to vote and hold office. And that you will enact laws securing to married women the full and entire control of all property originally belonging to them, and of their earnings during marriage; and making the rights of the wife over the children the same as a husband enjoys, and the rights of a widow, as to her children, and as to the property left by her husband the same that a husband has in the property and over the children of his deceased wife. (in Anthony [n.p.] 1837)

While the petitions collected and presented to the New York State Legislature took various forms from 1853 to 1859, they always pressed on the aporetic impasse of Womanhood and contract.

During the 1850s, woman's rights activists also published several newspapers. These papers were subscription-based, but reports suggest that in rural townships many often shared a single copy. Two of the most important woman's rights newspapers were *The Lily*, devoted to temperance at its founding in 1849 and expanding into all realms of the woman's rights movement from the 1850s through its 1856 demise, and the *Una*, devoted to woman's rights for its duration, from 1853 to 1855. *The Lily*'s annual subscription cost fifty cents, and circulation increased steadily over its first few years. Edited by Amelia Bloomer, the paper began by selling a couple hundred issues and by 1853 sold more than four thousand issues; by "early 1854, the *Lily* enjoyed a circulation of six thousand" (Hinck 1991, 31). The *Una* never achieved as broad a readership. It reached its peak in its first year of publishing with fewer than five hundred subscriptions, but the subscription rolls suggest that it served as a paper for woman's rights activists and their community (Tonn 1991, 52). In their public role, both of these papers reinscribed True Womanhood with alternative meanings and possibilities even as they interwove them with its popular understandings in an attempt to shift the field of social meanings of Womanhood. They deployed True Womanhood partly to focus on domesticity and motherhood, but also directly and indirectly to argue against the True Woman's confined sphere of activity and for a refiguring of Womanhood that would legitimate Woman's activity in realms not previously considered appropriate (Hinck 1991, 32; Tonn 1991, 63–64).

Without prominent national or regional organizations to define the woman's rights movement—organizations that did come to exist in the post–Civil War suffrage movement—the modern-day observer might not immediately recognize the workings of a social movement in woman's rights activities. To the extent that the antebellum woman's movement has been overlooked, it is in part a result of its purposeful rejection of familiar organizational forms. The movement certainly had continuity among its core activists and throughout its various strategies, such as petitioning, canvassing, holding conventions, and distributing printed materials. State and national convention bodies annually nominated and ratified a number of individuals to work collectively to organize the next conferences, to conduct and present research on specified topics, and to organize the year's petition drive, among many other critical tasks. And certainly some of the most active and dedicated women remained in frequent and lifetime correspondence. But members of the antebellum woman's movement absolutely refused, as a matter of principle, to concretize themselves into organizations. Numerous woman's rights activists had experienced the many frictions and fractures of organizations in recent abolition and temperance work—both of which often did not allow women full and active participation—and did not want to face in their new work what seemed to be intrinsic problems of organizations. Some even considered any institutional structure to be anathema to social movement progress. In fact, one of the ten widely distributed Woman's Rights Tracts concentrated on precisely this point. In it, Angelina Grimke Weld (1853, 3–4) contended that organization does not allow for change and does not respect the individual, explaining further that

> it is not to Organization that I object, but to an *Artificial one* only: one that must prove a burden, a clog, an incumbrance, rather than a help. Such an Organization as now actually exists among the women of America, I hail with heartfelt joy. We are bound together by the natural ties of a spiritual affinity; we are drawn to each other because we are attracted toward one common centre, the good of humanity. We need no external bonds to bind us together, no cumbrous machinery to keep our minds and hearts in unity of purpose and effort. We are not the lifeless staves of a barrel, which can be held together only by the iron hoops of an Artificial Organization. All we need, and all we ask, is freedom to think our own thoughts, and act out the promptings of our own inner being.

Reading history asunder—using a structural aporetic analysis—led to the conclusion that a social movement must have pressured the aporetic site in order that the impasse of Womanhood and contract foundational to modern democratic capitalism could fracture, fissure, and reshape itself in such a way that movement from the social order of the early to mid-1800s to our contemporary social order could occur. Faith in the theoretical power of the structural aporetic analytic—or rather, a more secular hunch—has led to a rereading of history, in part by investigating primary historical documents to trace the underlying intertwined social meanings and institutions constituting this particular modern structural aporia and to track the historical shape and pressures of such a social movement. This refigured history demonstrates the play of power and discourse within the aporetic site—the material and cultural power of its play. It provides not only a rewritten history of the past, but a newly understood history of the present by delineating particular irruptions of meanings and institutions as well as their prior, present, and future potential irruptions.

> From midcentury onward, antifeminist literature, cartoons, sermons, and caricatures increased in circulation. Typically they took the form of questioning the gender identity of women who spoke in public; that is to say, they made the woman's public voice the primary signifier of her problematic sexual being. . . .
>
> Certainly for an ambitious Victorian daughter, the stark disjunction between a paternal identification that validated her as speaking subject and a body that compelled her to identify with a devalued maternal object is repeatedly shown to provoke an unutterable rage.
>
> —Claire Kahane, *Passions of the Voice*
>
> We do not like to write hard words of any of the sex, but when women un-sex themselves, as it were, and glory in their shame, they lose their claim to leniency.
>
> —"Woman's Rights," *New York Sun,* May 17, 1853

An aporetic reading of U.S. history has shown that the troubled relation between Womanhood, contract, and the economy resides in a foundational impasse, defining Woman's very existence in the civil realm as abyssal. The antebellum woman's movement had to deploy fully discursive strategies to succeed because its success required shifting the multiple and fissured grounds of this structural aporia. That is, it had to apply simultaneous and intertwined pressure to the interimplicated workings of both institutions of Womanhood and the economy (such as legal regulation of marriage and of contract) and social meanings of Womanhood and the economy (such as True Womanhood, Republican Motherhood, Woman's Influence, the nation's morality, and legitimate contractual action and ownership as a right to public existence). The antebellum woman's movement did all of this by deploying a refigured True Womanhood in public speeches, writings, organized conventions, and petition drives, each of which simultaneously placed significant pressure on the legislature for legal change. Activists refigured True Womanhood complexly, dovetailing popularly accepted social meanings of Womanhood with shifts in meaning that placed education, financial independence, and the right to contract at the center of a radically altered True Woman. While aspects of the previous popular understandings of Womanhood retained some status in this process, the woman's movement's intricate deployment and redeployment radically reinscribed and reconfigured daily life's social meanings and institutions—a process that can occur only through a structural aporetic site.

As detailed in earlier chapters, Anglo-based democratic capitalism's discursive foundations had never truly allowed Woman to enter the civil or public realm that the social contract had initiated. Only the elision of the sexual contract created the semblance of Woman's entry. A precisely analogous disallowance of women in the economic and political realm *inhered* in nineteenth-century U.S. legal institutions and culture. True Womanhood's daily social practice was popularly understood as stabilizing and imparting a morality to the nation, but, by definition, it rested upon social and economic disorder and the same ejection from the economic and civil realm that Woman was subjected to by modernity's founding myths. In popular understandings, the True Woman's ejection from the public or civil realm centered around her means of imparting morality, her Woman's Influence, with which, by definition, she could only directly affect her intimate relations. If Woman deigned to enter the public realm, she *un-sexed* herself; she no longer bore any relation to the True Woman. By her civil action, she became something indefinable: not a Woman but *was a woman once* (T. Parker n.d., 21–22), *manish* (Mrs. Amelia Bloomer, in Woman's Rights Convention 1851/1973, 36) but not a man. In civil action, she endangered the nation's stability, which rested on True Womanhood's moral Influence, and lost her "claim to leniency" that was afforded Womanhood. And yet, to come into existence, a social movement's members must be recognized civilly in the institutions and culture they call their own; they must be able to call for community within their public. Legitimating the ability to speak in public as a respectable Woman was therefore critical for the 1850s woman's movement. The movement's strategic deployments of refigured Womanhood had to legitimate a True Woman who *properly* came to language in the public realm. In an 1851 speech, given at one of the earliest woman's rights conventions, Mrs. Amelia Bloomer pointed out this crucial problematic for the movement, even as she embodied a refigured version of the True Woman whose legitimacy could dismantle the problem: "[Women] may endure every hardship, labor in the most menial employments, expose themselves to the gaze of licentious men upon the theatrical stage, become paupers or public prostitutes, and nobody cares; 'they are within their sphere.' But let them come forth like true women, pleading in the name of God and humanity, that their wrongs may be redressed and their rights restored, and they are at once condemned. They have outstepped their sphere and become 'manish' " (Woman's Rights Convention 1851/1973, 36).

Not coincidentally, scientific attention to Victorian women's muted speech and expressive bodies also arose at this time, and quickly codified them as a medical problem rather than a social problem. J. M. Charcot's initial interest in hysteria—embodied, in his view, by the female patients residing at Paris's Salpêtrière—came at the same time as an outbreak of women's public speech in France, England, and the United States. Under his direction, Salpêtrière's women would serve as a medical model, enacting hysteria as medical theater for himself, other doctors, and medical students, who in one stroke studied, defined, and treated this culturally delimited medical condition. He would not direct the clinic until the 1880s, when he forever influenced Sigmund Freud and Josef Breuer, who published their joint studies on hysteria in the 1890s. Nonetheless, in his hands hysteria was first understood as an expressiveness of the female body which might be deciphered, beginning in the 1850s. In hysteria, a body that was for all other intents and purposes mute, or at least incoherent, might be made legible through medical intervention. Feminist rereadings of Freud's work on hysteria—work that could not have been done without Charcot's illustrious beginnings—have suggested that the various traveling paralyses and other bodily symptoms of hysteria can be understood as female resistance to a familial and social economy that operated on women in both a repressive and an oppressive manner. They read hysteria as female resistance to a set of closed economies that disallowed civil revolt (Bernheimer and Kahane 1985; Cixous and Clement 1986; Gallop 1982; Smith-Rosenberg 1985). In a classic rereading of hysteria, Hélène Cixous names the hysteric as

the one who resists the system, the one who cannot stand that the family and society are founded on the body of women, on bodies despised, rejected. . . . [She] is the nuclear example of women's power to protest. . . . The hysteric is, to my eyes, the typical woman in all her force. It is a force that was turned back against [her], but, if the scene changes and if woman begins to speak in other ways, it would be a force capable of demolishing those structures. . . . The hysteric is not just someone who has her words cut off, someone for whom the body speaks. . . . I see the hysteric saying: "I want everything." . . . In what she projects as a demand for totality, for strength, for certainty, she makes demands of the others in a manner that is intolerable to them and that prevents their functioning as they function (without their restricted little economy). She destroys their calculations. (in Cixous and Clement 1986, 154–55)

Over the next several decades, hysterics and woman's rights activists would embody and express True Womanhood's aporetic existence as conjoined twins on the social stage.

Women's "promiscuous" speech, or speech to mixed groups of men and women, only truly found the political spotlight in the 1850s. Prior to this time, women's attempts to speak in public forums were rare.[3] Political controversy over promiscuous speech had first arisen a bit earlier in response to the abolition work of two southern sisters, Angelina and Sarah Grimke. Their 1836 writings and oratory throughout the northeastern United States brought down upon them, and any other women who chose to so *unsex* themselves, a scathing religious denouncement. The 1837 "Pastoral letter of the General Association of Massachusetts to the churches under their care" was widely distributed and extensively discussed and lauded in the popular press; its explicit statement of the relation between intertwined social meanings of Womanhood and the society's institutional health reflected general understandings of the day. Its denouncement of promiscuous women's speech was suffused, on the one hand, with support for the propriety of Woman's Influence as channeled through Republican Motherhood and, on the other hand, with a derogation of Woman generally understood as inherent in her civil participation. The religious association wrote to pastors and the general public:

Brothers and friends . . .
We invite your attention to the dangers, which at present seem to threaten the female character, with widespread and permanent injury.

The appropriate duties and influence of women are . . . unobtrusive and private, but the sources of mighty power. When the mild, dependent, softening influence of woman upon the sternness of man's opinions is fully exercised, society feels the effects of it in a thousand forms. . . . There are social influences which females use in promoting piety and the great objects of Christian benevolence, which we cannot too highly commend. We appreciate the unostentatious prayers and efforts of woman in advancing the cause of religion at home and abroad; in Sabbath schools; in leading religious inquirers to the pastors for instruction; and in all such associated effort as becomes the modesty of her sex; and earnestly hope that she may abound more and more in these labors of piety and love.

But when she assumes the place and tone of man as a public reformer, our care and protection of her seem unnecessary; we put ourselves in self-defence against her; she yields the power which God has given her for protection, and her character becomes unnatural. If the vine, whose strength and beauty is to lean upon the trellis work and half conceal its clusters, thinks to assume the independence and the overshadowing nature of the elm, it will not only cease to bear fruit, but fall in shame and dishonor into the dust. We cannot, therefore, but regret the mistaken conduct of those who encourage females to bear an obtrusive and ostentatious part in measures of reform, and countenance any of that sex, who so far forget themselves as to itinerate in the character of public lecturers and teachers. We especially deplore the intimate acquaintance and promiscuous conversation of females with regard to things, "which ought not to be named;" by which that modesty and delicacy which is the charm of domestic life, and which constitutes the true influence of woman in society is consumed, and the way opened, as we apprehend, for degeneracy and ruin. (reprinted in *The Liberator,* August 11, 1837, in Anthony [n.p.] 1837)

The Pastoral letter effectively argued that the *true influence of woman in society* operated "unobtrusive[ly] and private[ly] . . . upon the sternness of man's opinions." And when respectable women used their Woman's Influence, *society felt the effect of it in a thousand forms.* Accordingly, the consequences of women acting in the civil realm—by definition *obtrusive and ostentatious* behavior—were dire both for individual women themselves and for the nation's stability. Women would "not only cease to bear fruit"— the biological and moral imperative of Republican Motherhood, through which she sustained the health of the nation by raising educated and moral citizen-sons—but would *fall in shame and dishonor*. Women's fall, out of Womanhood, and into an indefinable state in which *her character became unnatural*, endangered the nation by consuming the *true influence of woman in society* and, thereby, opening the way *for degeneracy and ruin*. The Pastoral letter's publicly persuasive claims on Womanhood unambiguously laid out the terrain that a fully discursive woman's movement would have to transform in order to successfully garner economic and contractual rights for women. And, since women's rights activists were themselves societal members, the terrain to be shifted would be internal as well as external.

Women activists were often terribly uncomfortable speaking and functioning in a public and "promiscuous" capacity at the beginning of the 1850s woman's rights movement, which strained their early activism. The *Proceedings of the Convention Held at Rochester, NY, Aug. 2, 1848* (Woman's Rights Convention 1848/1870b) depicts their unease with public action in the civil realm just two weeks after the initial Seneca Falls convention, at a meeting that was explicitly called "to Consider the Rights of Woman, Politically, Religiously and Industrially." In other words, the convention's very purpose was to consider woman's rights of civil action. And yet the women attending the meeting displayed distinct distress in their own attempts at civil action. When nominated, Elizabeth McClintock refused to serve as secretary of the Second Woman's Rights Convention "on the ground of being unprepared to have a woman the presiding officer" (3). Several other women central to the convention's operations felt similarly, and "at first, refused to take their seats upon the platform or otherwise co-operate with the Convention . . . but as the meeting proceeded, and they had listened to some opening remarks from our gentle but heroic President [Abigail Bush], their fears for the honor of the Convention subsided after which they worked nobly for the cause that had called us together" (3). Interestingly, even as the *Proceedings* recorded the women's fears regarding, and sometimes refusal of, civil action, it had already begun a redeployment of True Womanhood whereby women could work *nobly* in the civil realm. As the convention progressed, the attending crowd remonstrated for louder voices on the part of the speakers. In response, the President invoked the spectacle of the hysteric as one with the new woman's rights activists, asking the audience to bear with the female speakers' "trembling frames and faltering tongues . . . in the infancy of the movement" (4). Abigail Bush's remark presaged one aspect of the relation between woman's rights activists and convention attendees throughout the next decade.

During the 1850s, the public attended woman's rights conventions not only to listen to the substance of the debates, but also to see that content embodied. The spectacle of women arguing, debating, and philosophizing publicly—of women engaged in civil action, which would become only more spectacular with the advent of dress reform and the infamous Bloomer costume—could be had for a small fare if you were lucky enough to fit into the meeting space. This certainly accounted for many of the filled convention halls, yet, it also assured that their messages reached an audience beyond the already converted. Local coverage of the New York City 1859 National Woman's Rights Convention, which rivaled only the 1853 convention in tumult, depicts the active spectacle at a convention that had "some 1,700 persons gathered inside the hall" (*New York Times*, in Anthony [n.p.] 1837). The *New York Herald* reported: "IMMENSE AUDIENCE. Hisses, groans, whistling and boisterous laughter, principally from the galleries, at intervals interrupted all the speakers, which a portion of audience endeavored, but without success to suppress. It was evident, from the demonstrations all through the evening, that a large number of those present were not very ardent sympathisers with the object of the meeting, as they did not manifest the commonest respect due to woman, whether fanatical or philosophical, protected or unprotected" (in Anthony [n.p.] 1837). More commonly, a portion of convention audiences wanted to hear both the powerful female and male orators, but another part of the audience attempted to hoot down all male speakers, wishing to collapse the conventions into pure spectacle.

Success in the continuing battle over women's public speech was a necessary condition for success in refiguring True Womanhood in such a way that legitimate civil and contractual action, whether economic or political, was at its center. The 1850s woman's movement took on this battle in earnest, reimagining the True Woman in speeches and publications while personifying that newly amalgamated image for all to see. In their efforts, woman's rights activists simultaneously refigured True Womanhood, named themselves True Women, and publicly and "promiscuously" embodied this refigured

True Womanhood, making their very activity on a convention stage a spectacular cultural crucible. Their civil actions constituted them as spectacle not only for their detractors, but for themselves and their supporters as well, just as hysterics' bodily existence does to this day. As Reverend Samuel Longfellow told the 1860 National Woman's Rights Convention, speaking from the dais, "On a platform like this, when a woman speaks, her presence is not merely a plea and an argument, but also a proof. When a woman speaks, and speaks well, speaks so as to interest, and move, and persuade men, there is no need of any argument back of that to prove that she has the liberty and the right, and that it is a part of her sphere to do it. She *has* done it; and that of itself is the whole argument—both premise and conclusion in one" (National Woman's Rights Convention 1860, 59). At the beginning of the decade, woman activists' speech would more accurately have been called *premise and conclusion* and spectacle *in one*. But activists continually deployed this newly grounded True Woman, despite virulent reaction from the general public and press in the first years. Over the course of the 1850s, the movement succeeded in shifting the grounds of True Womanhood to include public speech as civil action to the extent that such a True Woman was conceivable and even legible to the general public, no longer just a spectacle.

The "strategy" of redeploying a True Woman who signified a positive and yet radical change for the future through her action in the civil realm began in the movement's founding moments, emerging from singular moments in individual speeches to a centerpiece of the movement. In a typical early example, Lucretia Mott felt the need to elucidate how and why she was refiguring True Womanhood in her 1849 "Discourse on Woman," explaining, "We would admit all the difference, that our great and beneficent Creator has made, in the relation of man and woman, nor would we seek to disturb this relation; but we deny that the present position of woman, is her true sphere of usefulness: nor will she attain to this sphere, until the disabilities and disadvantages, religious, civil, and social, which impede her progress, are removed out of her way. . . . So far from her 'ambition leading her to attempt to act the man,' she needs all the encouragements she can receive, by the removal of obstacles from her path, in order that she may become a 'true woman'" (1850, 7–8). By 1856, however, the woman's rights movement could place such a vision of the future True Woman at the center of its "Call for the Eighth National Convention" without the need to explain how it could exist: "We earnestly ask all those who believe our claims are just, who hope and look for a higher type of womanhood in the coming generations, to assert, now, their faith in the everlasting principles of justice, that have no respect for age, sex, color, or condition" (in Anthony [n.p.] 1837). By this time, a civilly active *earnest* and *higher type of womanhood* had become conceivable without explanation. While this successful refiguring of the True Woman as a speaking woman, and more specifically as an activist woman, was a necessary condition of Woman's and women's legitimate entry into the civil and economic realm, it did not happen easily. Over the decade, vitriolic public attacks based in normative deployments of Womanhood served as weapons in a battle to maintain a pious and privately influential True Womanhood, understood as the keeper of the nation's moral order in a time of increasing social and economic disorder. In a representative instance, partially quoted earlier, the *New York Sun* ran an article titled "Woman's Rights" on May 17, 1853, explicitly attacking female activism by relying on the normative code of True Womanhood:

> It is not so very wonderful after all, that some of the fair, and *not* fair, daughters of Mother Eve, should wish to be "as gods," receiving, on the public platform, the applauding homage of thousands, rather than be the presiding angels of humble and happy homes. . . . But while writing thus, let us not be misunderstood. We are in favor of woman's rights. We wish to see woman exercise her appropriate influence in every movement for social reform. She suffers most from the great evils which afflict Society; and every man of manly heart, will not only admit woman's right to all the protection that laws can afford, but join earnestly in the task of remedying her grievances and her wrongs. . . . We do not like to write hard words of any of the sex, but when women un-sex themselves, as it were, and glory in their shame, they lose their claim to leniency. (in Anthony [n.p.] 1837)

The article's able author turns woman's rights against itself by claiming to be "in favor of woman's rights," defined as *woman exercising her appropriate influence,* which he has already argued should be properly utilized as *the presiding angels of humble and happy homes.* The woman's rights movement successfully fought against such claims by repeatedly presenting a refigured

True Womanhood whose public speech and civil action did not "un-sex" her, but rather defined her active support for a better world, her looking forward to a world of ever greater justice carried out through her public speech and civil action.

The Lily published numerous such redeployments of True Womanhood throughout its tenure. A few representative examples follow. As early as 1850, Lydia A. Jenkins reimaged a woman *of true dignity* as one who recognized women's subjection by men, writing in *The Lily* that "every woman of self appreciation and of true dignity, must feel wounded, crushed, to know that whatever privileges she may enjoy, are not accorded to her as a *right* inherent in the constitution of every human being, but as a *privilege* conferred upon her by the gallantry of the opposite sex" (12). In July 1851, *The Lily* approvingly quoted the abolitionist *Cincinnati Nonpareil*'s comments on the May 1851 Akron, Ohio, Woman's Rights Convention, whose author nodded to popular meanings of True Womanhood and then explicitly redefined the True Woman as precisely she whom others denounced as unsexed. "The Convention is composed of a large number of talented females," he began. "They are the true women too—good wives, and excellent mothers." The author then declared, "It is said that these women are *masculine,* and their thoughts, feelings and desires are unfeminine. Be it known again, that if man's ideal of woman embraces those qualities which are most servicable to the race—that if anything useful entered into the divine plan in the creation of woman, then that class who are termed *masculine* come nearest the fulfilment of this plan, and are most truly *women*" (50). An 1853 article that specifically addressed "Property Rights and Business Qualifications of Woman" recognized woman's property rights activists as the day's *noble-minded women,* remarking that a "few clear-sighted noble-minded women have dared to think for themselves, and looked beyond the bounds of custom, and discovered that they have rights as well as men; and they have awakened the women of America to the subject, and now ask for liberty, freedom, and an equality with man" (Hotchkiss 1853).

The 1850s woman's rights movement actively deployed this refigured image of the True Woman in convention speeches and proceedings, in memorials to legislatures, in petition drives, and on speaking circuits, leading to further deployment in newspaper accounts of their activities. For instance, the 1853 public call to sign and distribute dual woman's rights petitions for the "JUST and EQUAL RIGHTS OF WOMAN" and for "WOMAN'S RIGHT OF SUFFRAGE," which were to be presented to the New York State legislature, equated *virtuous, noble and true* Womanhood with activism in the woman's rights movement, in direct contradiction to popular understandings of True Womanhood. The petition call "To the Women of the State of New York," signed by Elizabeth Cady Stanton, exhorted:

> If, in view of [legal disabilities] like these, there be women in this State so lost to self-respect, to all that is virtuous, noble and true, as to refuse to raise their voices in protest against such degrading tyranny, we can only say of that system which has thus robbed womanhood of all its glory and greatness, what the immortal Channing did of Slavery. "If," said he, "it be true that the slaves are contented and happy—if there is a system that can blot out all love of freedom from the soul of man, destroy every trace of his Divinity, make him happy in a condition so low and benighted and hopeless, I ask for no stronger argument against such a slavery as ours." (in Anthony [n.p.] 1837)

The petition call explicitly claimed here that the contemporary sets of social meanings and institutions of Womanhood that prevented woman's activism "robbed womanhood of all its glory and greatness."

In 1854, local press extensively covered the Woman's Rights Convention, held in Albany, New York, reporting on the proceedings both verbatim and in editorial form. At least three—the *Atlas,* the *State Register,* and one other paper—printed the entirety of fourteen resolutions presented at the start of the convention, which called in turn for woman's freedom to act in all spheres, for women's full property and contractual rights, and for women's suffrage. The tenth resolution summed up these prior demands with simplicity: "*Resolved,* therefore, That whether you regard woman as like or unlike man, she is in either case entitled to an equal joint participation with him in all civil rights and duties" (Woman's Rights Convention [n.p.]). The final resolution explicitly redeployed Womanhood, and Manhood as well, centering the newly refigured True Woman in her civil actions and specifically in civil struggle for woman's rights: "*Resolved,* That all true hearted men and women pledge themselves never to relinquish their unceasing efforts in behalf of the full and equal rights of women, until we have effaced the stigma resting on this Republic, that while it theoretically proclaims that all men are equal, deprives one half of its members of enjoyments of the rights and privileges possessed by the other" ([n.p.]).

One local paper, which remains untitled in the historical records, further assisted in deploying a newly imaged True Woman when it editorialized on the goals declared at the convention:

> The so called Woman's rights movement, is to make the appeal for "justice" earnest, imposing and effective, by showing how unequal are the laws of the country in regard to woman. They desire a reform in the civil government and a change of its laws. They contend that women are equal to men, and ask is anything irrational or revolutionary in the proposal that fathers, brothers, husbands, sons should treat their daughters, sisters, wives and mothers as their peers? This reform is designed, by its originators [sic], to make woman *womanly* in the highest sense of that term—to exalt, not to degrade—to perfect, not to impair her refining influence in every sphere. ([n.p.])

Here, in direct contradiction to the powerful Pastoral letter of 1837, women's *imposing and effective* activity is understood as *earnest* rather than "obtrusive and ostentatious" behavior that "un-sexes" her. In fact, the sets of social meanings entwined in True Womanhood are so reconfigured here that woman's public and civil activity is reconceived as based in her Woman's Influence, rather than degrading it, and constitutes her as an even truer True Woman. Her public and civil actions might then ensure an even more moral nation, rather than opening the way "for degeneracy and ruin." This Albany newspaper's commentary demonstrates some of the tangled and dovetailed aspects of the movement's successful refiguring of the True Woman. The aporetic site, by definition, consisted of unstable ground—fractures in which social meanings and institutions of Womanhood, contract, the economy, and the nation resided. Old meanings and institutions of True Womanhood and their relation to meanings and institutions of property, contract, and the nation could not simply be replaced with new, whether gradually or at once. Aporetic fissures and fractures shift and reshape social meanings and institutions into different configurations, entangling some of the older aspects with the newer in transformed relations. Differently interimplicated social meanings and institutions in an aporetic site create a radically new set of social relations employing strands of the old. How the woman's rights movement actively redeployed True Womanhood reflected this reality.

By the end of the decade, the movement's deployments of a refigured True Woman unproblematically assumed that a True Woman might exist as a speaking woman in the civil arena. Such a conception had become culturally legible, whether all members of the public agreed with it or not. The possibility of social meanings and institutions of Womanhood, contract, the economy, and the nation intertwining so that a True Woman might be defined by her civil action had been brought into existence. At the convention, held in New York City in 1858, Lucretia Mott spoke in the evening session of May 14, addressing the Pastoral letter of 1837 and the two battle-strewn decades following it. According to the *New York Tribune,* she argued that "woman had overstepped the limits which had been assigned her by a corrupt civilization and a perverted interpretation of the Scriptures. She had learned her own responsibilities, and to obey the higher law of a noble womanhood" (in Anthony [n.p.] 1837). Again, in this refiguration, the very act of speaking, of taking on activism in the woman's rights movement, cleared a path to True Womanhood, to *the higher law of a noble womanhood,* rather than obstructing it. But it could be stated directly and judiciously, without contextualizing it within arguments against more popular conceptions of Womanhood. On August 17, 1859, the *Daily Saratogian,* a temperance paper, summarized the extemporaneous speech made the night before by Antoinette Brown Blackwell at the Saratoga Springs Woman's Rights Meeting and spoke of *the true woman* in these terms: "Here in our own land and time, while she enjoys many privileges, equality with her brother man is denied. Instead of the true woman, we have our 'model woman' or 'type-lady,' who is restricted to the position which public opinion and the conventionalities of society have assigned to her. What she claimed for woman was the right to be whatever God has given her power to be. Woman should be the equal of man, legally, socially, politically" (in Anthony [n.p.] 1837). In this understanding, Woman's *legal, social, political*—in a word, civil—equality was the *true woman's* required ground. The *Daily Saratogian* put forth this conception directly and without explanation, expecting that the public was already familiar with it. Similarly, a local paper in Penn Yan, New York, reported on Susan B. Anthony's speech to the June 1860 Yates County Teacher's Association meetings: "Miss Susan B. Anthony, of Rochester, Lectured before the

Teacher's Association last Saturday on the 'True Woman.'—Her lecture was a radical appeal in behalf of woman's equality with men in all legal, social and political relations. It was ably written and impressively delivered" (in Anthony [n.p.] 1837). Again, this report unquestioningly grounds the *True Woman* in Woman's civil equality—in Woman as a legitimate civil actor. The circulation of True Womanhood conceived as a woman acting in and supporting a world of civil equality held within it several ongoing and more judicious refigurations. As each intertwined and dovetailed with the others, the "strategic effect"[4] was to refigure the True Woman as one who legitimately acted economically, contractually, and generally in the civic realm.

"THEN INDEED SHE WILL BE A WOMAN"

> There is a demand now for a new type of womanhood. We are daily assuming new positions—taking upon us new duties, and claiming the exercise of our civil and political rights.
> —Elizabeth Cady Stanton, "Letter from Mrs. Elizabeth C. Stanton to the Worcester Convention," 1851

> But she must do something to break the chains that ignorance and superstition have woven around her, and tied into a gordian knot. She must untie it with the sharp points of reason, dissolve the links by the light of knowledge, and thus bursting the unholy fetters, she must claim her rights equal with man, and then indeed she will be a woman. Her rights, and an education to develop all her powers, will strengthen her affections, purify her sympathies, refine her feelings, mature her judgment, and fit her for the vicissitudes of life as a companion to an intellectual man—a mother to train her children to become such—and above all, an honorable and useful member of society.
> —Ernestine L. Rose, "Speech of Mrs. Rose, A Polish Lady, at the Anniversary Paine Celebration," 1850

Throughout the 1850s, woman's rights activists simultaneously deployed the normative social meanings embedded in Republican Motherhood and Woman's Influence and asserted the emergence of *a new type of womanhood* that assumed an entirely different configuration of social meanings and institutions underlying it. On one hand, this new Womanhood expanded the traditional realm of the True Woman, making her not only a *pure* and *re-*

fined wife and mother who continued to impart morality to her husband and sons and, through them, to the nation, but also, *and above all, an honorable and useful member of society* who had *claim[ed] her rights equal with man.* On the other hand, this *new type of womanhood* completely transformed the realm of Womanhood and the True Woman herself by *claiming the exercise of her civil and political rights.* In other words, in its successful attempt to radically alter the shape and place of Woman in a modern democratic and capitalist society, the antebellum woman's movement at once deployed new and old, resistive and normative, social meanings of Womanhood. And it deployed these new and old, resistive and normative, social meanings as fully interimplicated with contemporary institutions. Conceiving of Womanhood involved, by definition, an entire imbricated set of social meanings and institutions of Womanhood, contract, the economy, and the nation. For a new or different invocation of Womanhood to make cultural sense, to be legible to the public, a different form and shape taken by the strings intertwining these social meanings and institutions, so to speak, had to be conceivable. These were the necessary conditions of the potential for change in the structural aporia. The antebellum woman's movement approached this complex task by overlapping popular understandings of Womanhood with an intricately refigured Womanhood, weaving their claims through three integral issues: access to education, availability of meaningful occupations, and rights to financial independence. Their powerful arguments for each issue began from a commonly accepted aspect of True Womanhood and inevitably led to *a new type of womanhood,* centrally defined by Woman's economic and contractual action. Essentially, they created a new culturally legible social compound—the new True Woman—by overlapping normative and resistive deployments in the aporetic crucible.

Members of the antebellum woman's rights movement staked their claims on these three sets of issues—education, occupations, and financial independence—from the very beginning. The "Call for the 1851 Woman's Rights Convention," to be held in Worcester, Massachusetts, delineated these issues as the critical components of the woman's rights struggle and included Woman's general civil and political rights as well: "Of the many points now under discussion and demanding a just settlement, the general question of Woman's Rights and Relations comprehends these:—Her EDUCATION, Literary, Scientific, and Artistic;—Her AVOCATIONS, Industrial, Commercial, and Professional;—Her INTERESTS, Pecuniary, Civil, and Political; in a word—Her RIGHTS as an Individual, and her FUNCTIONS as a Citizen" (Woman's Rights Convention 1851, 4). The call then detailed Woman's mistreatment by society at large and specifically through legal structures, invoking the refigured True Woman as an activist who would fulfill Womanhood's *noblest duties*:

> Woman has been condemned for her greater delicacy of physical organization, to inferiority of intellectual and moral culture, and to the forfeiture of great social, civil, and religious privileges. In the relation of marriage she has been ideally annihilated, and actually enslaved in all that concerns her personal and pecuniary rights; and even in widowhood and single life, she is oppressed with such limitation and degradation of labor and avocation as clearly and cruelly mark the condition of a disabled caste. . . . Manhood begins to feel the shame of muddying the springs from which it draws its highest life; and Womanhood is everywhere awakening to assert its divinely chartered rights, and to fulfil its noblest duties. (4–5)

The rest of this section outlines how the woman's rights movement reshaped contemporary social meanings of Womanhood to awaken this truer True Woman. Activists argued for three prongs of equal rights by: first, positing conceptions of the True Woman that fit with popular understandings of Womanhood, contract, the economy, and the nation; and, second, persuasively overlapping them with conceptions that radically reconfigured these aporetic relations. As the True Woman traveled along these paths, she *claimed her rights equal with man, and then indeed she became a woman.*

Refiguring Womanhood

From the beginning of the decade, activists demanded Woman's right to education. Convention speeches, resolutions, and pamphlets first argued that only a substantive education could provide a proper basis for Woman's moral influence on her sons and husband, truly fitting her to be a Republican Mother to the nation. Mrs. C. I. H. Nichols followed this line of reasoning in an 1851 speech to the Worcester Convention titled "On the Responsibilities of Woman," an example that deserves extended scrutiny because it would be published as No. 6 in the series of ten Woman's Rights Tracts and distributed widely throughout the Northeast. In fact, she explicitly staked her claim to Woman's rights as a claim for mother's rights:

> I would say in reference to the rights of woman, it is apt to be forgotten that, as the mother of the race, her rights are the rights of men also—the rights of her *sons*. As a mother, I may speak to you, freemen, *fathers* of the rights of my sons—of every mother's sons—to the most perfect and vigorous development of their energies, which the mother can secure to them by the application, and through the use of *all* her God-given powers of body or of mind. It is in behalf of our sons, the future men of the Republic, as well as for our daughters, its future mothers, that we claim the full development of our energies by education, and legal protection in the control of all the issues and profits of ourselves, called *property.* (1853, 3)

At the very end of this ode to the normative Republican Mother and non-normative plea for her educational rights, Mrs. Nichols snuck onto the tenuous terrain of property rights, presaging her next move: claiming Woman's economic rights by overlapping Republican Motherhood with a reconfigured True Woman. In this first mention, the need for Woman's property rights followed neatly from the True Woman's duty to protect her sons. If the general public and legislators recognized this as Woman's calling, then they had to consider what would happen when a True Woman and Republican Mother faced family tragedy, such as being widowed or having married a drunkard—being widowed in extremis. If society was true to the True Woman's duties as Republican Mother, Mrs. Nichols argued, then it had to grant Woman rights to education. Plucking on legislators' sentimental heartstrings as fathers and husbands, she asked

> how it happens that when you die your estates are cut up, and your children and the means for their support consigned to others' guardianship by laws, which yourselves have made or sworn to defend? Do you reply that women are not qualified by education for the business transactions involved in such guardianship? It is for this I ask that they may be educated. Yourselves must educate your wives in the conduct of your business. . . . Would it not soothe your sick bed, would it not pluck thorns from your dying pillow, to confide in your wife that she could conduct

the business, on which your family relies for support, and in case of your death, keep your children together and educate them to go out into the world with habits of self-reliance and self-dependence? . . . Do you know that they would only cling the closer to you in the stern conflict of life, if they were thus taught that you do not undervalue their devotion and despise their ability? Call woman to your side, in the loving confidence of equal interests and equal responsibilities, and she will never fail you. (4–5)

With these questions, she moved further onto the terrain of economic rights, claiming that widowed Republican Mothers ought to continue to educate their sons to be good citizens, imparting both morality and knowledge. In order to do so, though, they had to be able to support their families. To raise moral sons, moral citizens, a moral nation, women had to be educated. And here her argument turned. The True Woman, whom men had entrusted to raise moral sons and to sustain a moral nation, had to be able to maintain the family's finances in case of tragedy; otherwise, she would no longer be able to fulfill her calling, placing in peril the moral threads that bound the nation. She had to be able to engage knowledgeably in "the business trans-actions involved" in supporting a family if widowed. *It is for this I ask that they may be educated. Yourselves must educate your wives in the conduct of your business.* Passing through Woman's Influence and the Republican Mother's duty to educate and raise a nation of citizen-sons, Mrs. Nichols contended that the True Woman required full economic and property rights, and entreated the nation's men, "Call woman to your side, in the loving confidence of equal interests and equal responsibilities, and she will never fail you." She spelled out how "confid[ing] in your wife that she could conduct the business," which became conceivable and possibly even rea-sonable in light of her argument, would reshape Womanhood itself and all its relations. This trust would bring to a head the conflict between "wom-an's responsibilities and the laws that alienate her means to discharge them. And here let me call your attention to my position, that *the law which alien-ates the wife's right to the control of her own property, her own earnings, lies at the foundation of all her social and legal wrongs*" (5). In the rest of her speech, which filled an eighteen-page pamphlet, Mrs. Nichols continued si-multaneously to deploy the normative figure of Woman via her Influence and Republican Motherhood and to overlap it with her claims to education, property, and contract—transfiguring the True Woman so that she could truly fulfill her normative duties. Without this radically refigured Woman, Mrs. Nichols exhorted, "We are suffering; the race is suffering from the ill performance of our duties" (10).

Throughout her speech, Mrs. Nichols also deployed the popular temperance figure of the wife, whose drunkard husband literally haunted her, making her a widow in extremis. He returned from the wished-for grave (actually the bar, or the next state, or the western territories)—and repeatedly, at that—and with each return, he claimed what savings and personal effects she had amassed to support their children and herself in his absence. Each time, with horror, the drunkard's wife watched their children's sustenance swept back into a sea of alcohol with this ghost. Even the purest True Woman could make an unfortunate marital choice, and so the widow in extremis spoke to all women's precarious position. The image's haunting strength made it a favorite of woman's newspapers and magazines. The woman's rights movement strategically used it to support all three aspects of a refigured Womanhood: access to education, a wide availability of occupations, and financial independence. In typical form, Mrs. Nichols told the detailed story of a True Woman, Republican Mother, and wife whose drunkard husband had repeatedly wrested her earnings from her, leaving her penniless—without property or even clothing—and consequently forced her to flee with her children from New York to New Hampshire to escape his constant and malevolent haunting (11).

Interestingly, near the end of her speech, Mrs. Nichols explicitly stated that she was not pleading for Woman's political rights, proclaiming, "Now, my friends, you will bear me witness that I have said nothing about woman's right to vote, or make laws. I have great respect for manhood" (13). But the transfigured Woman she assumed only sentences later was implicitly defined by her civil rights, including in part her political rights: "If it be true, as all admit, that woman's responsibilities are equal to man's, I claim that God has endowed her with equal powers for their discharge" (14). By making a True Woman conceivable who could, by definition and in order to fulfill her noble calling, legitimately participate in the civil realm through education, work, and financial independence, woman's rights activists created a new social world and made possible radical shifts in the structural aporetic site. They did not just expand the bounds of social meanings and their interimplicated institutional relations, but transformed their very shape, even as they overlapped and re-embedded aspects of prior social meanings. Throughout the decade, activists continued this practice, strategically refiguring Womanhood by claiming that educational and economic rights had to be combined with legitimated access to work in order for her to truly rise to society's demands on True Womanhood, as seen in the poem recited by Mrs. Nowell at the 1859 Woman's Rights Meeting held at Mercantile Hall in Boston:

> But often—oh, how often!—do we see
> A woman rising from her misery
> To take the *father's* place! God hath decreed,
> That, in the hour of their utmost need,
> Her helpless little orphans still may prove
> How glows in woman's soul immortal love.
> Father and mother, nurse, bread-winner, all,—
> She shrinks from neither when her duties call;
> And, that she fills each sacred office well,
> Let the *good sons of noble mothers* tell!
> (11)

The simultaneous and complicated deployment of Woman's Influence, Republican Motherhood, True Womanhood, and Woman's rights to education, occupations, and financial independence inevitably led to a secondary question regarding Woman's access to education: Did the existing female academies provide an appropriate education for the True Woman? The answer, of course, depended on what particular configuration of Womanhood was in play. Already at the 1851 Akron, Ohio, Woman's Rights Convention, activists juxtaposed a refigured True Woman against the normative True Woman to declare the contemporary female academies gravely insufficient. In a "Report on Education," Mrs. E. Robinson declared that they were "got up on the principle of milk for babes, and as such ought to be rejected by every true woman" (Woman's Rights Convention 1851/1973, 22–23). That is, they *ought to be rejected by every true woman* who held occupational acumen and financial independence central to her duties as both Woman and Republican Mother. Further, Woman required access to a wide variety of occupations—the argument quickly took hold—if girls and their educators were to take their education seriously enough to fit the young girls for their calling as *a new type of womanhood*. For if they were only to become "angels of the home"—to fulfill the popular understanding of True Womanhood—then academies would provide education only in refined diversions for their leisure time that brought moral uplift, such as painting, playing the piano, or reading the evermore popular woman's novel and women's magazines. The antebellum woman's rights movement effectively deployed this line of reasoning, contending that a wide variety of occupations should be made available to women not only so they could care for their family if widowed or widowed in extremis, but equally so that girls would take their education seriously, ensuring their capacity to fulfill their future duties. Abby H. Price further complicated this particular argument in her report on behalf of the Committee on Industrial Avocations at the 1851 Woman's Rights Convention held in Worcester. She declared the normative conception of Womanhood to be but a maimed *true woman,* as disabled in body and form as she was legally:

> Giant Prejudice has palsied the hand that, long ere this, would have made sweet music on the discordant keys of human life, and the true woman now bleeds at the foot of a chained and helpless, yet petted idol! . . . Now what is the remedy for all these evils? We believe that Woman needs not only Education, equal and thorough, but that all industrial avocations should be thrown open to her. Give her a chance to see what she may find herself capable of *doing* and *being,* without the danger of making herself an outcast or a ridiculous eccentric. If she be by nature unfitted for anything in which the other sex excel, her attractions will lead her aright; while only by a liberty of choice can she establish and sustain true womanly dignity and independence. (Woman's Rights Committee 1852, 22)

Price averred that Woman required legitimated access to "all industrial avocations," not only so that her education would make her a True Woman capable of fulfilling her duties to the family and the nation, but for the good of the radically reshaped True Woman herself—so that in her *doing and being,* in her activities and existence in the realm of labor and the economy, she could *establish and sustain true womanly dignity and independence.*

Woman's rights activists deployed this same argument turned inside out, as demonstrated by E. Oakes Smith's proposed resolution at the Woman's Rights Convention held in Syracuse, New York, in 1852:

> Whereas, modern society is such that human freedom, in its best sense, can only be secured by pecuniary independence,
> Therefore—
> *Resolved,* That every woman should engage herself in Literature, the Fine Arts, Professions, Agriculture, Commerce, or whatever honorable occupation best adapted to her capabilities, that she may thus remove the stain from labor, and work out her own emancipation. (Woman's Rights Convention 1852b, 23–24)

Price had started from claims of Woman's right to education in order to deploy a refigured Womanhood who required occupational access, arguing that her economic participation would make the True Woman ever truer. In contrast, Smith started from the claim that "human freedom" was defined by "pecuniary independence" and Woman could only be a part of free and civil society if she had the right to financial independence, for which she required access to all "honorable occupation[s]." In turn, a refigured Womanhood who had occupational access would bring Woman's morality to labor and make Woman herself whole. Both Price's and Smith's arguments combined overlapping claims for Woman's access to education, occupations, and economic activity. And each argument combined an implicit deployment of the normative True Woman, who would morally educate the nation through her Republican Motherhood and would "remove the stain from labor," making all laboring occupations *honorable,* with an explicit deployment of a refigured True Woman, whose economic existence and activity provided the basis for her to *work out her own emancipation,* an *independence* conceived as *sustaining true womanly dignity.* By 1856, this complicated interweaving of financial independence, access to occupations, the purifying effect on labor of Woman's morality, and the elevating effect of labor on the True Woman had been firmly established as part of the woman's rights movement's strategic repertoire. An article titled "Practical Remedy for the Wrongs of Woman," published in the abolition and temperance paper the *New York Evangelist* on April 3, 1856, summarized: "To elevate the lot of woman, something more is needed than this legal protection [provided by the 1848 Married Woman's Property Act]. The practical remedy for the extremely dependent condition of the female sex, is to find out for them new means of support; to open new branches of industry, by which they can make a living, and become independent" (in Anthony [n.p.] 1837). Similarly, in her closing address as president of the Seventh National Woman's Rights Convention, held in New York City in 1856, Lucy Stone observed, "We must first be independent, pecuniarily, and to this end every occupation must be open to us. We must make our labor honored" (Woman's Rights Committee 1856, 86). In a series of three lectures on "The Market; or, Woman's Position as Regards Wages and Work," delivered in Boston in November 1859 as part of a northeast speaking tour on Woman's relations to education, law, and the market, the Englishwoman Caroline Dall (1867/1972, 185–86) defined these particular intertwined relations as implicit to contemporary Womanhood and the economy: "A want of respect for woman, and a want of respect for labor, latent and unacknowledged in the public mind, must be overcome before she can [take her proper place]. . . . Educated, respectable women should have the giving-out and the inspection of woman's work; but educated and respectable women will never stand in such a position till public opinion teaches them that all *labor* is honorable, and that no lady will ever sit with folded hands."

As noted earlier, the antebellum woman's movement usually mounted claims to legitimate the True Woman's financial and civil activity by, first, explicitly or implicitly establishing the duties of a normative True Woman and Republican Mother to her sons and her nation, and then moving to a claim for Woman's access to a wide variety of occupations so that she could: (a) fulfill her duties properly if widowed; (b) have true access to education and take it seriously; and (c) be more truly Woman as a refigured True Woman, defined in part precisely by her economic and civil capabilities. The demand for available occupations rested on these multiple bases, making the transfigured True Woman more and more conceivable, or culturally legible, by reshaping the relations between Womanhood, contract, the economy, and the nation. A letter read at the Woman's Rights Convention of 1851 conveyed this complex interweaving and overlapping of popular and reshaped figures of Womanhood and their relations to education, occupations, economic action, and marriage, on which activists would rely for the next decade:

We deprive the greater portion of woman-kind of the best influences of life. All women are more or less subjected to some of the following evils: They are deprived of liberal education, and if, in a few rare instances, such an education is given, they are deprived of all the opportunities of enjoying its benefits by giving their acquired talents and knowledge a proper sphere of operation. . . . They are deprived of all personal pecuniary independence—ENSLAVED by the inadequate wages of their toil—compelled to be dependent upon men, and deprived, by their restricted mode of life, even of the privilege of looking abroad sufficiently to make a judicious choice of the husband to whom they entrust their fate, and vow eternal submission in accordance with law and usage. (Dr. Joseph R. Buchanan, in Woman's Rights Convention 1851/1973, 48)

In his letter, Dr. Buchanan touched on one other way that activists spoke to the True Woman's aporetic foundations in the marriage contract. In its most common variant, activists claimed that Woman would be ensured true marital choice only if she held rights to economic and contractual action, removing financial pressures from her decision. Mrs. E. Oakes Smith provided a sophisticated example in her eight-page pamphlet on the "Sanctity of Marriage," published and distributed throughout the Northeast as No. 5 in the Woman's Rights Tract series. She posited that only Woman's equal legal rights to contractual action would ensure the marriage relation's sanctity by arguing that an honorable marriage's "terms of contract should be such as to secure its inviolability, and therefore I claim that there should be equality of character in the contracting parties—legal equality, at the very least" (1853, 2). Indeed, Mrs. Smith argued that society's recognition of Woman as a legitimate civil individual with contract and property rights would *honor* rather than degrade her because only these *rights to the dignities of property* would allow her to enter into *this divine relation of marriage* from a place of *honor* rather than desperation:

> In claiming a woman's right to be individual, and her right to the dignities of property, it was with the view that these might relieve her from the necessity of seeking in marriage that which society ought to award her as her right—that is, position, independent of her relation to one of the other sex; that she should be truly, nobly woman—marry or not marry, as her heart or her taste may dictate, and yet be honorable; . . . in all

things she should so comport herself that her best and truest womanhood should he [sic] developed, and she be honorable, and honored in it;
and finally, that if in the maturity of her beauty and the clearness of her
intellect she be disposed to carry all this affluence of nature into this divine relation of marriage, she should be still honorable, not as a reflex of
another's glory, but as of herself, lending and receiving. (4–5)

The marital institution was popularly regarded as the foundation on which
both society and Womanhood stood. Mrs. Smith explicitly deployed that
foundation's aporetic instability to reshape Woman's relation to contract
and civil society. In order to protect the honor of marriage, Womanhood,
and through them the nation, she "claim[ed] a woman's right to be individual" and imaged her *best and truest womanhood* as reflected, in part, in her
"lending and receiving" of herself in marriage. In other words, Smith refigured the True Woman as integrally defined by her contractual and economic
actions even in, and specifically in, the marital relation itself. In so doing,
she reshaped the imbricated relations between social meanings and institutions of Womanhood, contract, the economy, and the nation from the center of the aporetic space, even as she affirmed the centrality of marriage to
Womanhood, contract, and the nation.

At the same time that activists transfigured Womanhood's social meanings, they distributed petitions demanding women's legal and civil rights
and presented them annually to the New York State Legislature. The "material" politics of petitioning for legal rights and the "cultural" politics of refiguring Womanhood did not only occur simultaneously, but in fact were
mutually constitutive; neither would succeed without the other. In addition,
only a stirred-up aporetic site—produced in this instance by the combination of the nineteenth century's legal codification movement and its extreme economic and social flux—could provide the space for the woman's
movement's success by potentiating engagement with foundational social
structures. Such a movement, one that rests on a structural aporia, could
not succeed without a stirred-up structural aporia. Similarly, a stirred-up
structural aporia in no way guaranteed such a movement's emergence. And
only the confluence of a fully discursive movement—necessarily doubly
constituted of interimplicated cultural and material change—with an appropriately primed structural aporia could bring about radical cultural and

institutional social change. The next section returns to chapter 2's analysis of legal aporias to discern what changes to Woman's legitimated contractual and civil existence this particular confluence of historical events made possible.

"SO, GET READY, GENTLEMEN"

> But the wife who is so fortunate as to have inherited property, has, by the new [1848] law in [New York] State, been redeemed from her lost condition. She is no longer a legal nonentity. This property law, if fairly construed, will overturn the whole code relating to woman and property. The right to property implies the right to buy and sell, to will and bequeath, and herein is the dawning of a civil existence for woman, for now the *femme covert* must have their right to make contracts. So, get ready, gentlemen.
>
> —Elizabeth Cady Stanton, *Address to the Legislature of New-York, Adopted by the State Woman's Rights Convention*, 1854

In her 1854 address to the Joint Judiciary Committee of the New York Legislature, Elizabeth Cady Stanton imparted the consequences of property rights in modern democratic capitalist society. Just before Stanton's powerful address, the woman's rights movement had submitted dual petitions to the legislature, calling for the "Just and Equal Rights of Women" and "Woman's Right to Suffrage," the former signed by 5,931 men and women and the latter by 4,164 men and women (E. C. Stanton 1854, appendix). Stanton's speech would travel into the far corners of New York State, tracing the impressive breadth of the antebellum woman's rights movement. In a handwritten note attached to her copy of Stanton's speech, Susan B. Anthony commented that it "was not only laid on the table of every member of the Legislature—but delivered in the [Woman's Rights] Convention—and before a legislative committee—and I had printed 20,000 copies and scattered them throughout the state on my campaign of 1854–1855" (Woman's Rights Convention [n.p.]).

Stanton rhetorically based her prediction of Woman's movement into civil existence in an immediately prior and more moderate discussion, in which she considered the True Woman-Mother's contemporary social position via the figure of the drunkard's wife:

If she have a worthless husband, a confirmed drunkard, a villain, or a vagrant, he has still all the rights of a man, a husband, and a father. Though the whole support of the family be thrown upon the wife, if the wages she earns be paid to her by her employer, the husband can receive them again. If, by unwearied industry and perseverance, she can earn for herself and children a patch of ground and a shed to cover them, the husband can strip her of all her hard earnings, turn her and her little ones out in the cold northern blast, take the clothes from their backs, the bread from their mouths; all this by your laws may he do, and he has done, oft and again, to satisfy the rapacity of that monster in human form, the rum-seller. (10–11)

In quick succession, Stanton called forth: commonly accepted antebellum social meanings of Womanhood; a moderate woman's rights plea for retaining the sanctity of the Woman maltreated by an irresponsible husband; and a radical woman's rights argument for economic and contractual rights for all women, which would lead finally to *the dawning of a civil existence for woman*. Her rapid movement between these overlapping discourses of respectable Womanhood telescoped their intertwined deployment by the woman's rights movement during the 1850s. And her argument's contemporary legibility lay bare the intricate and contingent relations between social meanings of Womanhood and institutions of law and the economy on which the social movement's success would rest.

Unfortunately, all the original petitions submitted to the New York State Legislature by the 1850s woman's rights movement and pertinent legal documents were destroyed in 1911 when the New York State Library burned to the ground.[5] Luckily, copies of the Journals of the Assembly and Senate of the State of New York had been stored elsewhere and remained intact. As a result, the extant record of legislative response to the woman's rights movement consists solely of committee reports from 1854, 1855, and 1856; reports of votes in 1859 and 1860; and various newspaper reports of legislative debates found in scrapbooks kept by Susan B. Anthony. This limited historical record traces the legislature's direct confrontation of a structural aporia— what Spivak (1988a, 4) termed the *violent event* itself—*a functional change in a sign system that can only be operated by the force of a crisis*.[6] That is, it traces the operation of fundamental societal shifts, located and dislocated in society's foundational impasse, by detailing the legislature's confrontation with the unstable and contingent nature of the institutions and social meanings constituting this aporetic site. It traces the operation of fundamental societal shifts in the difficult contingencies between economic and contractual legislation, social meanings of Womanhood and the civil existence of women, and the pressures applied by the antebellum woman's rights movement.

Each year the woman's rights movement presented petitions to the New York State legislature; which committee reviewed the petitions in part determined the legislative response. Consequently, committee assignments were the subject of serious legislative debate. If, for instance, the petitions were sent to the Judiciary Committee, they would go no further. As Assemblyman D. P. Wood noted in 1854, "Let such a disposition be made of [the petitions], and there will then be no danger that any one will be fired up by it; for it will then be sure to sleep the sleep of death" (in Anthony [n.p.] 1837). Proving him correct, the Judiciary Committee of 1856 was assigned consideration of the petitions and produced an entirely sarcastic report, in which they made no substantive arguments and refused address of the issues raised. In 1854 and 1855, legislative members argued convincingly to keep the petitions from the Judiciary Committee, sending them to a Select Committee of the Whole instead. Mr. Wood's comment on the Judiciary Committee actually anchored a plea for full consideration of the petitions. Recognizing that the petitions' demands implied radical social change, he argued, "When a petition like this comes before the Legislature, it should not only be respectfully received, but courteously considered; particularly when it asks, as this petition does, a review of the entire of our civil statute law" (in Anthony [n.p.] 1837). As he wished, the Select Committee of the Whole responded to the 1854 and 1855 petitions to the Assembly with reports that finally confronted the aporetic abyss. Their reports moved Woman into the economic realm via the normative and dovetailed definitions of the Republican Mother and the True Woman, just as Stanton had pressed for in her speech of 1854.

The New York Assembly debates of 1854 over which committee should consider the woman's rights petitions were "Reported for the Evening Journal" (presumably of Albany) on February 20. Legislators deployed a range of definitions of Womanhood in the debate—from ones denying women any form of public speech to a variety of definitions embedded in the over-lapping and dovetailed figures of Republican Motherhood, True Woman-hood, and Woman's Influence. Mr. Burnett, Chair of the Judiciary Committee and Mr. Wood's opponent in this particular debate, imparted the former position, naming the women who dared to make public demands not a part of Womanhood at all, but *un-sexed*. He avowed, "It is well known that the object of these un-sexed women is to overthrow the most sacred of our in-stitutions, to set at defiance the divine law which declares man and wife to be one, and to establish on its ruins, what will be in fact and in principle but a species of legalized adultery" (in Anthony [n.p.] 1837). Mr. Burnett recog-nized, along with Mr. Wood, that the petitions' demands to redefine Woman such that a True Woman would hold economic and contractual rights, such that she would experience *the dawning of a civil existence,* called for social rupture. But where Assemblyman Wood asked the legislature to directly confront this aporetic site, which would require "a review of the entire of our civil statute law," Assemblyman Burnett refused address of the struc-tural aporia, invoking instead the danger of social irruption while affirm-ing the aporetic impasse across, between, and beyond the contingencies of Womanhood and the economy.

In a plea that at first glance seems to admit greater complexity than Mr. Burnett's denial, Assemblyman Peters called for serious consideration of the petitions, despite clear differences between his opinions and the pe-titions' requests. Grounding Woman's place in current social meanings of Republican Motherhood and the True Woman, Mr. Peters allowed for the possibility of expanding Woman's realm economically so that she could bet-ter fulfill her duties of Motherhood and Womanhood. He opined, "I do not believe it to be a part of the duty of women to sit in the jury box, to vote, or to participate in all the tumultuous strifes of life; but I do believe that those who differ from me in opinion should have a respectful hearing. Nor, be-cause women are not allowed to vote, do I admit that they are precluded from all agency in the direction of national affairs. They, more than their husbands, have power over the future history of the country, by impart-ing a correct fire-side education to their sons. But there are legal disabilities imposed upon women which I would be willing to see removed, in regard to property, &c" (in Anthony [n.p.] 1837). By conceiving that some rights of property and contract might be given to women without significantly changing the realm of Woman's Influence, let alone the shape of modern society as it congealed in and around economic and legal institutions and social meanings of Womanhood and the economy, Mr. Peters in fact discerned the surrounding social world with less complexity and accuracy than either Mr. Burnett or Mr. Wood.

Both Mr. Burnett and Mr. Wood could be said to have read their contemporary social order asunder. While one went apoplectic at the prospective horrors of social chaos, the other considered that perhaps it was time to confront an underlying and fundamental social abyss. But both recognized the site that comprised Woman's abyssal and abysmal contemporary existence as *an unstable assemblage of faults, fissures, and heterogeneous layers that threatened the fragile inheritor from within or from underneath* (Foucault 1977/1988, 146). One turned away in terror from the dangers of facing Medusa; the other considered that the site held the promise of the future and heard its ethical call for *the nonpassive endurance of the aporia as the condition of responsibility and of decision* (Derrida 1993, 16).[7] Meanwhile, Mr. Peters remained blithely unaware of the aporetic rumblings beneath his feet. In the end, the 1854 Select Committee's report did not refuse aporetic address but, like Mr. Peters, explicitly chose to remain unaware of the aporia's ethical call. It granted only the petitioners' argument for mothers' economic rights, figuring them as widows in extremis. Specifically, the report argued that

> where the husband neglects or refuses to provide for the support and education of his family, the wife should have the right to collect and receive her own earnings, and the earnings of her minor children, and apply them to the support and education of the family, free from the control of the husband, or of any person claiming the same through him. [However,] there are many other rules of law applicable to the relation of husband and wife, which in occasional cases bear hard upon the one or the other, but your committee do not deem it wise that a new arrangement of our laws of domestic relations should be attempted, to obviate such cases. They always have, and always will arise out of every subject of legal regulation. (Assembly Doc. No. 129, 1854, 4)

The Select Committee further "ask[ed] leave to introduce a bill corresponding with the suggestions hereinbefore contained" (4).

An Albany newspaper's coverage of the Select Committee's report printed the report verbatim and editorialized, welcoming the committee's argument to recognize women *qua* mothers and solely through that lens. With the Select Committee, the editor supported Motherhood as embedded in two distinct sets of meanings: first, via True Womanhood's basis in Republican Motherhood and Woman's Influence, understanding Motherhood and Womanhood as the providers of moral grounding for sons, families, and the nation; and second, via the figure of widowhood in extremis, presenting a spectacle of a repudiated Motherhood and Womanhood whose moral provisions were repeatedly denied. The editorial read: "The Committee report adversely to the Petitions, but recommend one or two changes in our existing law, which will, we think, commend themselves as well to the opponents as to the advocates of Women's Rights, viz: A voice, by the Mother, in the disposition of the child, either when apprenticed to service or placed under guardianship; and the right of the Wife to collect and control her own earnings and the earnings of her children, when the family is neglected by the Husband. These, we think, are reasonable and just propositions, which can hardly fail to receive the favorable consideration of the Legislature" (in Anthony [n.p.] 1837). Of course, the wife's right to her earnings did not pass the legislature at this time, but the form of the local press's favorable opinion is crucial. The editor deployed traditional meanings of Motherhood to extend women's economic rights within limits that seemed to leave intact the foundational impasse defining contemporary relations between social meanings of Womanhood and economic and contractual institutions of modern democracy. But, throughout the 1850s, the woman's rights movement smartly deployed these same widely accepted meanings of Motherhood in all their convolutions, demonstrating their irrevocable intertwining with a Womanhood that learned, labored, owned, and contracted in its fully recognized civil existence. Over a decade's time, they continually pressured the populace and the legislature to recognize and confront this intricate impasse that lay at the heart of modern democracy—the impasse in which the knot of Womanhood, the economy, and the nation resided. In their speeches, pamphlets, and petitions, the antebellum woman's rights movement meticulously refigured Womanhood by dovetailing popular understandings of True Womanhood and Motherhood with a respectable Womanhood that operated economically and contractually at its very base. According to the

Select Committee and the Albany newspaper editor, women should legally exist as economic actors, but only *qua* mothers, as figures of True Womanhood via the morality of Woman's Influence through Motherhood. Under their proposal, by no means would earnings legitimate women as economic and contractual actors *qua* women. By no means should women have the capacity for civil existence because, as Mr. Burnett had so clearly warned, that would endanger both Womanhood and the nation by *unsexing* women, leading to a nation bereft of morality and suffused with sacrilege. "That this is their real object—however it may be attempted to be disguised—is well known to every one who has looked . . . at the practical and inevitable result of the movement," proclaimed Assemblyman Burnett (in Anthony [n.p.] 1837) In fact, even as the Select Committee suggested that women *qua* mothers should have certain economic rights, it explicitly agreed with Mr. Burnett's charge of the dangers to the nation's "harmony of life" attendant upon the loss of Woman's morality. Their report declared: "A higher power than that from which emanates legislative enactments has given forth the mandate that man and woman shall not be equal; that there shall be inequalities, by which each in their own appropriate sphere shall have precedence to the other; and each shall be superior or inferior as they well or ill act the part assigned them. . . . We cannot obliterate [this inequality] if we would, and legal inequalities must follow. . . . Dissension and distraction quickly arise when this necessity is not answered. The harmony of life, the real interest of both husband and wife, and of all dependent upon them, require it" (Assembly Doc. 129, 1854, 2–3).

In her earlier speech to the Assembly, Elizabeth Cady Stanton (Stanton 1854/1989, 101) had delineated the legal aporia faced by women who contracted to marry and by that single contract "[had] no civil existence, no social freedom." She had argued that "the signing of this contract is instant civil death to one of the parties." On this point, the legislative report seemed to answer her directly:

> In the formation of governments, the manner in which the common interest shall be embodied and represented is a matter of conventional arrangement; but in the family an influence more potent than that of contracts and conventionalities, and which everywhere underlies humanity, has indicated that the husband shall fill the necessity which exists for a head.

. . . Your committee cannot regard marriage as a *mere contract,* but as something above and beyond—something more binding than records, more solemn than specialties; and the person who reasons as to the relations and rights of husband and wife as upon an ordinary contract, in their opinion, commits a fatal error in the outset; and your committee cannot recommend any action based upon such a theory. (Assembly Doc. 129, 1854, 2–3)

The committee's argument here pointed to their final decision. Even as they held out the possibility of legalizing limited economic rights for women— for a Womanhood understood only through the combining of Republican Motherhood and Woman's Influence—they closed their report with the determination, "Your committee do not deem it wise that a new arrangement of our laws of domestic relations should be attempted. . . . In conclusion your committee recommend, that the prayer of the petition be denied" (4). While the Assembly had begun the 1854 legislative session in a debate that tentatively confronted the abyss, they ended their discussion of the petitions with an explicit rebuke of any legal confrontation with Woman's aporetic state. The 1854 legislative session overall stood as a partial success by the woman's movement in pressing for a confrontation with the aporetic space on which the legislature itself was founded. Viewed alongside the earlier 1854 debates regarding whether the legislature should seriously consider the woman's rights movement's demands, the combination of the final legislative repudiation and arguments for women's limited financial independence further destabilized the aporetic site.

The movement again submitted petitions to the Assembly in its session of 1855, as they did in every session through 1860; again a Select Committee of the Whole reviewed them rather than the Judiciary Committee. This time, they "unanimously report[ed] adversely to the prayer of the petitioners" for woman's right to suffrage and "report[ed] favorably" on the "petition 'for the just and equal rights of woman,'" proposing a new bill to replace the current section of the Revised Statutes that regulated spousal inheritance of real property. If passed, the act would have given a surviving spouse ownership, for the rest of her or his natural life, of all real property that had been owned by a spouse who died intestate, as long as the deceased had no "lawful descendants, born or to be born of such marriage or of a prior marriage"

(Assembly Doc. No. 129, 1855, 1–2). No copy of the committee's report exists, so the detailed logic leading to the committee's recommendation cannot be analyzed. It cannot be known whether or not the proposed extension of property rights was explicitly couched in the language of Motherhood and True Womanhood, or what deployments of Womanhood the legislature put into play. But an aporetic analytic implies that such a change in the law overseeing the institutions of marriage and property could have operated only through social meanings of Womanhood.

The proposed act echoed New York State's Married Women's Property Act of 1848. The act of 1848 had primarily protected real property inherited by or given to a married woman, in the event of her spouse's death or indebtedness. In the event of death, it ensured that such property would remain the widow's own, if no children had been born to the marriage, rather than be distributed among her husband's family and creditors; if the marriage had borne children, the same real property would fall to them. In the event of profligacy, it protected this property as the wife's own, keeping it safe from creditors' claims. In this way, fathers' estates were protected from the families of sons-in-law and from creditors, allowing them to be passed on without fragmentation and the daughters' resultant poverty. While the act of 1848 granted women the right to hold certain delimited types of real property and real property only—excluding personal property and finances— it did not grant these same women any ability to act economically or contractually. The legislature's extension of 1849 allowing women to make contracts solely regarding such real property still did not give women *qua* women any economic or contractual rights. It only allowed wives to make a contract regarding the disposition of pieces of real property given to her in specific ways by men. These same wives could make no other economic or general contracts under their own name.[8] The act proposed by the 1855 Select Committee of the Whole extended the act of 1848 while remaining firmly within its parameters. It extended the property a widow inherited to include all real property owned by the husband as well as that set apart as hers—still excluding all personal property and finances—as long as the husband had not made a will with different provisions and no children had been born to this or any of the husband's prior marriages. And it expanded the concept of passing on intact the family's productive property to include all the nuclear family's real property rather than just the wife's father's estate. But in no way did the proposed legislation give women, or even these wives, any contractual rights. The right to inherit slightly more property as widows did not legitimate women as economic actors any more than the law of 1848 enabling inheritance of their father's real property had. Additionally, without the inheritance of personal property, women still would not inherit any monetary assets, including their own earnings that, as personal property, immediately became their husbands' legal possession. In other words, the Select Committee of the Whole responded to the petitions of 1855 by proposing an act that would expand the real property inherited by women *qua* widows, *qua* some-incarnation-of-the-True-Woman, but that specifically did not address women's economic and contractual rights. In doing so, their final response refused address of the aporetic site. Whether records of their debates or the full report itself would demonstrate some direct address, as they did in 1854, unfortunately cannot be known.

In December 1854, the indefatigable Susan B. Anthony, with the help of a few other women, embarked on a speaking tour and petition drive that covered every county in New York State by May 1855. Consisting "of 49 County Conventions at the County Seats—held Mondays, Wednesdays, and Fridays—at 4 and 7 PM," their canvass began at the far western tip of the state on December 26, 1854, in Chautauqua County, and ended at the far eastern edge on May 10, 1855, in Putnam County (in Anthony [n.p.] 1837). The organization of each county convention replicated the movement's three-pronged approach to refiguring Womanhood and combined with the early stages of the suffrage struggle. The female activists gave afternoon and evening speeches and distributed and collected dual petitions at each stop. Local papers along the canvass route invariably reported that the 4 o'clock afternoon speeches focused on Woman's lack of access to education and employment, while the 7 o'clock evening speeches focused on Woman's legal disabilities in marriage—with particular emphasis on economic and property rights—and obtaining suffrage rights (in Anthony [n.p.] 1837). The petition drive succeeded immediately. On January 10, 1855, the Bath *Advocate* reported that "over one hundred signatures to the petition for Woman's Rights of Suffrage [as well as to the petition for Just and Equal Rights], were obtained" at the convention there; a report from the Chenango convention noted that the previous year "six thousand names were sent in [to the legislature] for the Equal Rights of Woman, and four thousand for giving women the Right of Suffrage.—This winter [Susan B. Anthony] expected to get at least ten thousand names for each object" (in Anthony [n.p.] 1837). Public response to the speeches demonstrated a popular shift in understandings of the entwined social meanings of Womanhood and the economy and the institutions of marriage and contract. A local paper in Penn Yan explicitly accepted the speakers' redeployment of True Womanhood as a progressive and activist Womanhood, reporting on the Penn Yan convention, "What they contend for is not to compel woman to do all 'kinds of hard work,' but to give her the right. True womanhood, like true manhood, desires progress" (in Anthony [n.p.] 1837). In covering the evening speech made in Lockport, New York, the reporter for the *Lockport Daily Journal* was unable to distinguish between two sets of arguments made: those supporting the already existing limited rights of married women to hold real property separate from their husbands and to inherit their family's real property if their husband died, and those arguing for the civil existence of Womanhood that would come only with general economic and contractual rights. And, without distinction, the article granted the activists' argument for property rights: "Miss E. Rose . . . spoke eloquently in favor of many of the present laws relating to married ladies and their right to hold property. She also advocated with equal zeal and eloquence the right of female suffrage. The propriety of her claims under the first head were very generally conceded, but those under the second head did not probably meet with so general favor" (in Anthony [n.p.] 1837). As pressure on the aporetic site unsettled it more and more, those residing within it addressed it more and more; yet they still could not clearly articulate its imbricated relations precisely because they did reside within it.

Activists presented the petitions collected on the 1854–1855 canvass, as well as those collected through newspapers and the mail, to the 1856 New York State Legislature. Unfortunately, this was the one year that the petitions were sent to the Judiciary Committee rather than a Select Committee of the Whole. Only direct quotation can do justice to the level of sarcasm and dismissal found in the committee's final report, as they deployed the most traditional version of True Womanhood to support their case—figuring a True Woman who lacked the civic and educational grounding of even the Republican Mother:

The petitioners ask that there may be established by law an equality of rights between the sexes. The judiciary committee is composed of married and single gentlemen. The bachelors on the committee, with becoming diffidence, have left the subject pretty much to the married gentlemen. They have considered it with the aid of the light they have before them, and the experience married life has given them. Thus aided they are enabled to state, that ladies always have the best piece, and choicest titbit at table; they have their choice on which side of the bed they will lie, front or back. A lady's dress costs three times as much as that of a gentleman, and at the present time, with the prevailing fashion, one lady occupies three times as much space in the world as a gentleman.

It has thus appeared to the married gentlemen of your committee being a majority (the bachelors being silent for the reason mentioned, and also probably for the further reason that they are still suitors for the favors of the gentler sex), that if there is any inequality or oppression in the case, the gentlemen are the sufferers. They, however, have presented no petitions for redress, having doubtless made up their minds to yield to an inevitable destiny.

On the whole, the committee have concluded to recommend no measure, except, that as they have observed several instances in which husband and wife have both signed the petition. In such case, they would recommend the parties to apply for a law authorizing them to change dresses, so that the husband may wear the petty-coats, and the wife the breeches, and thus indicate to their neighbors and the public the true relation in which they stand to each other. (Assembly Doc. No. 114, 1856, 1–2)

Any legislative debate that would have demonstrated either the more general legislative sentiment toward granting women economic rights or their deployments of various understandings of Womanhood against each other was not recorded that year.

The extant legislative record does not refer again to the antebellum woman's movement's struggle for economic and property rights until 1859 and 1860, and those references remain brief, although significant. In 1859, the New York State Assembly almost unanimously passed "An act for the protection of the property in trade and earnings of married women" (102 votes for, 2 against; *Journal of the Assembly* 1859, 1147). In the next year's legislative session, on March 15, 1860, the Assembly again passed a bill of the same name, concurring with the Senate's prior amendments to it (92 for, 5 against; *Journal of the Assembly* 1860, 663). Finally, on March 16, 1860, the Senate passed the act into law, establishing the Married Women's Property Act known as the 1860 Earnings Act (*Journal of the Senate* 1860, 458). The paucity of the legislative and newspaper record of these years leaves much information to be desired regarding the final debates leading to its passage, since the 1860 Earnings Act meaningfully addressed the structural aporia swirling among Womanhood, marriage, property, contract, the economy, and the nation. Although more laws would be required in the next decades to fulfill the promise provided by this address of the aporetic site, the 1860 Earnings Act definitively marks the first true moment of successful societal address—an address that was made possible only by a redeployment of the social meanings of True Womanhood, a redeployment that reshaped True Womanhood so that it could include legitimate participation in the economic realm.

The act of 1860 gave a married woman control over her own earnings, or "that which she acquires by her trade, business, labor or services, [albeit] carried on or performed on her sole or separate account," and provided her with contractual rights and the legal ability to sue and be sued, which meant she could take legal action regarding the property she held and any other matter *(Laws of the State of New-York 1860,* chap. 90, § 1). When the Earnings Act passed almost unanimously, it granted the women of New York State a civil existence; it made them full economic, contractual, and thereby civil actors in the capitalist economy and polity. After 1860, demands for suffrage could rest on a reshaped ground of Womanhood—a ground that newly defined economic and civic participation through contract as a fundamental principle of Womanhood. The second section of the act of 1860 was explicit as to women's contractual rights over their personal property, including financial property such as earnings: "A married woman may bargain, sell, assign and transfer her separate personal property, and carry on any trade or business, and perform any labor or services on her sole and separate account, and the earnings of any married woman, from her trade, business, labor or services, shall be her sole and separate property, and may be used or invested by her in her own name" (chap. 90, § 2). Married women had never before been allotted any rights to personal property; at the moment of the marriage contract, control over all of a woman's personal and financial property had transferred to her husband. The Married Women's Property Acts of 1848 and 1849 and any legislation since had only allowed her to own some real property separate from her husband, thereby keeping it safe from creditors and untrustworthy husbands. Prior to the Assembly's attempted passage of this act in 1859, no law had broached women's rights to personal and financial property; hence all earnings were their husbands', including earnings from the real property that the law deemed legally owned by these women. Intertwined with this lack of address of personal property—of the ability to own in general in a capitalist democracy—no law had broached women's general rights of contract. But the 1860 Earnings Act gave married women full rights of contract over their personal and financial property as well as over their real property, declaring that all women who owned real property on their own account "may bargain, sell and convey such property, and enter into any contract in reference to the same" (chap. 90, § 3). Unfortunately, the Earnings Act legislated the requirement of a husband's written assent to all such contracts over real property, declaiming that those would not "be valid without the assent, in writing, of her husband," except as delimited in further sections of the act. But this requirement was repealed two years later in 1862 by a Married Women's Property Act (*Laws of the State of New-York 1862*, chap. 172, § 1). The Earnings Act of 1860 also legislated more general issues of women's rights of ownership and contract than those confined to economics; it made married women joint guardians of their children and equal inheritors to married men if a spouse died intestate (*Laws of the State of New-York 1860*, chap. 90, §§ 9, 10, 11). The Select Committees of the Whole of 1854 and 1855 had previously recommended portions of these reforms by deploying a shift in the social meanings of Womanhood, combining certain aspects of Republican Motherhood and Woman's Influence. The legislature had not passed them at that time. While these broader rights of ownership and contract were central to a full address of the structural aporia intertwining the social meanings and institutions of Womanhood, marriage, contracts, the economy, and the nation, they had as yet only been approached through social meanings of Womanhood that prohibited women from being civil actors.

The fate of the various sections of the Earnings Act of 1860 sheds light on how True Womanhood had and had not yet been successfully redeployed by the antebellum woman's movement and provides a comment on the inadequacy of negotiation when an aporetic site shifts beneath society's feet. Once the Civil War began, the woman's movement stopped its annual conventions and speaking tours, along with its annual pressure on the New York legislature. Without this continued pressure, portions of the 1860 act were quickly rescinded in 1862. However, the act of 1862 nullified none of the sections regarding married women's rights to economic property—real, personal, and financial—or their rights to contract in the economic realm. In fact, the 1862 act expanded these rights to provide married women full contractual control over their real property without their husbands' consent. In other words, by 1860, the New York State legislature had addressed seriously this particular structural aporia of modernity. By 1862, it had been sufficiently addressed that the terms defining a True Woman had dramatically changed shape, so that her legitimate interactions with the economic realm and contract were made part and parcel of her being. Interestingly, the 1862 act rescinded precisely those sections of the act of 1860 that granted married women rights based on more traditional deployments of True Womanhood while expanding the sections based on a radically new figure of Womanhood. Section 2 of the act of 1862 repealed married women's coguardianship of children and equal inheritance when a spouse died (*Laws of the State of New-York 1862*, chap. 172, § 2), replacing them with the more minimal right of a mother to prevent the binding of her children "to apprenticeship[s] or service or [the] part[ing] with the control of such child[ren]" by refusing to assent in writing (chap. 172, § 6). Under law prior to 1860, the husband had held absolute power over the disposal of children's lives, able to bind them in apprenticeships or for service even before their birth. Negotiating social meanings of Motherhood to expand understandings of Womanhood without radically changing Woman's shape, keeping the same delimitations on Woman, could not succeed in an aporetic site. These rights could be granted only to a radically refigured Womanhood as general rights of ownership and contract, constituting a Woman who was recognized as a legitimate civil actor. They could be granted only after their relationship to Womanhood, property, marriage, contract, and the nation had been redeployed on the newly shifted ground of the structural aporia. Meanwhile, the 1860 and 1862 Married Women's Property Acts clearly demonstrate the antebellum woman's movement's success in legitimating Woman's participation in the economic and contractual realm—and in redefining such participation as central to Womanhood itself.

In comparison with arguments that the 1860 Earnings Act defeated women's early radical claims for joint property rights in marriage, an analysis underscoring the refiguring of Womanhood and contract necessary to their passage suggests that they in fact achieved crucial aspects of the joint property demands. Proponents of the first spate of married women's property acts "had argued that wives should be allowed to hold assets they brought to or acquired during marriage as separate property in order to *protect women* from improvident, profligate, or intemperate husbands," Siegel (1994, 1116) writes; "those gathered at the Worcester conventions [in 1850] situated the argument for joint property rights on very different grounds. In their view, marital property reform was not about protecting economically dependent women from men, but instead was about empowering economically productive women to participate equally with men in managing assets both had helped to accumulate." While the second spate of married women's property acts, or earnings acts, did not recognize all assets accumulated during marriage as joint earnings, their passage signified a societal refiguring of Woman and contract that was the very condition of possibility for *economically productive women to participate equally with men* in the civil sphere, let alone the political sphere. Similarly, the fact that many of the second spate of acts confronted this particular structural aporia in the context of debates over the gendered form of freedpersons' contractual rights underscores the complex process of historical contingency at work in aporetic change. "The core of the problem was a wife's right to her own labor, wages, and person—a property right that the wage contract presumed but the marriage contract denied," Stanley (1998, 175) succinctly notes. Earnings acts "appeared to replicate the contract rights afforded to former [male] slaves. Yet the analogy was not so clear-cut, for the reforms did not nullify a husband's legal title to his wife's service at home." These historical impasses pinpoint aspects of the structural aporia that haunt us still today, on display in questions regarding women's self-ownership of and rights to their bodies as well as in questions of what constitutes fair recompense for women's productive labor. But that does not diminish the power of the antebellum woman's rights movement's accomplishments in refiguring Womanhood and thereby fundamentally reshaping the societal order. At a moment when the accidents of history combined to fulfill necessary but insufficient conditions for aporetic change, the 1850s woman's rights movement's fully discursive pressure succeeded in bringing forth from the aporetic site *the dawning of a civil existence for woman.*

Conclusion

STRUCTURAL APORIAS

Questions, Thoughts, and Contemporary Politics

> History is always in several places at once, there
> are always several histories underway; this is a
> high point in the history of women.
>
> —HÉLÈNE CIXOUS, IN CIXOUS AND CLEMENT,
> THE NEWLY BORN WOMAN

> In the instability and insecurity of global capital-
> ism, the economic actor, like the citizen in the
> modern nation, may become what is lost, and
> thus also the determining factor in new social
> consciousness.
>
> —SHANA COHEN, SEARCHING FOR A
> DIFFERENT FUTURE

IN THIS BOOK, I HAVE PROPOSED A NEW THEORETICAL
and methodological framework with which to analyze historically specific social orders and social movement, and I have
presented a detailed exemplar of its use. The structural aporetic analytic focuses on moments of societal rupture rather
than on social coherence—on the historically specific conditions of possibility for epistemic discontinuity inherent in any
social order's very constitution and on the historical process of

disruptive social change. And it suggests one way of analyzing the intricate imbrication of social meanings and institutions that constitute daily social life, not as separate analytic planes of ideas and practices but as a fully interimplicated system that constitutes our social world in its seeming solidity and its irruptive potential. Many questions remain and more will emerge as this theoretical framework is developed further. But three overarching questions linger regarding how structural aporias operate and what they offer, providing spurs for future thought and research. First, are structural aporias located outside of history, even as their very constitution and the *politics of the event* flowing through them can only be understood as the intricate and minute processes of history itself at work? Second, where might other structural aporias be located in the contemporary topography of the U.S. social order, and what current political movements reside in them and move through them? Third, what does a *history of the present* that investigates the social underpinnings of modern capitalist democracy—grounded in the nation-state, citizenship, and contract—offer present-day attempts to grapple with a future beyond: beyond the nation-state, beyond the modern subject?

The particular structural aporetic site and historical moment that I have interrogated came into existence with the social contract origin myths and political, economic, and legal institutions founding Western modernity. Based in particularly modern relations between Womanhood, contract, the economy, and the nation, this structural aporia partially constitutes and is constituted by a specific historical moment in a particular part of the world. Additionally, the complex process that enabled certain of modernity's conditions of possibility for disruptive change to be met and effectively put into play demonstrates history in process—the very movement of history. But, at a certain point in my analysis, the structural aporetic impasse comprising Womanhood and contract can seem to become a given. It is, after all, a *structural* aporia. Does this structural aporia change? And, if so, how and into what? These are difficult questions, and so far I have only incomplete answers: yes; it is not predetermined in any given case and depends on historical contingencies; and I do not know.

At any given time and place, structural aporias comprise the *always already there* parameters delimiting social meanings and institutions, but they equally comprise the contingent foundations that delineate daily life and through which radical social change is possible. For this reason, reading history asunder seeks the shape of a specific moment's particular contingent foundations, including their impasses, abysses, fissures. A structural aporia's shape provides a certain coherence to its social order's daily life while defining potential sites of disjunctive change for that same social order. As historical forces play in and move through a structural aporetic site, they can force epistemic social change of anywhere from minor to massive proportion. With each aporetic irruption, the shape of the structural aporia itself must shift. While a structural aporia composed of interimplicated relations between Womanhood, contract, the economy, and the nation still existed after the successes of the antebellum woman's rights movement, the form of their interimplications changed. How their strands intertwined changed form. Their very imbrication changed shape. In the first place, the social meanings and institutions themselves that constituted each of these components had changed. In the second place, the 1850s woman's movement for economic rights could not have succeeded if the form of their interimplications had not changed. But how were they newly imbricated? What new shape did the structural aporia take? And could this structural aporia, through further irruptions, eventually cease to exist? Or might it change into something entirely different, as the very concept of epistemic discontinuity implies? And would such a radical change be equivalent to its ceasing to exist? I have no full answer to these crucial questions. But I can suggest some of the ways this structural aporetic site has played out in the United States over the 150 years since the antebellum woman's rights movement as well as some distinct but related structural aporetic sites central to life in the United States today.

Three second-wave feminist causes—two lost in the legislature and one partially won—clearly engaged kernels of this structural aporia: comparable worth, the Equal Rights Amendment (ERA), and marital rape. Comparable worth would have restructured pay scales to reward equal pay for qualitatively equal work by evaluating and weighting all jobs against each other, thereby overcoming the problem of gender-specific occupations. If comparable worth had taken effect, it would have required economic restructuring on a national level. But it would also have required reconfiguring the social meanings and institutions that intertwined women's subjecthood, the family, the economy, labor, and the nation. Society's popular conception of women's relation to the family in the 1970s differed greatly from the 1850s understanding of Republican Womanhood, the True Woman, and Woman's Influence. And yet, clearly, comparable worth foundered in a reformulated version of the prior structural aporia. Its defeat marked one moment in a long genealogy that intrinsically links the 1850s woman's rights movement's demands for joint rights in family earnings, a husband's right to his wife's "performance of services to the family" (Kerber 1998, 121),[1] and the web of social meanings still entwining the nation's moral status with women's relations to motherhood and market labor. While, in practice, the radical economic restructuring required might have endangered the operations of the entire institutional web on which the American economy depended, this was not the flashpoint of the comparable worth struggle. Instead, it ignited the long-standing crucible of women's appropriate relation to the family, the economy, and the nation, with opponents arguing vociferously that it would be the downfall of all these institutions, taking the country down with them.

The overlapping struggle to enact the ERA, which would have ensured equal political and civil rights for women, was fired in almost the same crucible. Certainly the relations between womanhood, the family, and the (hetero)sexual-social contract were central to the contest. One of the major anti-ERA organizers, Phyllis Schlafly, "mobilized opponents of the ERA by arguing that it would constitutionalize abortion and homosexuality, which she condemned as potent symbols of the new family forms that the ERA would entrench" (Post and Siegel 2007, 418). In this fight, though, women's relation to physicality, citizenship, and the nation became an additional flashpoint. Much to my dismay, a group of my female senior honors classmates attending a high school soccer game in 1983 mirrored contemporary discourse when they bargained for sticks of gum from a similar group of male honors students with the following exchange: "Could we have some gum too?" "Do you support the ERA?" "No, I don't want to be drafted!" the girls replied in chorus. "Okay, then, you can have some," the boys demurred, as they handed the chewing gum around. As reflected in this anecdote, ERA politics stirred up kernels of a foundational aporia whose relations took on a slightly different shape than they did for comparable worth. This particular web of social meanings and institutions informs the aporetic location of certain late twentieth- and early twenty-first-century gay politics as well, engaging "what J. G. A. Pocock has called 'the [American] language of myth and metahistory' [that] connects citizenship to military service" (Kerber 1998, 242). It brought to the fore structured-in social meanings and institutions comprising the citizen-soldier, which ground legitimate citizenship in the modern nation-state. When the fundamental aporetic site constituting the citizen-soldier is put in peril, certain imbricated structural foundations of the modern nation are in turn endangered: homosocial bonding, citizenship, manhood, and the military. By placing these impassable foundations in jeopardy, the ERA threatened to make visible this societal abyss. In fact, when first-wave feminists fought their earlier battle for the ERA in 1921, the knotty entanglements of womanhood, economic labor, and military service proved to be central to their debates. For instance, a prominent feminist historian at that time, Mary Beard, explained why she opposed the ERA by referring to her experiences in postwar Europe, where she had witnessed "so much industrial equality that women sweep the streets and till the land while men drink in the cafés. I believe that women will be conscripted for war in the future" (cited in Kerber 1998, 245). The form the struggles over comparable worth and the ERA took in the 1970s stemmed in part from the earlier structural aporia analyzed in this book, but they entwined aspects of the aporia differently and combined them with other interimplicated societal categories. In other words, they resided in slightly different but entirely interrelated aporetic sites.

Over the past thirty-five years women have also fought to make marital rape illegal. The battle itself stems from and resides in the same Anglo-based democracy's structural aporia that I analyzed in this book, interimplicating women's civil subjecthood, marriage, contract, and property. Indeed, the antebellum woman's rights movement first fought this battle, demanding "woman's right of self-possession" and, not surprisingly, arguing for this right by deploying various figures of motherhood (Hasday 2000, 1414). But coverture's subjugation of Woman's civil existence to her husband continued to include property in her body and the ability to contract regarding use of her physical body, other than as market labor, long after the 1860s. Reading history aporetically helps to make sense of how the marital rape exemption outlasted the antebellum woman's movement as well as the first wave of feminism, and how the second and third waves of feminism have only gained "a confusing mix of victory and defeat" in courts and legislatures

(1375). Married woman's legal capacity to consent, the centerpiece of rape law to this day, could not exist until she had the right to contract, both socially and privately. Gaining that right, however, was a necessary but insufficient condition for her consent always being considered relevant, necessary, or legitimate regarding what happened to her own body and subject. As a result of women's movement pressure from the 1970s onward, states began to change the marital rape exemption, but frequently qualified its removal in the name of the family and the nation. For instance, under new laws, forcible sex between spouses often was considered rape only if it occurred in the presence of children or if the wife incurred clear bodily harm. Additionally, numerous states considered marital rape prosecutable only if the husband and wife lived separately; otherwise, "the [marital rape] exemption applie[d] in full force" (West 1989, 56–57). Consequently, in 1989, after legal reform, a woman still could not legally be raped by a husband she lived with in Kentucky, Louisiana, Maryland, Mississippi, Missouri, Montana, New Mexico, North Carolina, Oklahoma, South Carolina, South Dakota, Tennessee, and Utah (56–57). By 2006, "a majority of states still retain[ed] some form of the rule exempting a husband from prosecution for raping his wife . . . [whether] requir[ing] a couple to be separated at the time of the injury . . . [or] only recogniz[ing] marital rape if it involve[d] physical force and/or serious physical harm . . . [or] provid[ing] for vastly reduced penalties if a rape occurs in marriage, or creat[ing] special procedural requirements for marital rape prosecutions" (Hasday 2000, 1484–85).

A history of seemingly illogical state legislative debates and actions and judicial decisions also makes sense once read through this structural aporia. For instance, over the last course of feminist pressure on this particular aporetic site, legislatures actually extended the marital rape exemption to cohabitants in Pennsylvania, New Mexico, Minnesota, Montana, Kentucky, Louisiana, and Connecticut, and even further to "voluntary social companions" in New Hampshire (West 1989, 58; Hasday 2000, 1484). Minnesota's 1987 criminal statutes declared, "A person does not commit criminal sexual conduct . . . if the actor and complainant were adults cohabiting in an ongoing voluntary sexual relationship at the time of the alleged offense" (Minn. Stat. 609.349 [1987], cited in Hasday 2000, n. 408). Beyond that, single men accused or convicted of rape argued in court that their prosecution and conviction denied them equal protection under the Fourteenth Amendment. In other words, they argued that since a marital rape exemption existed, single men were being denied the rights of married men.[2]

In these ways, the marital rape exemption and the politics of date rape have engaged one of the structural aporia's final kernels. Battles over reproductive rights are still engaging it as well. But what new forms will it take? Again, only close historical analysis of its genealogical palimpsest can answer this question. Recent historical works have usefully traced intertwined histories of marriage, labor, race and racial construction, immigration, prostitution, and citizenship, all in relation to rights of consent and contract (see Cott 2000; Stanley 1998). Reading these histories asunder—renarrating them through a structural aporetic analytic—would undoubtedly provide some answers. But, while I analytically separated out certain relations to explore a particular structural aporia, it must not be forgotten that those relations are always intricately implicated with many others. For instance, when reading the histories of marriage, race, and immigration asunder, the process of locating and analyzing the relevant structural aporia would focus on contemporary and related, but slightly different, categories from women's subjecthood, contract, the economy, and the nation. A contemporary and related, but somewhat different, structural aporia would be implicated, even as all the prior categories remain relevant to it. In other words, multiple structural aporias are always operative and interlinked, even as they irrupt and shift shape. *History is always in several places at once; there are always several histories underway.*

In this vein, I would venture that the past decade's battles over gay rights to marriage reside in and flow through a related structured-in foundational impasse of modern capitalist democracies that interimplicates contract, marriage, and legitimated subjecthood in the polity and civil society. Proponents of the Defense of Marriage Act of 1996 made its relation transparent in the House debates.[3] In eerie similarity to legislative declarations from the 1850s, Representative James M. Talent of Missouri pronounced, "It is an act of hubris to believe that marriage can be infinitely malleable, that it can be pushed and pulled around like silly-putty without destroying its essential stability and what it means to our society, and if marriage goes, then the family goes, and if the family goes, we have none of the decency or ordered liberty which Americans have been brought up to enjoy and to appreciate. That is what this bill is about" (7446). In opening the debate, Representative

Charles T. Canady of Florida proclaimed that the question of gay marriage "is far from a trivial political issue." He asked, "What is at stake in this controversy? Nothing less than our collective moral understanding— as expressed in the law—of the essential nature of the family—the fundamental building block of society. . . . I believe that the traditional family structure—centered on a lawful union between one man and one woman—. . . is one of the essential foundations on which our civilization is based" (7441). Yet the underlying structural aporia has some different focal points from the one analyzed in this book. The structural aporia relevant to gay marriage politics imbricates these categories with heteronormative requirements of citizenship, which I suggest stem in part from the underlying homosociality of male citizenship and its relationship to manhood and military bonding in both origin myths[4] and contemporary conceptions and institutions. From those intertwined relations, what I suspect is the underlying focal site comes into view, illuminated additionally and even more clearly in the flashpoints of battles over gays in the military.

Again, read asunder, some right-wing pundits' seeming incoherence on the subject—their insistence that (legibly) allowing gays into the military would cause chaos in the very foundations of military order and the nation—portrays an accurate sense of the aporetic nature of the site. Discursive underpinnings of modern nationhood and citizenship relate intense male homosocial bonding—kept in check by heteronormativity and yet more powerful than any heterosexual bonding—to manhood, military service, and the very constitution of citizens whose cohesion defines a nation. These, in turn, hold a specific relation to the social meanings and institutions surrounding the family. I do not in any way agree with right-wing pundits' political positions on the issue. But I do believe that reshaping these aporetic sites is a necessary condition for winning these battles. In other words, progressive forces must address these foundational aporetic sites head on, refiguring their various internal relations that together constitute our contemporary tropes of family, citizenship, and the nation.

Ironically, Representative Bob Barr of Georgia declared his opposition to gay marriage in the 1996 House debates by exhorting its supporters to do just this: "Marriage does not mean two men or two women getting married. It just does not mean that. You can say it does, but it does not. You are talking about something completely different. If that is what you want, then come up with legislation and say, that is what we want. We want to redefine the basic building block on which our society was founded, and then let us have a debate about it" (7445). Recognizing the structural aporetic analytic and practicing reading history asunder obliges us to heed Derrida's ethical call to experience the aporetic promise of democracy—*to nonpassively endure the aporia as the condition of responsibility and of decision*—and to place pressure on society at large to do the same. In this case, such resistance requires refiguring society's systematic relations between the citizen-soldier, the family, the nation, manhood, and womanhood. The political manifesto and petition "Beyond Same-Sex Marriage: A New Strategic Vision for All Our Families and Relationships" (2006), written by queer activists and theorists, does just this. It argues for a restructuring of the very institutions composing civil society: "All families, relationships, and households struggling for stability and economic security will be helped by separating basic forms of legal and economic recognition from the requirement of marital and conjugal relationship." And it makes this argument by refiguring the web of social meanings that imbricates the family, positing that "marriage should be one of many avenues through which households, families, partners, and kinship relationships can gain access to the support of a caring civil society." Its analytically cogent list of demands points directly at the aporetic site studied in this book, as it is entangled with citizenship and heteronormativity:

> Legal recognition for a wide range of relationships, households, and families, and for the children in all of those households and families, including same-sex marriage, domestic partner benefits, second-parent adoptions, and others. . . .
> The separation of benefits and recognition from marital status, citizenship status, and the requirement that "legitimate" relationships be conjugal. . . .
> Recognition of interdependence as a civic principle and practical affirmation of the importance of joining with others (who may or may not be LGBT) who also face opposition to their household and family compositions, including old people, immigrant communities, single parents, battered women, prisoners and former prisoners, people with disabilities, and poor people.

But even without recognizing the aporetic site, the more narrow same-sex marriage battle does force a crack in the societal regulation of an appropriately gendered, sexed, raced, classed, citizen-ed family by pushing that regulation into the open and into debate. The legislative debates and public hoopla surrounding the Defense of Marriage Acts voted on in numerous states remove the veil from the aporetic site and its impassable, impossible, foundational heteronormativity. "It is for this reason that marriage matters" (Brandzel 2005, 179).

As we press toward the future, invoking democracy's inherent promise of justice-not-yet-reached, economic and political institutions and meanings are in the throes of global reorganization. Whether we live in a new modernism or a postmodernism, we enter it from a particular point, or, actually, many particular points. Each nation or region operates through particular interimplicated cultural, political, and economic frames—through particular imbricated sets of social meanings and institutions—and these found and structure its move into global relations. They equally found and structure the formation of global subjects. The United States and Morocco, for example, enter a world of increasingly global economic, political, and cultural relations with very different genealogical palimpsests, with very different *histories of the present.* Americans and Moroccans experience a global subjecthood delimited by very different present histories of subjecthood, and they influence the formation of a new global subject from their grounding in these very different sites. At a time often experienced as movement into the beyond—beyond the nation-state, beyond the local economic and political actor, beyond the subject, beyond the cohesive self—an analysis of the modern nation-state's and citizen's figuring, refiguring, disfiguring, and transfiguring can seem stuck in the old world. But such structural aporetic analyses delineate the shifting grounds from which we step into the beyond, providing us a necessary starting point for responsible engagement with the future. For if, in the trajectory of globalization, the modern economic actor and national citizen *might become what is lost,* the precise moment and shape of the various national and regional sites from which they were lost will *thus also be the determining factor in new social consciousness,* in new social orders. It will be a determining factor in the history of the future.

NOTES

PART I

1. Women's role in representing ethnic differences is, of course, directly related to and intertwined with the racial aspects of True Womanhood's social meanings. Only the Truly pure, the Truly pious, could become True Women. All others were *beyond* Womanhood. Given immigration numbers and ethnic differences in the population at the time, the "others" were Catholics and non-English immigrants from northern and western Europe, as well as, of course, African slaves and freedpersons and Native Americans. Mass immigration from south and central Europe remained minimal until the 1870s and 1880s (Lieberson 1980).

1. TRUE WOMANHOOD

1. This same pamphlet was reissued by the author in 1880 under the title of *Industrial Independence of Women; Through Their Equal Income, and Equal Suffrage.* Bryan J. Butts was a resident of the religious community of Hopedale, Massachusetts, where most of his pamphlets were published. The community as a whole "recogniz[ed] and accept[ed] the obligations imposed upon [them by their Charter, or 'Standard,' and] had heartily espoused the Anti-Slavery, Temperance, and Peace movements, and had borne faithful witness in the pulpit and elsewhere against the great evils they were designed to overcome and banish from the world" (Ballou 1897, 13). The Standard, or Declaration of Sentiments, of the community was signed upon its founding, and was explicitly religious, antigovernment, pacifist, and activist: "We hold ourselves bound to do good as we have opportunity unto all mankind, to feed the hungry, clothe the naked, minister to the sick, visit the imprisoned, entertain the stranger, protect the helpless, comfort the afflicted, plead for the oppressed, seek the lost, lift up the fallen, rescue the ensnared, reclaim the wandering, reform the vicious, enlighten the benighted, instruct the young, admonish

the wayward, rebuke the scornful, encourage the penitent, confirm the upright, and diffuse a universal charity" (4–5). Butts's many pamphlets (1856, 1860, 1871, [post-1873], 1880), also delivered as speeches and inspirational discourses on various occasions, addressed the political issue of slavery and expanded the community's politics to include woman's rights as well as discussing economic and moral principles.

2. In other words, the antebellum woman's rights movement was significant *not* because "its mature critique was not confined to women's issues," as Nancy Isenberg (1998, 204) posits, but because "its mature critique" demonstrated that women's issues were one with the fundamental issues of the economy and the nation.

3. Jonathan Arac (1979, 31–32) created the term "reading asunder" specifically to refer to a process of literary close reading that he juxtaposes against "try[ing] to hold the lines [of a text] ever more closely together . . . engag[ing] in a glossing that knits parts into a comprehensive totality. . . . Such a reading [asunder] might open a space between parts of the poem . . . point[ing] toward problems within any state of the text, [toward] lines that run in different directions to form a 'palimpsest.'"

4. As Mary Jo Buhle and Paul Buhle (1978, xviii) remark in their preface to an edited and severely pared-down version of the classic work, "The *History of Woman Suffrage* is neither a comprehensive record of the struggle for women's enfranchisement nor a historical interpretation of the movement's course. Rather, the six volumes compiled over forty years by a series of editors offer a vast compendium of reminiscences, reports, propagandistic arguments, and commentaries unevenly shaped by the logic of the suffrage cause and its leading intellectuals."

5. In the past few decades, feminist historians have also written numerous individual and collective autobiographies of female activists from this era (for instance, Lerner 1967; Painter 1996; Sklar 1973; Yee 1992). While they begin from the lives of individual women to highlight contemporary social formations, this study moves in the other direction, examining social formations to highlight the historical and cultural conditions of possibility within which individuals interacted. Consequently, I draw on them here only to provide discrete pieces of historical data.

6. Linda K. Kerber and Jane Sherron De Hart's sixth edition (2004) of their rightly influential seven-hundred-plus-page compendium of American women's history from 1600 to the present day, *Women's America: Refocusing the Past,* provides a telling example. In section II of the book, "The Many Frontiers of Industrializing America, 1820–1900" (129–296), they cover the period from 1848 to the Civil War with the following articles and documents: an article on social networks and the 1848 Seneca Falls Convention by Judith Wellman, the entirety of the 1848 Declaration of Sentiments from Seneca Falls, one page that has brief snippets of the New York State Married Women's Property Acts from 1848 and 1860, and a two-page note considering Sojourner Truth's iconic 1851 statements and status by Nell Irvin Painter. Women's activism in the 1850s remains unwritten. More worrisome, since

space always constrains and forces choices of inclusion on editors, is that the Married Women's Property Acts are presented solely as representations of the limits placed on antebellum women (and as providing some extensions of those limits): "Note the limits of the 1848 New York law and the ways in which women's rights were extended by the 1860 revision. In 1860 married women were also confirmed in the joint guardianship of their children" (217). Please note that the 1860 law "extended" the 1848 law and, even in its extensions, it "also confirmed [married women] in [their] joint guardianship." In other words, the laws were active; their passage and the women on whom they acted were both passive. The accompanying text that Kerber and De Hart provide makes no mention, suggestion, or even implicit reference to any active struggle or meaningful social change embedded in the passage of these laws.

7. This is not to suggest that participation in capitalism is in and of itself a libratory goal, but rather that legitimate civil participation in a social order is desirable for anyone who is subject to it.

8. To clarify, by "strategic effect," I do not refer to conscious strategizing in the sense in which the word is usually used. Rather, I refer to the historical result of discursive—cultural, political, and economic—conjunctures that are specifically *not* the result of individual, or even collective, actors' decisions. I do not mean to suggest that the actors involved had no strategy of their own in mind; I simply mean that, even though this was not necessarily their conscious tactic for systems-level struggle, it is analytically useful to view their actions *as if* it were, given the relevant historical effects.

9. There has been some debate as to the historical significance of the Earnings Act's passage in 1860. Even as she argues that the 1850s woman's movement attempted to radically resituate women's economic and contractual position, Reva B. Siegel (1994, 1079, 1104) positions the Earnings Act of 1860 as a defeat of that attempt in that passage of legislation that reflected their strongest formulations of women's equality in economic life was not achieved (1136). She also notes that judges tended to interpret the act as narrowly as possible for years to come. On the other hand, Carole Shammas (1994, 21) points out that women's share of wealth and, more specifically, married women's share of women's wealth (as measured through probate documents in Massachusetts) increased more "between the 1860s and the 1890s than had transpired in the previous two hundred years of American history." The details are telling:

> Massachusetts had passed its principal legislation in the 1840s and in 1855. Back in 1829–31, 16 percent of probated estates belonged to women and they accounted for about 7 percent of total probated wealth. These percentages were not terribly different from the 9 percent of probated decedents who were women in late seventeenth-century Essex County, Massachusetts and their 4.3 percent of total probated wealth. In the post-legislation period, 1859–61,

over one quarter of probated estates belonged to women, and they had doubled
their share of wealth. In 1880, the proportion of probate participation and
of total wealth continued to rise. And by the 1890s, the results are striking:
42.8 percent of probates were women and they owned over one quarter of total wealth. (20)

As I note later, Siegel's position is not counter to mine, as it first appears. I believe
our arguments complement each other. I argue that, in their struggle for economic
equality, woman's rights activists dramatically shifted the very ground on which
Woman could be thought in relation to the economy. So, while they may not have
been able to gain the strongest legislation at this time, or even ensure the strongest
enforcement of the legislation they did gain, their fight to radically resituate wom-
en's economic position had in fact succeeded in ways that would affect life in the
United States to this day. The ways in which they did not succeed would also affect
daily life to this day.

10. Interestingly, according to federal census data, more than 90 percent of women
married between 1835 and 1980, excluding those born during the period 1860
to 1880. Women born in these two decades saw the highest percentage of never
marrying, ranging from 10 to 11.1 percent. These would have been precisely those
women born into a newly emerging order of Womanhood—an order not yet fully
gelled as they grew up (Degler 1980a, 152).

11. While Basch (1982), Thurman (1966), and Warbasse (1987) all inform the discussion in the next two paragraphs, Basch provides a particularly useful summary of
married women's legal disabilities under coverture (51–55).

12. What now seems a strange, almost nonsensical, legal regulation of land inheritance is in fact a symptom of the maelstrom of change concurrent with the shift
from an economy based in landed capital to one based in financial capital. This
same jolting transformation affected relations between the historical institutions
of property and marriage and the social meanings of the economy and Womanhood, as detailed in chapters 2–4.

13. See note 9 above.

2. READING ANTEBELLUM HISTORY APORETICALLY

1. The grammatical and figural dimensions of language are further discussed below.

2. It is entirely relevant that even within this "relatively simple" discussion of aporetic
form, the figure of Woman serves only and importantly as an unnamed signifier.
The example cannot exist without Woman and simultaneously exists precisely
only with/out Woman, as I suggest is also the case in the aporetic space of democracy's founding myth and symbolic representation, the social contract.

3. In this effort, I maintain a modified view of what is meant by "ideology" and prefer
to draw on the concept as little as possible. The power of Foucault's conception of
discourse and my use of discursive politics is precisely that they deploy their "pro-

ductions, discriminations, censorship, interdictions, and invalidations . . . at the level of base, not of superstructure," as opposed to traditional and classical Marxist uses of "ideology" (Said 1978, 705).

4. Jonathan Culler (1982) addresses the reaction in the humanities that interprets the concept of unknowability as nihilism. His point remains just as applicable for the social sciences: "In mathematics, for example, Gödel's demonstration of the incompleteness of metamathematics (the impossibility of constructing a theoretical system within which all true statements of number theory are theorems) does not lead mathematicians to abandon their work. The humanities, however, often seem touched with the belief that a theory which asserts the ultimate indeterminacy of meaning makes all effort pointless. The fact that such assertions emerge from discussions that propose numerous particular determinations of meaning, specific interpretations of passages and texts, should cast doubts upon an impetuous nihilism" (133).

5. Such a *history of the present* offers a new and critical basis for strategic decision making by both hegemonic and counterhegemonic groups and forces.

6. Culler's translation (1982, 277).

7. Reasons for this delimitation are detailed below.

8. While the specifics of the state of nature and civil society differ within the various theories, feminist political theorists have focused on the extent to which they position women similarly. For instance, Linda K. Kerber (1997, 205) points out that while the "great texts of the Enlightenment—notably those of Rousseau . . . and of Montesquieu . . . —addressed directly and with great subtlety the problem of how to invent a state that has the power to preserve order yet in which it is also possible for individuals to preserve their own integrity and authenticity," these individuals were always specifically and only male.

9. Here, reading aporetically suggests another reason that second-wave feminist analysis focused on the public/private divide: it is the site of a key gendered structural aporia in Anglo-based democracies. See, for instance, Rosaldo and Lamphere's (1974) anthology for classic, early feminist discussions of the public/private distinction theorizing women's realm, the private and domestic realm, as intermediary between culture and nature and perceived as closer to nature than the public realm; see especially the Rosaldo, Chodorow, and Ortner triumvirate of articles. See also Elshtain (1981) and Okin (1979). Anne Phillips's (1991) more recent investigations implicate how liberal democracy, participatory democracy, and civic republicanism each gender spheres of societal activity and participation, thereby delimiting the potential for women's legitimate civic and political subjecthood under each democratic form.

10. Concomitant with second-wave feminism's focus on the concept of a public/private divide, feminist lesbian theory proposed clear resistive myths to the heterosexual "traffic in women" embedded within that divide. Again, a structural aporetic

reading of gender in Western democracies suggests that the focus of this response is not surprising, which does not detract from the many important insights gained therein. See Rubin (1985) for the classic feminist theorization of the gendered and patriarchal institutional and psychological structures involved in the mythical move from nature to culture, with results convergent with Pateman's. See, for instance, Irigaray (1980) for a provocative second-wave lesbian feminist response to these societal structures of "traffic in women."

11. On state laws granting feme sole status to married women, see Warbasse (1987, 20); Salmon (1986, 46–49).

12. Although these questions are not further engaged in this book, a structural aporetic analytic might provide new approaches to the historical record when developed along these lines, allowing scholars to tease out the relations of single heterosexual women and lesbians to the economy and polity in new ways.

13. See *Frazier v. State* 86 S.W. 854 (Texas 1905), in which the marital rape exemption stood despite separate abodes of residence because the court had refused the wife's petition for divorce, or *Regina v. Miller* [9154] 2 All E.R. 529, in which the marital rape exemption stood even after the wife had filed for divorce. By 1980, a number of states still had "[made] no exceptions for separation agreements or interlocutory decrees of divorce" (Barry 1980, 1099). While today a woman's choice to leave her husband and live separately without consulting the state has to some extent been recognized as abrogating the husband's marital rape exemption, limitations on what can be charged as rape in these cases still exist. For example, in South Carolina, even when residing apart from the spouse, "a person cannot be guilty of criminal sexual conduct . . . if the victim is the legal spouse unless . . . the offending spouse's conduct constitutes criminal sexual conduct in the first degree or second degree" (S.C. Code Ann. 16–3–659 [Law. Co-op Supp. 1999], cited in Hasday 2000, n. 408).

14. See Barry (1980, 1088); Freeman (1981–1982, 8–17). Beyond this, some courts have suggested that if a woman refuses to perform both acts legally constituting the marriage contract, the husband should force her to do so, that is, rape her, so that they will be married and he will then have immunity from rape. For example, in a 1974 English case, Lord Dunedin ruled, "If the wife is adamant in her refusal the husband must choose between letting his wife's will prevail, thus wrecking the marriage, and acting without her consent" (in *G. v. G.* Crim. App. 357, cited in Freeman 1981–1982, 21).

15. Even in the less than desirable free labor contracts of the nineteenth-century United States, the legal power given to the employer was that of wage forfeiture; that is, the employer could withhold the promised wages if he claimed the laborer had breached the contract, but he could not legally physically force labor from the worker (Steinfeld 2001, 10).

16. This word is partly unreadable in the original document.

17. Some historians have argued that "domestic feminism" enabled women to move outward into the social realm as they successfully redefined social issues as do-

mestic issues, as issues that they as mothers and domestic caretakers should have charge over. These included issues such as poverty, housing, social welfare, and birth control (Degler 1980a; Riley 1988; D. S. Smith 1979). However, I am aware of no similar discussion of women's movement into the economic realm, which required a shift from Woman's Influence through benevolence and charity work that "domestic feminism" did not. Elizabeth Bowles Warbasse (1987) does argue that women's attainment of "financial and legal independence within the home" was necessary prior to obtaining extradomestic political rights such as suffrage. She conceptualizes legal and economic rights as domestic relations, though, as opposed to relations defining women's position within society at large (ii). She does suggest that becoming "an individual recognized by law" was extremely important to women's "happiness," but does not suggest any changes in the broader social meaning or understanding of women's position concomitant with or in relation to women's new legal status (307).

3. GENDERED ECONOMIES

1. Barbara Leslie Epstein (1981) provides a detailed analysis of this historical moment and process.
2. Historians generally place literacy among the native-born middling and upper classes at over 90 percent at this time. New York State censuses of 1855 and 1865 certainly support this statistic and, in fact, suggest that this statistic might be generalized to the population as a whole. (Of course, eastern and southern European immigration had hardly begun at this point; most immigrants still came from Anglophone countries; Lieberson 1980.) Statistics I have culled and estimated from the 1855 New York State census suggest that of a total population over the age of twenty-one of 1,788,037 (estimated), 92.03 percent could read and write. Only 46,509 (2.60 percent) were reported as able to read but not write; 96,489 (5.40 percent) were reported unable to read or write ("Recapitulation of Population, Colors, Sexes, Civil Condition, &c.," "Recapitulation of Ages and Sexes," in New York State, Secretary's Office 1857). Statistics from the 1865 New York State census suggest that of a total population of 1,953,786 (estimated) over the age of twenty-one, 93.76 percent were able to read and write. It reports that 26,093 (1.34 percent) could read and not write, and only 95,865 (4.91 percent) could neither read nor write (New York State, Secretary's Office 1867, lvii, lxxxiv–lxxxv).
3. All data on business incorporations are culled from Evans (1948). Unless otherwise noted, the data cited are from page 17.
4. All data on Erie Canal tonnage reported in this paragraph and the next come from North (1961, 251).
5. I do not consider the data reliable enough to derive changes in share of production or share of market from them. Production for market was still too volatile and data collection was still too rudimentary to have successfully included all relevant

categories of production or to accurately reflect market production's changing entanglements with domestic production.

6. Temin (1969) makes this claim in the context of arguing that prices were more flexible than production in large eastern cities and that therefore short panics with fairly stable production in the East and decreased prices meant that real income may not have fallen as precipitously as unemployment figures for eastern cities make it appear.

7. Expected return is used here in the legal sense of the calculation of expectation damages rather than in the economic sense of rational decision-making functions over time. While they are somewhat related, they are not the same.

8. I am, of course, not discounting the operation and effects of economic regularities that can be traced with any growth of capitalist markets or of technological innovations. They simply do not pertain to the questions that I am addressing as I narrate these moments of social dislocation that are inherent in transformative social change, whether it is progressive or regressive, revolutionary or reactionary.

9. Changes in legal institutions are investigated further in chapter 4.

10. Data from before 1855 are not well standardized across county censuses in New York State.

11. The *Census of the State of New York, for 1865* includes a 123-page introduction consisting entirely of compiled data comparing the 1855 and 1865 census results. It should be noted that the 1865 census inspired fear in some of the populace that it would be used in connection with military service (since the Civil War was an overwhelming reality at the time) or taxation (see "Preface," in New York State, Secretary's Office 1867). This should not make my use of the comparative data any less persuasive, however, for these fears would have led to undercounting in 1865 relative to 1855. The disorder experienced in the rapid economic transformation of this time would therefore be underestimated, and not overestimated, by these figures.

12. All the following figures are calculated from comparative occupational data provided in the preface to the 1865 census (New York State, Secretary's Office 1867, lxxv).

13. Reported total New York State population rose from 3,466,212 to 3,831,777 over the course of this decade—an increase of only 10.5 percent, significantly less than that experienced by any of the occupational categories above or following (New York State, Secretary's Office 1867, xlii–xliii).

14. For a discussion of guard labor, see Bowles et al. (1990, 195).

15. Some speculators also gambled on newly changing land prices.

16. The pamphlet press proliferated during this era and served as one aspect of a public debate over pressing issues. It is not well documented or studied, however. As a major bibliographic effort of the historic pamphlet press notes, "Despite the historic significance of pamphlets in shaping and reflecting our past, they have rarely

flowed into channels sifted by scholars. The reasons are not difficult to discern. Most pamphlets were privately printed, in limited editions, with local, uncertain distribution. Major universities and institutions have been unable to collect more than a fraction of the total, and even these collections have been difficult to organize. Indeed, most collections are incomplete, uncataloged, and inaccessible, leaving the scholar at sea" (Barnard 1979).

17. Popular conceptions and legal understandings are clearly not the same entity sociologically, although they are equally clearly intertwined. During this period, jurists were being forced to negotiate changing popular practice in relation to landed property through their opinions. Consequently, and without drawing any specific conclusions about the flow dynamics between legal meanings and larger social meanings, jurists' negotiations of cases brought at common law (by nonlegal members of the populace) can serve as a broad marker of the shifts in meaning of property that were occurring in the 1800s and the extent of their impact on concurrent refiguring of the social. That is, they provide a broad marker of the extent to which these changes are intertwined in a changing web of social meanings, in particular with meanings of the economy, Womanhood, and the nation.

18. The legal history outlined in this paragraph is drawn primarily from Horwitz (1977, 31–62), which provides a rigorous and detailed study of jurists' shifting conceptions of property from 1780 to 1860.

19. I rely heavily on Linda K. Kerber's (1980, 1997) two book-length studies for my description of the figure of the Republican Mother and its emergence.

20. By focusing on True Womanhood's rise to hegemony from 1820 to the 1850s, I do not mean to suggest that it was the only existing way of thinking about Womanhood. Implicit in the concept of hegemony is contestation, no matter how minimal—contestation not merely reactive, but also specifically proactive. For instance, Frances B. Cogan (1989) demonstrated that a cogent notion of Real Womanhood arose from 1840 to 1880 in advice and health literature, providing women with an alternative to True Womanhood. Real Womanhood "advocated intelligence, physical fitness and health, self-sufficiency, economic self-reliance, and careful marriage" (4). In addition, in chapter 5, I analyze the significant ways in which the antebellum woman's movement rearticulated and refigured the very image of True Womanhood to include economic and contractual relations as a central aspect of the True Woman's sphere, reworking the imbrications of Womanhood, contract, property, the economy, and the democratic nation. These challenges do not diminish the fact of True Womanhood's hegemony from 1820 to the 1850s; rather, they were challenges precisely to its hegemony.

21. *Woman's Mission* actually ends by calling for women's equal political rights, attempting the sort of refiguring of Womanhood that I detail in chapter 5.

22. This would serve as one of a number of iconic representations of slavery's oppression (see, for instance, Newman 1999).

23. See chapter 1.

24. Theories of civilization as race-based and biologically hereditable also presumed nongendering of populations not considered white. "In 1897, William I. Thomas, a social scientist at the University of Chicago, specified with utmost clarity the concept of the evolutionary connection between sexual difference and racial progress: 'The less civilized the race the less is the physical difference of the sexes.' Or to put the same relationship another way around: the more civilized the race, the more the men and women of that race [differed] from one another" (Newman 1999, 34).

25. Hazel Carby (1987) was first to renarrate Cooper's remark in a similar manner. Charles Lemert's (1998) later and much fuller tracing of Cooper's activist deployment of social meanings and other scholars' various narrations of their meaning comes closest to my reading. He remarks:

> Today, it is well understood that whenever voice is seized by a formerly silent people, the terms of political representation in the social whole also change. Both liberal and Left ideals of democratic participation have been severely challenged in the past quarter century, mostly by the emergence of formerly colonized peoples in the arena once controlled univocally by the Euro-American dominant classes. While Cooper could not have had access to our understandings, she was in her day, at the end of the nineteenth century, attempting to do just what the decolonizing and related social movements have done in the last generations of the twentieth—and this is surely what Hazel Carby is driving at in her interpretation of Cooper as a virtual decolonizer before the fact. Cooper was, most self-consciously, seeking to give voice to black women in America by creating, then assuming, the representative position of the Black Woman of the South. (34)

26. See, for instance, DuCille (1994).

4. GENDERED LAW

1. Or, at least, this reformulation of what was a national discourse of Womanhood should be considered equally as important as the history of lingering court refusals to succumb to changes that new discursive formulations and legislation offered women. See Siegel (1994) for a compelling argument that the married women's property acts should not be considered watersheds for women's rights as they did not legislate activists' strongest demands for economic equality (joint property statutes) and frequently were not upheld in court decisions in the following decades.

2. This note relies on a combined reading of several of Durkheim's works. See Durkheim (1915/1965, 1982, 1984) and Durkheim and Mauss (1963). As Jeffrey C. Alexander (2004) has pointed out, this process of societal integration is decidedly more complex in today's modern and secular societies.

3. When published, his speech filled eighty-three pamphlet pages.

4. For Blackstone's theory of legal unity, see chapter 2.

5. In this section, I rely primarily on Basch (1982) and Warbasse (1987) for information on the common law disabilities of wives in the United States.

6. I rely heavily on Warbasse (1987, 29–50) for the early history of Chancery, or the Equity Court.

7. Interestingly, the history of petitioning Equity Courts with pleas to correct individual injustices can be seen as an aspect of the battle over whether women activists had the right of petition over political issues in the nineteenth century. In her study of women's antislavery petitioning, Susan Zaeske (2003, 1) notes that an antislavery petition sent to Congress by a group of Ohio women in 1834 marked the first time American women had "collectively petition[ed] Congress on a political issue. In so doing they defied the long-standing custom of females limiting their petition of Congress to individual prayers regarding personal grievances," which had been women's right under Anglo law for a number of centuries.

8. I rely heavily on Cook's (1981) seminal study for the history of the codification movement.

9. The New York State Constitutional Convention of 1846 was covered in its entirety by two pairs of reporters for competing Albany newspapers: William G. Bishop and William H. Attree for *The Evening Atlas* and S. Croswell and R. Sutton for *The Albany Argus.* Since Bishop's and Attree's report contains some information that Croswell and Sutton's does not, I cite Bishop and Attree in the text throughout. For all historical details included in both reports, I include the Croswell and Sutton citations in the endnotes. Croswell and Sutton 1846, 794–95.

10. Croswell and Sutton, 812.

11. Croswell and Sutton, 795.

12. Croswell and Sutton, 811.

13. Croswell and Sutton, 812.

14. Croswell and Sutton, 813.

15. In this section, I rely primarily on Thurman (1966) and Warbasse (1987) for information on married women's property acts through 1848.

16. "Debates over the rights of creditors played an important part in the development of married women's law" throughout the century, not just with the early acts (Chused 1985, 5). But legislatures' continued negotiation of relations between creditors and debtors does not in any way negate the point that the early acts negotiated *only* this issue, while an address of women's aporetic relation to Womanhood, property, and contract was fundamental to the later acts.

5. THE ANTEBELLUM WOMAN'S MOVEMENT

1. Lori D. Ginzberg (2005) traces myriad earlier stirrings of the woman's movement through a heretofore ignored 1846 petition for woman's rights in New York State. John F. McClymer (1999) refocuses attention on the 1850 National Woman's Rights Convention as a starting point for a truly active movement.

2. This and other similarly cited references refer to materials found in the scrapbooks of Susan B. Anthony, which she donated to the Library of Congress at the turn of the twentieth century. The scrapbooks are not paginated, but all references here come from Scrapbook No. 1.

3. With the notable exception of members of a few religious minorities, such as Hicksite Quakers.

4. As I indicated in chapter 1, this term refers to the result of fully discursive—cultural and institutional—conjunctures rather than to conscious strategizing. I simply mean that, even though it was not the singular actors' conscious tactic, it can be analytically useful to view their actions *as if* this was their strategy, given the relevant historical effects.

5. Personal communication, Jim Folts, Reference Librarian, New York State Records at New York State Archives, January 1997.

6. See chapter 2.

7. See chapter 2.

8. See chapter 4 for a detailed discussion.

CONCLUSION: STRUCTURAL APORIAS

1. As late as 1995, damages for a husband's loss of his wife's performance of services were still a viable part of an accident liability suit covering injuries sustained by the wife.

2. See, for example, *People v. Liberta* 474 N.E. 2d 567 (New York 1984).

3. All references to this debate rely on "Defense of Marriage Act" (1996).

4. For instance, see social contract origin myths and Sigmund Freud's (1991a, 1991b) reading of narcissism and paranoia.

BIBLIOGRAPHY

MANUSCRIPTS AND SPECIAL COLLECTIONS

Brown University, John Hay Library

Library of Congress
- Manuscript Division
  - Papers of Susan B. Anthony
- Rare Books and Special Collections Division
  - Miscellaneous Pamphlets Collection
  - National American Woman Suffrage Association Collection
  - Susan B. Anthony Collection

New York Public Library
- Uncatalogued Pamphlets, Woman—Legal Status

New York State Library
- Manuscripts and Special Collections

Vassar College Library
- Alma Lutz Collection

PUBLIC DOCUMENTS

"Beyond Same-Sex Marriage: A New Strategic Vision for All Our Families and Relationships." July 26, 2006. Text of petition located at www.beyondmarriage.org/full_statement.html.

"Defense of Marriage Act" (H.R. 3396). 1996. *Congressional Record* 142, no. 102 (July 11): H7441. Available from LexisNexis Congressional, Accessed September 20, 2006.

Documents of the Assembly of the State of New-York, 1840–60.

Documents of the Senate of the State of New-York, 1847.

Journal of the Assembly of the State of New-York, 1835–60.

Journal of the Convention of the State of New-York, Begun and Held at the Capitol in the City of Albany, on the First Day of June, 1846. Albany: Carroll and Cook.

Journal of the Senate of the State of New-York, 1848–60.

Laws of the State of New-York, 1848–62.

New York State, Secretary's Office. 1857. *Census of the State of New-York, for 1855; taken in pursuance of article third of the constitution of the state, and of chapter sixty-four of the laws of 1855. Franklin B. Hough, Superintendant of the Census.* Albany: Charles Van Benthuysen.

———. 1867. *Census of the State of New York, for 1865. Taken in pursuance of article third of the constitution of the state, and of chapter sixty-four of the laws of 1855, and chapter thirty-four of the laws of 1865. Franklin B. Hough, Superintendant of the Census.* Albany: Charles Van Benthuysen and Sons.

PRIMARY DOCUMENTS

1848. "The First Convention Ever Called to Discuss the Civil and Political Rights of Women, Seneca Falls, NY, July 19, 20, 1848." Call for convention. Seneca County Courier, July 14.

1853. *Declaration of Sentiments, Put forth at Seneca Falls, July 19th and 20th, 1848. Bound with Speech of Mrs. E. L. Rose, at the Woman's Rights Convention, Held at Syracuse, Sept. 1852. Bound as Woman's Rights Tracts, . . . No. 9 in Woman's Rights Commensurate with Her Capacities and Obligations. A Series of Tracts.* Syracuse, N. Y.: J. E. Masters.

Alcott, William A. 1850. *Letters to a Sister; or Woman's Mission.* Buffalo, N. Y.: Geo. H. Derby.

Anon. 1840. *Woman's Mission.* New York: Wiley and Putnam.

———. 1850a. "The Appropriate Sphere of Woman." *The Lily* 2 (June): 44.

———. 1850b. *Debtor and Creditor.*

———. 1850c. "Have Women Souls?" *The Lily* 2 (March): 21.

———. 1852. "Woman's Rights." *The Lily* 4 (December): 104.

———. 1854. "The Rochester Woman's Rights Convention." *The Lily* 6 (January).

Anthony, Susan B. [n. p.] 1837. *Scrap books containing the history of the woman movement from 1837 to 1900. Vol. 1.* 1848–64. In Susan B. Anthony Collection, Rare Books and Special Collections Division, Library of Congress.

———. 1852. "Delivered for the first at Batavia, May 1852." Unpublished speech. In Container 7, Papers of Susan B. Anthony, Manuscript Division, Library of Congress.

———. 1853. "Expediency." Unpublished speech. In Container 7, Papers of Susan B. Anthony, Manuscript Division, Library of Congress.

———. 1859. "Make the Slaves' Case Our Own." Unpublished speech. In Container 7, Papers of Susan B. Anthony, Manuscript Division, Library of Congress.

B., A. 1854. "What Woman Needs." *The Lily* 6 (July 1): 95.

Ballou, Adin. 1897. *History of the Hopedale Community, from its Inception to its Virtual Submergence in the Hopedale Parish.* Lowell, Mass.: Vox Populi Press.

Beecher, Catherine E. 1841. *A Treatise on Domestic Economy.* Boston.

———. 1846. *The Evils Suffered by American Women and American Children: The Causes and the Remedy. Presented in an Address by Miss C. E. Beecher, to Meetings of Ladies in Cincinnati, Washington, Baltimore, Philadelphia, New York, and Other Cities.*

Beecher, Henry Ward, and James T. Brady. 1859. "Addresses on Mental Culture for Women, Delivered in New York, October Twenty-Sixth, 1858." *The Pulpit and Rostrum. Sermons, Orations, Popular Lectures, &c.* January 15, 21–44.

Beman, Nathan Sydney Smith. 1850. *Female Influence and Obligations.* New York: American Tract Society Publications.

Bishop, William G., and William H. Attree. 1846. *Report of the Debates and Proceedings of the Convention for the Revision of the Constitution of the State of New-York, 1846.* Albany: Evening Atlas.

Blackstone, William. 1969 [1803]. *Commentaries on the Laws of England. With notes of reference to the Constitution and laws of the Federal Government of the United States, and of the Commonwealth of Virginia. By St. George Tucker.* Vol. 2. South Hackensack, N.J.: Rothman Reprints.

Britten, Emma (Hardinge). 1859. *The Place and Mission of Woman. An inspirational discourse, delivered by Miss Emma Hardinge, at the Melodeon, Boston, Sunday afternoon, Feb. 13, 1859. Phonographically reported by James M. W. Yerrinton.* Boston: H. W. Sweet.

Butts, Bryan J. 1856. *A Knotty Theme: or The Angel and the Bigot.* Hopedale, Mass.: Wm. B. Reed.

———. 1860. *The Angel and the 'Slaver'; A Radical Poem.* Hopedale, Mass.: Self-published.

———. 1871. *Material Independence of Woman.* January. Hopedale, Mass.: Self-published.

———. [post-1873]. *The Bigot's Dream; or A Disagreeable "Call to Preach."* Hopedale, Mass.: Self-published.

———. 1880. *Industrial Independence of Women; through Their Equal Income, and Equal Suffrage.* Hopedale, Mass.: Self-published.

Child, Lydia Maria Francis. 1972 [1829]. *The American Frugal Housewife.* New York: Harper and Row.

———. 1992 [1831]. *The Mother's Book.* Bedford, Mass.: Applewood Books.

Cincinnati Nonpareil. 1851. "Woman's Rights Convention." Reprinted in *The Lily* 3 (July): 50.

Coe, Mrs. 1853. *Extract from the Speech of Mrs. Coe. Bound with Speech of Wendell Phillips, Esq., at the Convention, Held at Worcester, Oct. 15 and 16, 1851 and Speech of Abby Kelly Foster. Bound as Woman's Rights Tracts, . . . No. 2 in Woman's Rights*

Commensurate with Her Capacities and Obligations. A Series of Tracts. Syracuse, N.Y.: J. E. Masters.

Cooper, Anna Julia. 1998a [1892]. "The Status of Woman in America." Pp. 109–17 in *The Voice of Anna Julia Cooper,* ed. Charles Lemert and Esme Bhan. New York: Rowman and Littlefield.

———. 1998b [1886]. "Womanhood: A Vital Element in the Regeneration and Progress of a Race." Pp. 53–71 in *The Voice of Anna Julia Cooper,* ed. Charles Lemert and Esme Bhan. New York: Rowman and Littlefield.

Courier. 1848. "The First Convention Ever Called to Discuss the Civil and Political Rights of Women, Seneca Falls, NY, July 19, 20, 1848." Seneca County, July 14.

Croswell, S., and R. Sutton. 1846. *Debates and Proceedings in the New-York State Convention, for the Revision of the Constitution.* Albany: Albany Argus.

Curtis, George William. 1858. *An Address, vindicating the rights of woman to the elective franchise, delivered at the Woman's Rights Convention, May 15, 1858.* New York: S. T. Munson.

Dall, Caroline H. 1972 [1867]. *The College, the Market, and the Court; or, Woman's Relation to Education, Labor, and Law.* New York: Arno Press.

Davis, Paulina W. 1853. *On the Education of Females. Read at the Convention in Worcester, Mass., October 16th, 1851. Bound with Letter from Harriet Martineau. Read by Mrs. Coe, at the Convention held in Worcester, Oct. 16, 1851. Bound as Woman's Rights Tracts, . . . No. 3 in Woman's Rights Commensurate with Her Capacities and Obligations. A Series of Tracts.* Syracuse, N.Y.: J. E. Masters.

———, compiler. 1971 [1871]. *A History of the National Woman's Rights Movement, for Twenty Years, With the Proceedings of the Decade Meeting held at Apollo Hall, October 20, 1870, from 1850 to 1870, With an Appendix Containing the History of the Movement During the Winter of 1871, in the National Capitol.* New York: Kraus Reprinting.

Declaration of Sentiments. 1853. *Put forth at Seneca Falls, July 19th and 20th, 1848. Bound with Speech of Mrs. E. L. Rose, at the Woman's Rights Convention, Held at Syracuse, Sept. 1852. Bound as Woman's Rights Tracts, . . . No. 9 in Woman's Rights Commensurate with Her Capacities and Obligations. A Series of Tracts.* Syracuse, N. Y.: J. E. Masters.

Editors. 1863. "The Legal Rights of Married Women." *New Englander,* January, 22–36.

Fairchild, James Harris. 1852. *The Joint Education of the Sexes: A Report Presented at a Meeting of the Ohio State Teachers' Association, Sandusky City, July 8th.* Oberlin: James M. Fitch.

Farrar, Eliza W. R. 1974 [1836]. *The Young Lady's Friend. By a Lady.* New York: Arno Press.

Foster, Abby Kelly. 1853. *Speech of Abby Kelly Foster. Bound with Speech of Wendell Phillips, Esq., at the Convention, Held at Worcester, Oct. 15 and 16, 1851 and Extract from the Speech of Mrs. Coe. Bound as Woman's Rights Tracts, . . . No. 2 in*

Woman's Rights Commensurate with Her Capacities and Obligations. A Series of Tracts. Syracuse, N. Y.: J. E. Masters.

Foster, R. W. 1854. *Women's Rights and Servants' Rights According to the Bible.* January.

Fuller, Margaret. 1971 [1855]. *Woman in the Nineteenth Century.* Boston: John P. Jewett.

Gage, M. E. J. 1853. *Speech of Mrs. M. E. J. Gage, at the Women's Rights Convention, Held at Syracuse, Sept. 1852. Woman's Rights Tracts, . . . No. 7 in Woman's Rights Commensurate with Her Capacities and Obligations. A Series of Tracts.* Syracuse, N. Y.: J. E. Masters.

Garrison, William Lloyd. 1858. Statement. In *Consistent Democracy. The Elective Franchise for Women. Twenty-five Testimonies of Prominent Men.* Worcester, Mass.

Grimke, Sarah. 1988 [1838]. *Letters on the Equality of the Sexes.* New Haven, Conn.: Yale University Press.

Herttell, Thomas. 1839. *Remarks Comprising in Substance Judge Herttell's Argument in the House of Assembly of the State of New-York, in the Session of 1837, in Support of the Bill to Restore to Married Women "The Right of Property," as Guarantied by the Constitution of this State.* New York: Henry Durell.

Higginson, Thomas Wentworth. 1857. *The Woman's Rights Almanac for 1858. Containing Facts, Statistics, Arguments, Records of Progress, and Proofs of the Need of It.* Worcester, Mass.: Z. Baker.

——. 1859. *Ought Women to Learn the Alphabet? Abridged from the Atlantic Monthly, for February, 1859.*

——. n.d. *Remarks of Rev. T. W. Higginson Before the Committee of the Constitutional Convention on the Qualification of Voters, June 3, 1853. Bound with Woman and Her Wishes. An Essay. Bound as Woman's Rights Tracts. . . . No. 4 in Speeches and Essays on Woman's Rights.*

——. n.d. *Woman and Her Wishes. An Essay. Bound with Remarks of Rev. T. W. Higginson Before the Committee of the Constitutional Convention on the Qualification of Voters, June 3, 1853. Bound as Woman's Rights Tracts. . . . No. 4 in Speeches and Essays on Woman's Rights.*

Hotchkiss, A. 1853. "Property Rights and Business Qualifications of Woman." *The Lily* 5 (March).

Hovey, William A. 1860. *Woman's Rights. An Essay Delivered at the Exhibition of the English High School, Monday, July 16, 1860.* Boston: Yerrinton and Garrison.

Jenkins, Lydia A. 1850. "Woman—Civil Rights." *The Lily* 2 (February): 12.

Lovett, William. 1856. *Woman's Mission.* London: Simpkin, Marshall.

Mansfield, Edward D. 1845. *The Legal Rights, Liabilities and Duties of Women; with an Introductory History of Their Legal Condition in the Hebrew, Roman and Feudal Civil Systems. Including the Law of Marriage and Divorce, the Social Relations of Husband and Wife, Parent and Child, of Guardian and Ward, and of Employer and Employed.* Salem, Mass.: John P. Jewett.

Marke, Desdemona. 1858. *An Appeal to the Women of America.* Philadelphia: Wm. S. Young.

Martin, William R. 1871. *Civil Rights of Women. Lecture before the University Law School, by William R. Martin; Freedom the Only Solution—English vs. American Theory and Practice of Law.* Albany: Weed, Parsons and Company.

Martineau, Harriet. 1853. *Letter from Harriet Martineau. Read by Mrs. Coe, at the Convention held in Worcester, Oct. 16, 1851. Bound with On the Education of Females. Read at the Convention in Worcester, Mass., October 16th, 1851 by Paulina W. Davis. Bound as Woman's Rights Tracts, . . . No. 3 in Woman's Rights Commensurate with Her Capacities and Obligations. A Series of Tracts.* Syracuse, N.Y.: J. E. Masters.

May, Samuel J. 1853a. *Letter from Rev. Samuel J. May, to the Woman's Rights Convention, Held at Worcester, Mass., Oct., 1850. Bound with Letter from Angelina Grimke Weld, to the Woman's Rights Convention, Held at Syracuse, Sept., 1852. Bound as Woman's Rights Tracts, . . . No. 8 in Woman's Rights Commensurate with Her Capacities and Obligations. A Series of Tracts.* Syracuse, N. Y.: J. E. Masters.

———. 1853b. *The Rights and Condition of Women; A Sermon, Preached in Syracuse, Nov., 1845 by Samuel J. May. Woman's Rights Tracts, . . . No. 1 in Woman's Rights Commensurate with Her Capacities and Obligations. A Series of Tracts.* Syracuse, N. Y.: J. E. Masters.

Mill, Harriet Taylor. 1853a. *Enfranchisement of Women. Reprinted from the "Westminster and Foreign Quarterly Review," for July, 1851. Bound with Taxation Without Representation. Bound as Woman's Rights Tracts, . . . No. 4 in Woman's Rights Commensurate with Her Capacities and Obligations. A Series of Tracts.* Syracuse, N. Y.: J. E. Masters.

———. 1853b. *Taxation Without Representation. Bound with Enfranchisement of Women. Reprinted from the "Westminster and Foreign Quarterly Review," for July, 1851. Bound as Woman's Rights Tracts, . . . No. 4 in Woman's Rights Commensurate with Her Capacities and Obligations. A Series of Tracts.* Syracuse, N. Y.: J. E. Masters.

Mott, Lucretia. 1850. *Discourse on Woman. Delivered at the Assembly Buildings, December 17, 1849. Being a Full Phonographic Report, Revised by the Author.* Philadelphia: T. B. Peterson.

National Woman's Rights Convention. 1859. *Proceedings of the Ninth National Woman's Rights Convention Held in New York City, Thursday May 12, 1859, with a Phonographic Report of the Speech of Wendell Phillips, by J. M. W. Yerrinton.* Rochester, N.Y.: A. Strong.

———. 1860. *Proceedings of the Tenth National Woman's Rights Convention, Held at the Cooper Institute, New York City, May 10th and 11th, 1860. Phonographic report by J. M. W. Yerrinton.* Boston: Yerrinton and Garrison.

————. 1866. *Proceedings of the Eleventh National Woman's Rights Convention, Held at the Church of the Puritans, New York, May 10, 1866. Phonographic report by H. M. Parkhurst.* New York: Robert J. Johnston.

New York State Woman's Rights Committee. 1860. *Appeal to the Women of New York.*

New York Sun. 1853. "Woman's Rights." May 17. In Susan B. Anthony [n.p.] 1837. *Scrap books containing the history of the woman movement from 1837 to 1900.* Vol. 1. 1848–64. Susan B. Anthony Collection, Rare Books and Special Collections Division, Library of Congress.

Nichols, C. I. H. 1853. *On the Responsibilities of Woman. A Speech by Mrs. C. I. H. Nichols, Worcester, Oct. 15, 1851. Woman's Rights Tracts, . . . No. 6 in Woman's Rights Commensurate with Her Capacities and Obligations. A Series of Tracts.* Syracuse, N. Y.: J. E. Masters.

Ohio Women's Convention. 1850. *Proceedings of the Ohio Women's Convention, Held at Salem, April 19th and 20th, 1850; with an Address by J. Elizabeth Jones.* Cleveland: Smead and Cowles' Press.

Parker, Theodore. n.d. *A Sermon of the Public Function of Woman, Preached at the Music-Hall, Boston, March 27, 1853. Woman's Rights Tracts. . . . No. 2 in Speeches and Essays on Woman's Rights.*

Phillips, Hester V. 1826–57. Diary. In Manuscripts and Special Collections, New York State Library.

Phillips, Wendell. 1853. *Speech of Wendell Phillips, Esq., at the Convention, Held at Worcester, Oct. 15 and 16, 1851. Bound with Extract from the Speech of Mrs. Coe and Speech of Abby Kelly Foster. Bound as Woman's Rights Tracts, . . . No. 2 in Woman's Rights Commensurate with Her Capacities and Obligations. A Series of Tracts.* Syracuse, N. Y.: J. E. Masters.

Preston, Ann. 1855. *Introductory Lecture, to the Course of Instruction in the Female Medical College of Pennsylvania, for the Session 1855–6.* Philadelphia.

Richardson, Joseph. 1833. *A Sermon, on the Duty and Dignity of Woman, Delivered April 22, 1832, by the Minister of the First Parish in Hingham.*

Rose, Ernestine L. 1850. *Speech of Mrs. Rose, A Polish Lady, at the Anniversary Paine Celebration, in New York, Jan. 29, Year of Independence, 74th—Christian Era, 1850.*

————. 1851. *An Address on Woman's Rights, Delivered Before the People's Sunday Meeting, in Cochituate Hall, on Sunday Afternoon, Oct. 19th 1851.* Boston: J. P. Mendum.

————. 1852. *Review of Horace Mann's two lectures: delivered in New York, February 17th and 29th, 1852.*

————. 1853. *Speech of Mrs. E. L. Rose, at the Woman's Rights Convention, Held at Syracuse, Sept. 1852. Bound with Declaration of Sentiments, Put forth at Seneca Falls, July 19th and 20th, 1848. Bound as Woman's Rights Tracts, . . . No. 9 in Woman's Rights Commensurate with Her Capacities and Obligations. A Series of Tracts.* Syracuse, N. Y.: J. E. Masters.

Severance, Caroline Maria. 1852. *Woman's Rights*. Cleveland: Press of Harris, Fairbanks and Company.

Sigourney, Lydia H. 1838. *Letters to Mothers*. Hartford, Conn.: Hudson and Skinner.

———. 1841 [1836]. *Letters to Young Ladies*. 6th ed. New York: Harper and Brothers.

Smith, E. Oakes. 1851. *Woman and Her Needs*. New York: Fowlers and Wells.

———. 1853. *Sanctity of Marriage. Woman's Rights Tracts, . . . No. 5 in Woman's Rights Commensurate with Her Capacities and Obligations. A Series of Tracts*. Syracuse, N. Y.: J. E. Masters.

Smith, Henry. 1846. *The Mission of Woman. An Address Delivered on the Evening of the Anniversary of Putnam Female Seminary; August 11, 1846*. Zanesville, Ohio.

Smith, Jonathan. 1884. *The Married Women's Statutes, and Their Results Upon Divorce and Society. An Essay Read Before the Social Science Club, at Clinton, February 19, 1884*. Clinton, Mass.: Clinton Printing Company.

Stanton, Elizabeth Cady. 1851. "Letter from Mrs. Elizabeth C. Stanton to the Worcester Convention." *The Lily* 3 (November): 82.

———. 1853a. *It Is So Unlady-Like*.

———. 1853b. *Letter from Mrs. Elizabeth C. Stanton, to the Woman's Rights Convention, Held at Worcester, Oct., 1850. Bound with Letter from Mrs. Elizabeth C. Stanton, to the Woman's Rights Convention Held at Syracuse, Sept. 1852. Bound as Woman's Rights Tracts, . . . No. 10 in Woman's Rights Commensurate with Her Capacities and Obligations. A Series of Tracts*. Syracuse, N. Y.: J. E. Masters.

———. 1853c. *Letter from Mrs. Elizabeth C. Stanton, to the Woman's Rights Convention Held at Syracuse, Sept. 1852. Bound with Letter from Mrs. Elizabeth C. Stanton, to the Woman's Rights Convention, Held at Worcester, Oct., 1850. Bound as Woman's Rights Tracts, . . . No. 10 in Woman's Rights Commensurate with Her Capacities and Obligations. A Series of Tracts*. Syracuse, N. Y.: J. E. Masters.

———. 1854. *Address to the Legislature of New-York, Adopted by the State Woman's Rights Convention, Held at Albany, Tuesday and Wednesday, February 14 and 15, 1854*. Albany: Weed, Parsons and Company.

———. 1858. *I Have All The Rights I Want*.

———. 1861. *Address of Elizabeth Cady Stanton, on the Divorce Bill, before the Judiciary Committee of the New York Senate, in the Assembly Chamber, Feb. 8, 1861*. Albany: Weed, Parsons and Company.

———. 1870. *Address of Mrs. Elizabeth Cady Stanton, Delivered at Seneca Falls and Rochester, NY, July 19th and August 2d, 1848. Bound with the Report of the Convention Held at Seneca Falls, NY, July 19, 20, 1848, and Proceedings of the Convention Held at Rochester, NY, Aug. 2, 1848. Bound in Proceedings of the Woman's Rights Conventions, Held at Seneca Falls & Rochester, NY, July & August, 1848*. New York: Robert J. Johnston.

———. 1989 [1854]. "Address to the Joint Judiciary Committee, New York Legislature, 1854." In *The Search for Self-Sovereignty: The Oratory of Elizabeth Cady Stanton*, ed. Beth M. Waggenspack. New York: Greenwood Press.

Stanton, Elizabeth Cady, Susan B. Anthony, and Matilda Joslyn Gage, eds. 1970
[1889]. *History of Woman Suffrage*. Vol. 1. New York: Source Book Press.

Stanton, Henry B. 1851. Letter to Elizabeth Cady Stanton, February 15. In Biographical box 7, Elizabeth Cady Stanton folder. Alma Lutz Collection, Vassar College Library.

Stewart, Ellen. 1858. *Life of Mrs. Ellen Stewart, Together with Biographical Sketches of Other Individuals. Also A Discussion with Two Clergymen, and Arguments in Favor of Woman's Rights; Together with Letters on Different Subjects. Written By Herself.* Akron, Ohio: Beebe and Elkins.

Todd, John. 1867. *Woman's Rights*. Boston: Lee and Shepard.

Tuthill, Louisa C. 1848. *The Young Lady's Home*. Philadelphia: Lindsay and Blakiston.

Walker, Timothy. 1849. *Legal Condition of Women*. Reprinted from *Western Law Journal*.

Weld, Angelina Grimke. 1853. *Letter from Angelina Grimke Weld, to the Woman's Rights Convention, Held at Syracuse, Sept., 1852. Bound with Letter from Rev. Samuel J. May, to the Woman's Rights convention, Held at Worcester, Mass., Oct., 1850. Bound as Woman's Rights Tracts, . . . No. 8 in Woman's Rights Commensurate with Her Capacities and Obligations. A Series of Tracts.* Syracuse, N. Y.: J. E. Masters.

Whole World's Temperance Convention. 1853. *The Whole World's Temperance Convention Held at Metropolitan Hall in the City of New York on Thursday and Friday, Sept. 1st and 2d, 1853.* New York: Fowlers and Wells.

Woman's Rights Committee. 1850. "Woman's Rights Convention." *The Lily* 2 (October): 76.

———. 1852. *The Proceedings of the Woman's Rights Convention, Held at Worcester, October 15th and 16th, 1851.* New York: Fowlers and Wells.

———. 1853. *Proceedings of the Woman's Rights Convention, Held at the Broadway Tabernacle, in the City of New York, on Tuesday and Wednesday, Sept. 6th and 7th, 1853.* New York: Fowlers and Wells.

———. 1854. "Justice to Women: Convention at Albany Tuesday and Wednesday, Feb. 14 and 15." *The Lily* 6 (February): 24.

———. 1856. *Proceedings of the Seventh National Woman's Rights Convention, Held in New York City, at the Broadway Tabernacle, on Tuesday and Wednesday, Nov. 25th and 26th, 1856.* New York: Edward O. Jenkins.

Woman's Rights Convention. [n. p.] "Reports: 1848–1870." In Susan B. Anthony Collection, Rare Books and Special Collections Division, Library of Congress.

———. 1851. *The Proceedings of the Woman's Rights Convention, Held at Worcester, October 23d and 24th, 1850.* Boston: Prentiss and Sawyer.

———. 1852a. *The Proceedings of the Woman's Rights Convention Held at West Chester, PA. June 2d and 3d, 1852.* Philadelphia: Merrihew and Thompson.

———. 1852b. *The Proceedings of the Woman's Rights Convention, Held at Syracuse, September 8th, 9th & 10th, 1852.* Syracuse, N.Y.: J. E. Masters.

———. 1854. *Proceedings of the National Women's Rights Convention, Held at Cleveland, Ohio, on Wednesday, Thursday, and Friday, October 5th, 6th, and 7th, 1853, phonographically reported by T. C. Leland.* Cleveland: Gray, Beardsley, Spear, and Company.

———. 1855. *Reports on the Laws of New England, Presented to the New England Meeting Convened at the Meionaon, Sept. 19 and 20, 1855.*

———. 1870a [1848]. *Proceedings of the Convention Held at Rochester, NY, Aug. 2, 1848. Bound with the Report of the Woman's Rights Convention, Held at Seneca Falls, NY, July 19th and 20th, 1848 and the Address of Elizabeth Cady Stanton. Bound as Proceedings of the Woman's Rights Conventions, Held at Seneca Falls and Rochester, NY, July and August, 1848.* New York: Robert J. Johnston.

———. 1870b [1848]. *Report of the Woman's Rights Convention, Held at Seneca Falls, NY, July 19th and 20th, 1848. Bound with the Proceedings of the Convention Held at Rochester, NY, Aug. 2, 1848 and the Address of Elizabeth Cady Stanton. Bound as Proceedings of the Woman's Rights Conventions, Held at Seneca Falls and Rochester, NY, July and August, 1848.* New York: Robert J. Johnston.

———. 1973 [1851]. *The Proceedings of the Woman's Rights Convention, Held at Akron, Ohio. May 28 and 29, 1851.* New York: Burt Franklin.

Woman's Rights Meeting. 1859. *Report of the Woman's Rights Meeting, at Mercantile Hall, May 27, 1859.* Boston: S. Urbino.

GENERAL BIBLIOGRAPHY

Alexander, Jeffrey C. 2004. "Cultural Pragmatics: Social Performance between Ritual and Strategy." *Sociological Theory* 22, no. 4: 527–73.

Althusser, Louis. 1971. "Ideology and Ideological State Apparatuses (Notes towards an Investigation)." Pp. 127–86 in *Lenin and Philosophy.* Trans. Ben Brewster. New York: Monthly Review Press.

Anderson, Bonnie S. 2000. *The First International Women's Movement, 1830–1860.* New York: Oxford University Press.

Appiah, Anthony. 1991. "Tolerable Falsehoods: Agency and the Interests of Theory." Pp. 63–90 in *Consequences of Theory,* ed. Jonathon Arac and Barbara Johnson. Baltimore: Johns Hopkins University Press.

Arac, Jonathan. 1979. "Bounding Lines: The Prelude and Critical Revision." *Boundary 2,* 7, no. 3: 31–48.

———. 2006. *Call It Sleep: The Tongs Set Free.* Lecture. Center for the Humanities, Wesleyan University, February 20.

Austin, J. L. 1961a. "Performative Utterances." Pp. 220–39 in *Philosophical Papers.* Oxford: Oxford University Press.

———. 1961b. "A Plea for Excuses." Pp. 123–52 in *Philosophical Papers.* Oxford: Oxford University Press.

———. 1962. *How to Do Things with Words.* Cambridge, Mass.: Harvard University Press.

Baker, Paula. 1984. "The Domestication of Politics: Women and American Political Society, 1780–1920." *American Historical Review* 89 (June): 620–47.

Balleisen, Edward J. 2001. *Navigating Failure: Bankruptcy and Commercial Society in Antebellum America.* Chapel Hill: University of North Carolina Press.

Barnard, Henry, ed. 1979. *Pamphlets in American History, Group I: A Bibliographic Guide to the Microform Collection.* Sanford, N.C.: Microfilming Corporation of America.

Barrett, Michele. 1985. "Ideology and the Cultural Production of Gender." Pp. 65–85 in *Feminist Criticism and Social Change: Sex, Class and Race in Literature and Culture,* ed. Judith Newton and Deborah Rosenfelt. New York: Methuen.

———. 1992. "Words and Things: Materialism and Method in Contemporary Feminist Analysis." Pp. 201–19 in *Destabilizing Theory: Contemporary Feminist Debates,* ed. Michele Barrett and Anne Phillips. Stanford: Stanford University Press.

Barry, Susan. 1980. "Spousal Rape: The Uncommon Law." *American Bar Association Journal* 66 (September): 1088–1091.

Barthes, Roland. 1972. *Mythologies.* Trans. Annette Lavers. New York: Hill and Wang.

Basch, Norma. 1982. *In the Eyes of the Law: Women, Marriage, and Property in Nineteenth-Century New York.* Ithaca, N.Y.: Cornell University Press.

———. 1983. "Equity vs. Equality: Emerging Concepts of Women's Political Status in the Age of Jackson." *Journal of the Early Republic,* September: 297–318.

Beard, Mary Ritter. 1986. *Woman as Force in History: A Study in Traditions and Realities.* New York: Octagon Books.

Bennington, Geoffrey. 1989. "Aberrations: de Man (and) the Machine." Pp. 209–22 in *Reading de Man Reading,* ed. Lindsay Waters and Wlad Godzich. Minneapolis: University of Minnesota Press.

Berg, Barbara. 1978. *The Remembered Gate: Origins of American Feminism, the Woman and the City, 1800–1860.* New York: Oxford University Press.

Bernheimer, Charles, and Claire Kahane, eds. 1985. *In Dora's Case: Freud—Hysteria—Feminism.* New York: Columbia University Press.

Berthoff, Rowland. 1971. *An Unsettled People: Social Order and Disorder in American History.* New York: Harper and Row.

Bolt, Christine. 1993. *The Women's Movements in the United States and Britain from the 1790s to the 1920s.* Amherst: University of Massachusetts Press.

Bourdieu, Pierre. 1991. *Language and Symbolic Power.* Cambridge, Mass.: Harvard University Press.

Bowles, Samuel, David M. Gordon, and Thomas E. Weisskopf. 1990. *After the Wasteland: A Democratic Economics for the Year 2000.* Armonk, N.Y.: M. E. Sharpe.

Brandzel, Amy L. 2005. "Queering Citizenship? Same-Sex Marriage and the State." *GLQ* 11, no. 2: 171–204.

Brown, Ira V. 1965. "The Woman's Rights Movement in Pennsylvania, 1848–1873." *Pennsylvania History* 32 (April): 153–65.

Brownlee, W. Elliot. 1988. *Dynamics of Ascent: A History of the American Economy.* 2nd ed. Chicago: Dorsey Press.

Buhle, Mary Jo, and Paul Buhle, eds. 1978. *The Concise History of Woman Suffrage: Selections from the Classic Work of Stanton, Anthony, Gage and Harper.* Urbana: University of Illinois Press.

Burchfield, R. W., ed. 1972. *A Supplement to the Oxford English Dictionary.* Oxford: Oxford University Press.

Butcher, Patricia Smith. 1989. *Education for Equality: Women's Rights Periodicals and Women's Higher Education, 1849–1920.* New York: Greenwood Press.

Butler, Judith. 1990. *Gender Trouble: Feminism and the Subversion of Identity.* New York: Routledge.

———. 1991. "Imitation and Gender Insubordination." Pp. 13–31 in *Inside/Out: lesbian theories, gay theories,* ed. Diana Fuss. New York: Routledge.

———. 1992. "Contingent Foundations: Feminism and the Question of 'Postmodernism.'" Pp. 3–21 in *Feminists Theorize the Political,* ed. Judith Butler and Joan W. Scott. New York: Routledge.

———. 1995a. "'Conscience Doth Make Subjects of Us All.'" *Yale French Studies* 88: 6–26.

———. 1995b. "Contingent Foundations." Pp. 35–58 in *Feminist Contentions: A Philosophical Exchange,* by Judith Butler, Drucilla Cornell, Nancy Fraser, and Seyla Benhabib. New York: Routledge.

———. 1995c. "For a Careful Reading." Pp. 127–44 in *Feminist Contentions: A Philosophical Exchange,* by Judith Butler, Drucilla Cornell, Nancy Fraser, and Seyla Benhabib. New York: Routledge.

———. 1997. *Excitable Speech: A Politics of the Performative.* New York: Routledge.

Campbell, Karlyn Kohrs. 1989. *Man Cannot Speak for Her.* Vol. 1. New York: Greenwood Press.

Carby, Hazel V. 1987. *Reconstructing Womanhood: The Emergence of the Afro-American Woman Novelist.* New York: Oxford University Press.

Carroll, Berenice A. 1976. "Mary Beard's *Woman as Force in History:* A Critique." Pp. 26–41 in *Liberating Women's History: Theoretical and Critical Essays,* ed. Berenice A. Carroll. Urbana: University of Illinois Press.

Caruth, Cathy. 1995a. "The Claims of Reference." Pp. 92–105 in *Critical Encounters: Reference and Responsibility in Deconstructive Writing,* ed. Cathy Caruth and Deborah Esch. New Brunswick, N.J.: Rutgers University Press.

———. 1995b. "Introduction: The Insistence of Reference." Pp. 1–8 in *Critical Encounters: Reference and Responsibility in Deconstructive Writing,* ed. Cathy Caruth and Deborah Esch. New Brunswick, N.J.: Rutgers University Press.

Chodorow, Nancy. 1974. "Family Structure and Feminine Personality." Pp. 43–66 in *Woman, Culture, and Society,* ed. Michelle Zimbalist Rosaldo and Louise Lamphere. Stanford: Stanford University Press.

Christ, Carol. 1977. "Victorian Masculinity and the Angel in the House." Pp. 146–62 in *A Widening Sphere: Changing Roles of Victorian Women,* ed. Martha Vicinus. Bloomington: Indiana University Press.

Chused, Richard H. 1983. "Married Women's Property Law: 1800–1850." *Georgetown Law Journal* 71: 1359–1425.

———. 1985. "Late Nineteenth Century Married Women's Property Law: Reception of the Early Married Women's Property Acts by Courts and Legislatures." *American Journal of Legal History* 29: 3–35.

Cixous, Hélène. 1983. "The Laugh of the Medusa." Pp. 279–97 in *The Signs Reader: Women, Gender and Scholarship,* ed. Elizabeth Abel and Emily Abel. Chicago: University of Chicago Press.

Cixous, Hélène, and Catherine Clement. 1986. *The Newly Born Woman.* Trans. Betsy Wing. Minneapolis: University of Minnesota Press.

Clark, Elizabeth. 1987. "Religion, Rights and Difference: The Origins of American Feminism, 1848–1860." *Working Papers,* 2 (February): 2. Institute for Legal Studies, University of Wisconsin, Madison, Law School.

Clinton, Catherine. 1984. *The Other Civil War: American Women in the Nineteenth Century.* New York: Hill and Wang.

Cogan, Frances B. 1989. *All-American Girl: The Ideal of Real Womanhood in Mid-Nineteenth-Century America.* Athens: University of Georgia Press.

Cohen, Shana. 2004. *Searching for a Different Future: The Rise of a Global Middle Class in Morocco.* Durham, N.C.: Duke University Press.

Coleman, Peter J. 1974. *Debtors and Creditors in America: Insolvency, Imprisonment for Debt, and Bankruptcy, 1607–1900.* Madison: State Historical Society of Wisconsin.

Conway, Jill K. 1982. *The Female Experience in Eighteenth- and Nineteenth-Century America: A Guide to the History of American Women.* New York: Garland.

Cook, Charles M. 1981. *The American Codification Movement: A Study of Antebellum Legal Reform.* Westport, Conn.: Greenwood Press.

Copjec, Joan. 1994. *Read My Desire: Lacan against the Historicists.* Cambridge, Mass.: MIT Press.

Cornell, Drucilla. 1991. *Beyond Accommodation: Ethical Feminism, Deconstruction, and the Law.* New York: Routledge.

Cott, Nancy F. 1977. *The Bonds of Womanhood: "Woman's Sphere" in New England, 1780–1835.* New Haven, Conn.: Yale University Press.

———. 1987. *The Grounding of Modern Feminism.* New Haven, Conn.: Yale University Press.

———. 1998. "Marriage and Women's Citizenship in the United States, 1830–1934." *American Historical Review* 103, no. 5: 1440–74.

———. 2000. *Public Vows: A History of Marriage and the Nation.* Cambridge, Mass.: Harvard University Press.

Crosby, Christina. 1991. *The Ends of History: Victorians and "The Woman Question."* New York: Routledge.

Cross, Whitney R. 1950. *The Burned-over District: The Social and Intellectual History of Enthusiastic Religion in Western New York, 1800–1850*. Ithaca, N.Y.: Cornell University Press.

Culler, Jonathan. 1982. *On Deconstruction: Theory and Criticism after Structuralism*. Ithaca, N.Y.: Cornell University Press.

Davidson, Harriet. 1995. "'I Say I Am There': Siting/Citing the Subject of Feminism and Deconstruction." Pp. 241–61 in *Critical Encounters: Reference and Responsibility in Deconstructive Writing*, ed. Cathy Caruth and Deborah Esch. New Brunswick, N.J.: Rutgers University Press.

Degler, Carl N. 1980a. *At Odds: Women and the Family in America from the Revolution to the Present*. New York: Oxford University Press.

———. 1980b. "Women and the Family." Pp. 308–26 in *The Past Before Us: Contemporary Historical Writing in the United States*, ed. Michael Kammen. Ithaca, N.Y.: Cornell University Press.

de Lauretis, Teresa. 1987. *Technologies of Gender: Essays on Theory, Film, and Fiction*. Bloomington: Indiana University Press.

de Man, Paul. 1979. *Allegories of Reading: Figural Language in Rousseau, Nietzsche, Rilke, and Proust*. New Haven, Conn.: Yale University Press.

———. 1986. "The Resistance to Theory." Pp. 3–20 in *The Resistance to Theory*. Minneapolis: University of Minnesota Press.

Derrida, Jacques. 1977. "Limited Inc. a b c . . ." *Glyph* 2, supplement: 162–254.

———. 1986a [1982]. "Différance." Pp. 1–27 in *Margins of Philosophy*. Trans. Alan Bass. Chicago: University of Chicago Press.

———. 1986b [1982]. "Signature Event Context." Pp. 307–30 in *Margins of Philosophy*. Trans. Alan Bass. Chicago: University of Chicago Press.

———. 1989. *Memoires for Paul de Man*. Trans. Eduardo Cadava. New York: Columbia University Press.

———. 1993. *Aporias*. Stanford: Stanford University Press.

Dicey, Albert Venn. 1981 [1914, 2nd ed.]. *Lectures on the Relation between Law and Public Opinion in England during the Nineteenth Century*. New Brunswick, N.J.: Transaction Books.

Donovan, Herbert D. A. 1925. *The Barnburners: A Study of the Internal Movements in the Political History of New York State and of the Resulting Changes in Political Affiliation, 1830–1852*. New York: New York University Press.

Douglas, Ann. 1977. *The Feminization of American Culture*. New York: Knopf.

DuBois, Ellen Carol. 1978. *Feminism and Suffrage: The Emergence of an Independent Women's Movement in America, 1848–1869*. Ithaca, N.Y.: Cornell University Press.

———. 1998. *Woman Suffrage and Women's Rights*. New York: New York University Press.

DuBois, Ellen Carol, Mari Jo Buhle, Temma Kaplan, Gerda Lerner, and Carroll Smith-Rosenberg. 1980. "Politics and Culture in Women's History: A Symposium." *Feminist Studies* 6 (March): 26–63.

DuCille, Ann. 1994. "The Occult of True Black Womanhood: Critical Demeanor and Black Feminist Studies." *Signs* 19, no. 3: 591–629.

Durkheim, Emile. 1965 [1915]. *The Elementary Forms of the Religious Life.* Trans. Joseph Ward Swain. New York: Free Press.

———. 1966 [1951]. *Suicide: A Study in Sociology.* Trans. John A. Spaulding. New York: Free Press.

———. 1982. *The Rules of Sociological Method and Selected Texts on Sociology and Its Method.* Trans. W. D. Halls. New York: Free Press.

———. 1984. *The Division of Labor in Society.* Trans. W. D. Halls. New York: Free Press.

Durkheim, Emile, and Marcel Mauss. 1963. *Primitive Classification.* Trans. Rodney Needham. Chicago: University of Chicago Press.

Elam, Diane. 1994. *Feminism and Deconstruction: Ms. en Abyme.* New York: Routledge.

Elshtain, Jean Bethke. 1981. *Public Man, Private Woman: Women in Social and Political Thought.* Princeton: Princeton University Press.

Epstein, Barbara Leslie. 1981. *The Politics of Domesticity: Women, Evangelism, and Temperance in Nineteenth-Century America.* Middletown, Conn.: Wesleyan University Press.

Evans, George Herberton, Jr. 1948. *Business Incorporations in the United States, 1800–1943.* New York: National Bureau of Economic Research.

Fitzpatrick, Peter. 1992. *The Mythology of Modern Law.* New York: Routledge.

Flexner, Eleanor. 1959. *Century of Struggle: The Woman's Rights Movement in the United States.* New York: Atheneum.

Foucault, Michel. 1972. *The Archaeology of Knowledge and the Discourse on Language.* Trans. A. M. Sheridan Smith. New York: Pantheon Books.

———. 1973 [1970]. *The Order of Things: An Archaeology of the Human Sciences.* New York: Vintage Books.

———. 1975 [1973]. *The Birth of the Clinic: An Archaeology of Medical Perception.* Trans. A. M. Sheridan Smith. New York: Vintage Books.

———. 1979 [1977] *Discipline and Punish: The Birth of the Prison.* Trans. Alan Sheridan. New York: Vintage Books.

———. 1980a [1978]. *The History of Sexuality, Vol. 1: An Introduction.* Trans. Robert Hurley. New York: Vintage Books.

———. 1980b. *Power/Knowledge: Selected Interviews and Other Writings, 1972–1977,* ed. and trans. Colin Gordon. New York: Pantheon Books.

———. 1982. "The Subject and Power." Pp. 208–26 in *Michel Foucault, Beyond Structuralism and Hermeneutics,* ed. Hubert L. Dreyfus and Paul Rabinow. Chicago: University of Chicago Press.

———. 1988 [1977]. "Nietzsche, Genealogy, History." Pp. 139–64 in *Language, Counter-memory, Practice: Selected Essays and Interviews,* ed. and trans. Donald Bouchard. Ithaca, N.Y.: Cornell University Press.

———. 1991. "Politics and the Study of Discourse." Pp. 53–72 in *The Foucault Effect: Studies in Governmentality,* ed. Graham Burchell, Colin Gordon, and Peter Miller. London: Harvester Wheatsheaf.

Freeman, Michael D. A. 1981–82. "'But If You Can't Rape Your Wife, Who[m] Can You Rape?': The Marital Rape Exemption Re-examined." *Family Law Quarterly,* 15: 1–29.

Freud, Sigmund. 1991a. "On the Mechanism of Paranoia." Pp. 29–48 in *General Psychological Theory: Papers on Metapsychology,* ed. Philip Rieff. New York: Simon and Schuster.

———. 1991b. "On Narcissism: An Introduction." Pp. 56–82 in *General Psychological Theory: Papers on Metapsychology,* ed. Philip Rieff. New York: Simon and Schuster.

Friedman, Lawrence M. 1985. *A History of American Law.* 2nd ed. New York: Simon and Schuster.

Fuss, Diana. 1989. *Essentially Speaking: Feminism, Nature and Difference.* New York: Routledge.

Gallop, Jane. 1982. *The Daughter's Seduction: Feminism and Psychoanalysis.* Ithaca, N.Y.: Cornell University Press.

Ginzberg, Lori D. 1986. "'Moral Suasion Is Moral Balderdash': Women, Politics, and Social Activism in the 1850s." *Journal of American History* 73 (December): 601–22.

———. 1990. *Women and the Work of Benevolence: Morality, Politics, and Class in the Nineteenth-Century United States.* New Haven, Conn.: Yale University Press.

———. 2000. *Women in Antebellum Reform.* Wheeling, Ill.: Harlan Davidson.

———. 2005. *Untidy Origins: A Story of Woman's Rights in Antebellum New York.* Chapel Hill: University of North Carolina Press.

Godzich, Wlad. 1983. "The Domestication of Derrida." Pp. 20–40 in *The Yale Critics: Deconstruction in America,* ed. Jonathon Arac, Wlad Godzich, and Wallace Martin. Minneapolis: University of Minnesota Press.

Gordon, Ann D., and Mari Jo Buhle. 1976. "Sex and Class in Colonial and Nineteenth-Century America." Pp. 278–300 in *Liberating Women's History: Theoretical and Critical Essays,* ed. Berenice A. Carroll. Urbana: University of Illinois Press.

Gordon, Avery F. 1997. *Ghostly Matters: Haunting and the Sociological Imagination.* Minneapolis: University of Minnesota Press.

Gould, Timothy. 1995. "The Unhappy Performative." Pp. 19–44 in *Performativity and Performance,* ed. Andrew Parker and Eve Kosofsky Sedgwick. New York: Routledge.

Groneman, Carol, and Mary Beth Norton, eds. 1987. *"To Toil the Livelong Day": America's Women at Work, 1780–1980.* Ithaca, N.Y.: Cornell University Press.

Hall, Stuart. 1978. "Some Problems with the Ideology/Subject Couplet." *Ideology and Consciousness* 3: 113–21.

Haraway, Donna. 1992. "Ecce Homo, Ain't (Ar'n't) I a Woman, and Inappropriate/ d Others: The Human in a Post-Humanist Landscape." Pp. 86–100 in *Feminists Theorize the Political,* ed. Judith Butler and Joan W. Scott. New York: Routledge.

Hasday, Jill Elaine. 2000. "Contest and Consent: A Legal History of Marital Rape." *California Law Review* 88 (October): 1373–1505.

Haskell, Thomas L. 1985a. "Capitalism and the Origins of the Humanitarian Sensibility, Part 1." *American Historical Review* 90, no. 2: 339–61.

———. 1985b. "Capitalism and the Origins of the Humanitarian Sensibility, Part 2." *American Historical Review* 90, no. 3: 547–66.

Hewitt, Nancy A. 1984. *Women's Activism and Social Change: Rochester, New York, 1822–1872.* Ithaca, N.Y.: Cornell University Press.

Hillenbrand, Laura. 2003. "A Sudden Illness." *The New Yorker,* July 7, 56–65.

Hinck, Edward A. 1991. "*The Lily,* 1849–1856: From Temperance to Woman's Rights" Pp. 30–47 in *A Voice of Their Own: The Woman Suffrage Press, 1840–1910,* ed. Martha M. Solomon. Tuscaloosa: University of Alabama Press.

Hirst, Paul Q. "Althusser and the Theory of Ideology." *Economy and Society* 5: 385–412.

Hoff, Joan. 1991. *Law, Gender and Injustice: A Legal History of U.S. Women.* New York: New York University Press.

Hoffert, Sylvia D. 1995. *When Hens Crow: The Woman's Rights Movement in Antebellum America.* Bloomington: Indiana University Press.

Horwitz, Morton J. 1977. *The Transformation of American Law, 1780–1860.* Cambridge, Mass.: Harvard University Press.

Hurst, James Willard. 1964. *Law and the Conditions of Freedom in the Nineteenth-Century United States.* Madison: University of Wisconsin Press.

Irigaray, Luce. 1980. "When the Goods Get Together." Pp. 107–10 in *New French Feminisms: An Anthology,* ed. Elaine Marks and Isabelle de Courtivron. New York: Schocken Books.

Isenberg, Nancy (Gale). 1990. " 'Coequality of the Sexes': The Feminist Discourse of the Antebellum Women's Rights Movement in America." Ph.D. diss., University of Wisconsin, Madison.

———. 1998. *Sex and Citizenship in Antebellum America.* Chapel Hill: University of North Carolina Press.

Jerry, E. Claire. 1991. "The Role of Newspapers in the Nineteenth-Century Woman's Movement." Pp. 17–29 in *A Voice of Their Own: The Woman Suffrage Press, 1840–1910,* ed. Martha M. Solomon. Tuscaloosa: University of Alabama Press.

Jordan, Winthrop. 1969. *White over Black: American Attitudes toward the Negro, 1550–1812.* Baltimore: Penguin Books.

Kahane, Claire. 1995. *Passions of the Voice: Hysteria, Narrative, and the Figure of the Speaking Woman, 1850–1915.* Baltimore: Johns Hopkins University Press.

Kerber, Linda K. 1980. *Women of the Republic: Intellect and Ideology in Revolutionary America.* Chapel Hill: University of North Carolina Press.

———. 1989. "Separate Spheres, Female Worlds, Woman's Place: The Rhetoric of Women's History." *Journal of American History* 75 (March): 9–39.

———. 1997. *Toward an Intellectual History of Women.* Chapel Hill: University of North Carolina Press.

———. 1998. *No Constitutional Right to Be Ladies: Women and the Obligations of Citizenship.* New York: Hill and Wang.

Kerber, Linda K., and Jane Sherron De Hart, eds. 2004. *Women's America: Refocusing the Past.* 6th ed. New York: Oxford University Press.

Kessler-Harris, Alice. 1981. *Women Have Always Worked: A Historical Overview.* Old Westbury, N.Y.: Feminist Press.

———. 1982. *Out to Work.* New York: Oxford University Press.

Kraus, Natasha Kirsten. 1996. "Desire Work, Performativity, and the Structuring of a Community: Butch/Fem Relations of the 1940s and 1950s." *Frontiers: A Journal of Women Studies* 7, no. 1: 30–56.

Kugler, Israel. 1987. *From Ladies to Women: The Organized Struggle for Women's Rights in the Reconstruction Era.* Westport, Conn.: Greenwood Press.

Lacan, Jacques. 1977. "The Mirror Stage as Formation of the Function of the I." Pp. 1–7 in *Ecrits: A Selection.* Trans. Alan Sheridan. London: Tavistock.

Landes, Joan B. 1988. *Women and the Public Sphere in the Age of the French Revolution.* Ithaca, N.Y.: Cornell University Press.

Lebergott, Stanley. 1984. *The Americans: An Economic Record.* New York: Norton.

Leitch, Vincent B. 1986. "Deconstruction and Pedagogy." Pp. 45–56 in *Theory in the Classroom,* ed. Cary Nelson. Chicago: University of Illinois Press.

Lemert, Charles. 1998. "Anna Julia Cooper: The Colored Woman's Office." Pp. 1–43 in *The Voice of Anna Julia Cooper,* ed. Charles Lemert and Esme Bhan. New York: Rowman and Littlefield.

Lerner, Gerda. 1967. *The Grimké Sisters from South Carolina: Rebels against Slavery.* Boston: Houghton Mifflin.

———. 1979. "The Lady and the Mill Girl: Changes in the Status of Women in the Age of Jackson, 1800–1840." Pp. 182–96 in *A Heritage of Her Own: Toward a New Social History of American Women,* ed. Nancy F. Cott and Elizabeth H. Pleck. New York: Simon and Schuster.

Lieberson, Stanley. 1980. *A Piece of the Pie: Blacks and White Immigrants Since 1880.* Berkeley: University of California Press.

Matthaei, Julie A. 1982. *An Economic History of Women in America: Women's Work, the Sexual Division of Labor, and the Development of Capitalism.* New York: Schocken Books.

McClymer, John F. 1999. *This High and Holy Moment: The First National Woman's Rights Convention, Worcester, 1850.* Fort Worth: Harcourt Brace.

McGrane, Reginald Charles. 1924. *The Panic of 1837: Some Financial Problems of the Jacksonian Era.* Chicago: University of Chicago Press.

Melder, Keith Eugene. 1964. "The Beginnings of the Women's Rights Movement in the United States, 1800–1840." Ph.D. diss., Yale University.

Mohanty, Chandre Talpade. 1991. "Under Western Eyes: Feminist Scholarship and Colonial Discourses." Pp. 51–80 in *Third World Women and the Politics of Feminism,* ed. Chandre Talpade Mohanty, Ann Russo, and Lourdes Torres. Bloomington: Indiana University Press.

Murray, James A. H., Henry Bradley, W. A. Craigie, and C. T. Onions, ed. 1933. *The Oxford English Dictionary.* Oxford: Oxford University Press.

Newman, Louise Michele. 1999. *White Women's Rights: The Racial Origins of Feminism in the United States.* New York: Oxford University Press.

Newmark, Kevin. 1989. "Paul de Man's History." Pp. 121–35 in *Reading de Man Reading,* ed. Lindsay Waters and Wlad Godzich. Minneapolis: University of Minnesota Press.

Nietzsche, Friedrich. 1969 [1967]. *On the Genealogy of Morals.* Trans. Walter Kaufmann. New York: Vintage.

Norris, Christopher. 1982. *Deconstruction: Theory and Practice.* New York: Methuen.

North, Douglass C. 1961. *The Economic Growth of the United States, 1790–1860.* Englewood Cliffs, N.J.: Prentice-Hall.

Norton, Mary Beth. 1979. "The Paradox of 'Women's Sphere.'" Pp. 139–49 in *Women of America: A History,* ed. Carol Ruth Berkin and Mary Beth Norton. Boston: Houghton Mifflin.

Okin, Susan Moller. 1979. *Women in Western Political Thought.* New York: Virago.

O'Neill, William L. 1969. *Everyone Was Brave: A History of Feminism in America.* Chicago: Quadrangle Books.

Ortner, Sherry B. 1974. "Is Female to Male as Nature Is to Culture?" Pp. 67–87 in *Women, Culture, and Society,* ed. Michelle Z. Rosaldo, Sherry B. Ortner, and Louise Lamphere. Stanford: Stanford University Press.

Painter, Nell Irvin. 1996. *Sojourner Truth: A Life, a Symbol.* New York: Norton.

Parker, Gail Thain, ed. 1972. *The Oven Birds: American Women on Womanhood, 1820–1920.* Garden City, N.Y.: Doubleday.

Pateman, Carole. 1980. "Women and Consent." *Political Theory* 8, no.2: 149–68.

———. 1988. *The Sexual Contract.* Stanford: Stanford University Press.

———. 1989. *The Disorder of Women: Democracy, Feminism and Political Theory.* Stanford: Stanford University Press.

Pathak, Zakia, and Rajeswari Sunder Rajan. 1992. "'Shahbano.'" Pp. 257–79 in *Feminists Theorize the Political,* ed. Judith Butler and Joan W. Scott. New York: Routledge.

Patton, Cindy. 1995. "Performativity and Spatial Distinction: The End of AIDS Epidemiology." Pp. 173–96 in *Performativity and Performance,* ed. Andrew Parker and Eve Kosofsky Sedgwick. New York: Routledge.

Pêcheux, Michel. 1982. *Language, Semantics and Ideology.* New York: St. Martin's Press.

Phillips, Anne. 1991. *Engendering Democracy.* University Park: Pennsylvania State University Press.

Poovey, Mary. 1988. *Uneven Developments: The Ideological Work of Gender in Mid-Victorian England.* Chicago: University of Chicago Press.

———. 1995. "Feminism and Deconstruction." Pp. 128–42 in *Feminist Cultural Studies,* vol. 2, ed. Terry Lovell. Brookfield, Vt.: Edward Elgar.

Post, Robert, and Reva Siegel. 2007. "Roe Rage: Democratic Constitutionalism and Backlash." *Harvard Civil Rights–Civil Liberties Law Review* 42 (summer): 373–433.

Przeworski, Adam. 1985. *Capitalism and Social Democracy.* New York: Cambridge University Press.

Rabkin, Peggy A. 1975. "The Origins of Law Reform: The Social Significance of the Nineteenth-Century Codification Movement and Its Contribution to the Passage of the Early Married Women's Property Acts." *Buffalo Law Review* 24, no. 3: 683–760.

———. 1980. *Fathers to Daughters: The Legal Foundations of Female Emancipation.* Westport, Conn.: Greenwood Press.

Riley, Denise. 1988. *"Am I That Name?": Feminism and the Category of 'Women' in History.* Minneapolis: University of Minnesota Press.

———. 1992. "A Short History of Some Preoccupations." Pp. 121–29 in *Feminists Theorize the Political,* ed. Judith Butler and Joan W. Scott. New York: Routledge.

Rosaldo, Michelle Zimbalist. 1974. "Woman, Culture, and Society: A Theoretical Overview." Pp. 17–42 in *Woman, Culture, and Society,* ed. Michelle Zimbalist Rosaldo and Louise Lamphere. Stanford: Stanford University Press.

Rosaldo, Michelle Zimbalist, and Louise Lamphere, eds. 1974. *Woman, Culture, and Society.* Stanford: Stanford University Press.

Rosenberg, Rosalind. 1982. *Beyond Separate Spheres: Intellectual Roots of Modern Feminism.* New Haven, Conn.: Yale University Press.

Rubin, Gayle. 1985. "The Traffic in Women: Notes on the 'Political Economy' of Sex." Pp. 157–210 in *Toward an Anthropology of Women,* ed. Reyna Reiter. Boston: Monthly Review Press.

Russo, Ann, and Cheris Kramarae, eds. 1991. *The Radical Women's Press of the 1850s.* New York: Routledge.

Ryan, Mary P(atricia). 1971. "American Society and the Cult of Domesticity, 1830–1860." Ph.D. diss., University of California, Santa Barbara.

———. 1975. *Womanhood in America: From Colonial Times to the Present.* New York: Franklin Watts.

———. 1981. *Cradle of the Middle Class: The Family in Oneida County, New York, 1790–1865.* New York: Cambridge University Press.

———. 1990. *Women in Public: Between Banners and Ballots, 1825–1880.* Baltimore: Johns Hopkins University Press.

———. 1997. *Civic Wars: Democracy and Public Life in the American City during the Nineteenth Century.* Berkeley: University of California Press.

Said, Edward. 1978. "The Problem of Textuality: Two Exemplary Positions." *Critical Inquiry* 4 (June): 673–714.

Salmon, Marylynn. 1979. "Equality or Submersion? Feme Covert Status in Early Pennsylvania." Pp. 92–113 in *Women of America: A History,* ed. Carol Ruth Berkin and Mary Beth Norton. Boston: Houghton Mifflin.

———. 1986. *Women and the Law of Property in Early America.* Chapel Hill: University of North Carolina Press.

Scott, Anne Firor. 1984. *Making the Invisible Woman Visible.* Urbana: University of Illinois Press.

Scott, Joan W(allach). 1989. *Gender and the Politics of History.* New York: Columbia University Press.

———. 1992. "Experience." Pp. 22–40 in *Feminists Theorize the Political,* ed. Judith Butler and Joan W. Scott. New York: Routledge.

Shammas, Carole. 1994. "Re-assessing the Married Women's Property Acts." *Women's History* 6, no. 1: 9–30.

Shanley, Mary Lyndon. 1979. "Marriage Contract and Social Contract in Seventeenth Century English Political Thought." *Western Political Quarterly* 32, no. 1: 79–91.

Siegel, Reva B. 1994. "Home as Work: The First Woman's Rights Claims Concerning Wives' Household Labor, 1850–1880." *Yale Law Journal* 103 (March): 1073–1217.

———. 1996. "In the Eyes of the Law: Reflections on the Authority of Legal Discourse." Pp. 225–31 in *Law's Stories: Narrative and Rhetoric in the Law,* ed. Peter Brooks and Paul Gewirtz. New Haven, Conn.: Yale University Press.

———. 1999. "Collective Memory and the Nineteenth Amendment: Reasoning about 'the Woman Question' in the Discourse of Sex Discrimination." Pp. 131–82 in *History, Memory, and the Law,* ed. Austin Sarat and Thomas R. Kearns. Ann Arbor: University of Michigan Press.

Sklar, Kathryn Kish. 1973. *Catherine Beecher: A Study in American Domesticity.* New Haven, Conn.: Yale University Press.

———. 2000. *Women's Rights Emerges within the Antislavery Movement, 1830–1870: A Brief History with Documents.* New York: St. Martin's Press.

Smith, Daniel Scott. 1979. "Family Limitation, Sexual Control, and Domestic Feminism in Victorian America." Pp. 222–45 in *A Heritage of Her Own: Toward a New Social History of American Women,* ed. Nancy F. Cott and Elizabeth H. Pleck. New York: Simon and Schuster.

Smith, Paul. 1988. *Discerning the Subject.* Minneapolis: University of Minnesota Press.

Smith-Rosenberg, Carroll. 1985. *Disorderly Conduct: Visions of Gender in Victorian America.* New York: Oxford University Press.

Solomon, Martha M. 1991. "The Role of the Suffrage Press in the Woman's Rights Movement." Pp. 1–16 in *A Voice of Their Own: The Woman Suffrage Press, 1840–1910,* ed. Martha M. Solomon. Tuscaloosa: University of Alabama Press.

Speth, Linda E. 1982. "The Married Women's Property Acts, 1839–1865: Reform, Re-action, or Revolution?" Pp. 69–91 in *Women and the Law: A Social Historical Perspective*, vol. 2, ed. D. Kelly Weisberg. Cambridge, Mass.: Schenkman.

Spillers, Hortense J. 1987. "Mama's Baby, Papa's Maybe: An American Grammar Book." *diacritics*, summer, 65–81.

Spivak, Gayatri Chakravorty. 1988a. "Can the Subaltern Speak?" Pp. 271–313 in *Marxism and the Interpretation of Culture*, ed. Cary Nelson and Lawrence Gross-berg. Chicago: University of Illinois Press.

———. 1988b. "Subaltern Studies: Deconstructing Historiography." Pp. 3–32 in *Selected Subaltern Studies*, ed. Ranajit Guha and Gayatri Chakravorty Spivak. Lon-don: Oxford University Press.

———. 1993. *Outside in the Teaching Machine*. New York: Routledge.

Stanley, Amy Dru. 1998. *From Bondage to Contract: Wage Labor, Marriage, and the Market in the Age of Slave Emancipation*. New York: Cambridge University Press.

Steinfeld, Robert J. 2001. *Coercion, Contract, and Free Labor in the Nineteenth Cen-tury*. New York: Cambridge University Press.

Temin, Peter. 1969. *The Jacksonian Economy*. New York: Norton.

Thurman, Kay Ellen. 1966. "The Married Women's Property Acts." Master's thesis, University of Wisconsin Law School.

Tonn, Mari Boor. 1991. "The Una, 1853–1855: The Premiere of the Woman's Rights Press." Pp. 48–70 in *A Voice of Their Own: The Woman Suffrage Press, 1840–1910*, ed. Martha M. Solomon. Tuscaloosa: University of Alabama Press.

Van Vleck, George W. 1967. *The Panic of 1857: An Analytical Study*. New York: AMS Press.

Warbasse, Elizabeth Bowles. 1987. *The Changing Legal Rights of Married Women, 1800–1861*. New York: Garland.

Warminski, Andrzej. 1995. "Ending Up/Taking Back (with Two Postscripts on Paul de Man's Historical Materialism)." Pp. 11–41 in *Critical Encounters: Reference and Responsibility in Deconstructive Writing*, ed. Cathy Caruth and Deborah Esch. New Brunswick, N.J.: Rutgers University Press.

Weigman, Robyn. 1995. *American Anatomies: Theorizing Race and Gender*. Durham, N.C.: Duke University Press.

Weiner, Lynn Y. 1985. *From Working Girl to Working Mother: The Female Labor Force in the United States, 1820–1980*. Chapel Hill: University of North Carolina Press.

Weitzman, Lenore J. 1981. *The Marriage Contract: A Guide to Living with Lovers and Spouses*. New York: Free Press.

Welter, Barbara. 1966. "The Cult of True Womanhood: 1820–1860." *American Quar-terly* 18 (June): 151–74.

———. 1976. *Dimity Convictions: The American Woman in the Nineteenth Century*. Athens: Ohio University Press.

West, Robin. 1989. "Equality Theory, Marital Rape, and the Promise of the Four-teenth Amendment." Unpublished manuscript.

Williamson, Chilton. 1960. *American Suffrage: From Property to Democracy, 1760–1860*. Princeton: Princeton University Press.

Yee, Shirley J. 1992. *Black Women Abolitionists: A Study in Activism, 1828–1860*. Knoxville: University of Tennessee Press.

Zaeske, Susan. 2003. *Signatures of Citizenship: Petitioning, Antislavery, and Women's Political Identity*. Chapel Hill: University of North Carolina Press.

INDEX

Pateman, Carole, 58–60, 63–67
Price, Abby H., 33–34, 189–90
Property law, 111–13; social meanings of, 111, 229 nn. 17–18

Queer politics: civil rights and, 219–20; family policies and, 219–20; marriage rights and, 217–20; military service and, 218

Reading asunder, 19, 92–93, 168, 222 n. 3
Real womanhood, 118, 229 n. 20
Refigured womanhood: African American women and, 120–22; antebellum woman's rights movement and, 37, 41–42, 68–71, 75–76, 80–81, 167, 169, 175–93, 199–200, 209–10; married women's property acts and, 72–76, 131, 208–10; Republican Mother and, 164, 184–86, 199; True Womanhood and, 34–37, 68–71, 90–91, 120–23, 167, 169–70, 174–93
Republican Mother, 113–18, 123. *See also* Refigured womanhood
Richardson, Joseph, 29, 123–24
Riley, Denise, 21, 36–37
Robinson, Mrs. E., 188–89
Rochester. *See* New York State, central and western
Rose, E. (Ernestine), 204
Rousseau, Jean Jacques, 49, 54–58
Ryan, Mary Patricia, 9–12, 28, 83–88, 91–92, 104–5, 113

"Sanctity of Marriage" (E. Oakes Smith, 1853), 192–93
Second Bank of the United States, 93
Second Great Awakening, 86–88
Separate spheres: feminist scholarship and, 7–13; institutional spheres and, 8–13; social meanings and, 7–13,

27–29; True Womanhood and, 27–32, 35–36, 69–71, 80
Sermon, on the Duty and Dignity of Woman, A (Joseph Richardson, 1833), 123–24
Siegel, Reva B., 21, 41–42, 56–57, 69, 209, 223 n. 9, 230 n. 1
Sigourney, Lydia H., 31, 115–16
Smith, E. Oakes, 190–93
Social contract: freedpersons and, 60–61; heterosexuality and, 60–63, 225 n. 10, 226 n. 12; Native Americans and, 60–61; marriage contract and, 58–61, 72; as promise, 54–58; as sexual-social contract, 58–63, 72; *The Social Contract*, 49, 54–58; as structural aporia, 23–24, 54–63
Social movement: conditions of possibility for success, 23–25, 80, 227, 241; as fully discursive, 22, 32, 41–42, 80–81, 169–70, 193–94; organization and, 167–68; performativity and, 41; social meanings and, 13, 36–38, 41–42, 80–81, 158, 169–70, 193–94, 213–20. *See also* Antebellum woman's rights movement
Spillers, Hortense, 120
Spivak, Gayatri Chakravorty, 67–68, 195
Stanley, Amy Dru, 21, 57–61, 122, 209
Stanton, Elizabeth Cady, 158, 179, 194–96, 200–201
Stone, Lucy, 191
"Strategic effect," 37, 182, 223 n. 8
Structural aporias: as analytic frame, 22–25, 46–58, 75–76, 211–12; discursive systems and, 13, 22–24, 52–54, 67–68, 74–76, 125–26, 211; promise and, 54–58, 219–20; social movements and, 75–76, 168, 213–20; subjectivation through, 61–63, 125–26. *See also* Aporia; Language; Marriage contract; Social contract

Natasha Kirsten Kraus has taught sociology and women's studies at the University at Buffalo, SUNY, has been a Research Fellow at the Center for the Humanities, Wesleyan University, and is currently a Scholar in Residence at the Center for Cultural Sociology, Yale University.

Library of Congress Cataloging-in-Publication Data
Kraus, Natasha Kirsten
A new type of womanhood : discursive politics and social change in antebellum America / Natasha Kirsten Kraus.
p. cm.
Includes bibliographical references and index.
ISBN 978-0-8223-4333-2 (cloth : alk. paper)
ISBN 978-0-8223-4368-4 (pbk. : alk. paper)
 1. Women—United States—History—19th century. 2. Women—United States—Social conditions—19th century. 3. Women—Legal status, laws, etc.—United States—History—19th century. I. Title.
 HQ1418.K73 2008
 305.420973'09034—dc22   2008013877